PRAISE FOR

I LIVE FOR THIS!

• • •

"Tommy Lasorda is one of the greatest managers his sport
—or any sport—has ever seen. *I Live for This!* takes readers inside his world, where honor, loyalty, hard work, and
heart are not just part of the game plan but essential to life.
He has succeeded where many would have failed, and this
book tells you how—and why."

— JOE PATERNO,
head football coach,
Pennsylvania State University

"Everyone knows Tommy Lasorda bleeds Dodger Blue, but
after reading this remarkable book, you realize he bleeds
red, white, and blue. He is baseball's best ambassador."

— JOE MORGAN,
ESPN sportscaster and member
of the Baseball Hall of Fame

"From Jackie Robinson to Sandy Koufax to Fernando Valenzuela, from Brooklyn to Chavez Ravine to Sydney to Hon-
shu, Lasorda has lived a baseball life like no other. Finally,
he shares—with humor, insight, and pathos—his memories of all that he has borne witness to. *I Live For This!* takes
its place alongside *The Glory of Their Times* and *Ball Four*
on the short list of indispensable baseball books."

— JEREMY SCHAAP,
ESPN sports correspondent and author
of *Cinderella Man* and *Triumph*

"Plaschke wades into Tommy Lasorda's eighty-year-old stream of consciousness, fishes out the best of the best, and stuffs and mounts the outrageous quotes, opinions, and tales of Dodger Blue on a solid, engaging background of prose. Very nice work indeed . . . a winner."

— LEIGH MONTVILLE,
author of *The Big Bam*

"*I Live for This!* takes readers on an unforgettable ride through the world of Tommy Lasorda. Here is where baseball's good will is done on a day-to-day basis by a guy who defied all odds to become something in the sport he loved, and who succeeded like a true champion. Tommy is one-of-a-kind, a master motivator, a great and gutsy manager, and an outrageous storyteller. This book has it all."

— PAT RILEY,
president of the Miami Heat and author
of *Showtime* and *The Winner Within*

"Tommy Lasorda is a Hall of Fame manager. And if there were a Hall of Fame for colorful characters and great storytellers, he would be in those too. It's all here—enjoy."

—BOB COSTAS,
NBC Sports and HBO Sports

I LIVE FOR THIS!

I LIVE
FOR THIS!

Baseball's Last True Believer

BILL PLASCHKE
with TOMMY LASORDA

Mariner Books · Houghton Mifflin Harcourt

BOSTON · NEW YORK

First Mariner Books edition 2009
Copyright © 2007 by Bill Plaschke and Tommy Lasorda

www.hmhbooks.com

Library of Congress Cataloging-in-Publication Data
Plaschke, Bill.
  I live for this! : baseball's last true believer / Bill Plaschke with
Tommy Lasorda.
     p. cm.
  Includes index.
  ISBN 978-0-618-65387-4
  1. Lasorda, Tommy. 2. Baseball managers—United States—
Biography. 3. Los Angeles Dodgers (Baseball team) I. Lasorda,
Tommy. II. Title.
  GV865.L33P53 2007
  796.357092—dc22
  [B]   2007018306

  ISBN 978-0-547-23788-6 (pbk.)

Book design by Melissa Lotfy

Printed in the United States of America

DOC 10 9 8 7 6 5 4 3 2 1

To T-Berry, Boy-Boy, and G-Dog
You are my strength, my spirit, my soul
— B. P.

To my family
— T. L.

Contents

Foreword

I t is a glorious summer Sunday morning at Los Angeles's Dodger Stadium. I am walking through a dark tunnel. It leads from a glistening green field that smells delightfully of summer into a dank clubhouse that reeks like an old sock.

Outside, fans are buzzing and Nancy Bea Hefley's organ music is playing and athletes in brightly colored uniforms are jogging on the perspiring grass. The four bases are impossibly white, the two chalk lines are amazingly straight, and even the dirt seems to have been shaped and tinted like a socialite's hair. This is baseball. This is America.

Once inside that tunnel, the world turns. Everything in the Dodger clubhouse feels close and cramped and confusing. A heavy-eyed kid in a stained blue golf shirt is pushing a laundry cart. A lumpy older man in his underwear is filling a plastic tub with bubble gum. Two players in long johns and T-shirts are arguing over queens and hearts. Another player, in jeans and a jersey, is studying a truck-trader magazine. Three guys in the corner are cursing one another in Spanish. This is also baseball. This is also America.

I think, If only fans on the outside could see the inside. I wonder, What if all those who sat in this charming ballpark were exposed to the quirkiness of its depths? Would it ruin this splendid piece of American culture if folks knew that Dodger Stadium has more than one level, more than one angle, many crooked shadows? Or would it simply make it more real?

I walk underneath low ceilings, past ancient cubbyholes, up a chipped concrete walkway, through a wobbly blue door, and into the office of a similarly splendid piece of Americana named Tommy Lasorda.

It is 1990, and he is the legendary manager of the renowned Los Angeles Dodgers baseball team. In the past thirteen seasons he has won two world championships and four National League pennants and has captured the imagination of the jaded American baseball fan with everything from his crooked smile to his jiggling belly to his innate ability to create magic.

He howls, he hugs, he screams, he cries, he hikes his giant belt above his skinny legs, and sometimes he literally chases his players to greatness, running over anyone who dares to step in their path. He bumps bellies with umpires, exchanges curses with opponents, argues with sportswriters, taunts fans, and somehow makes them all laugh while doing it.

Tommy Lasorda is baseball's Santa Claus, and Americans are clamoring for his lap. Aging Dodger Stadium is usually filled to capacity because of the energy around him. A little-known diet product called Slim-Fast is making millions because of the salesman within him. Thousands in the military and in business and countless students have been motivated listening to speeches by him. Folks from Asia to South America have swooned during visits from him. He once went to the White House as a tourist, and within ninety minutes he met with President Reagan, his chief of staff, and the vice president without having an appointment to see any of them. This country's leaders heard he was there and went looking for him. He is not only one of baseball's best managers, but, in a crude yet lovably blustery way, he is also baseball's best ambassador.

Yet on this summer day in Chavez Ravine, he is just Tommy. He is the same man I see almost every day for six months every year. He is my assignment. He is my job. I am the Dodger beat reporter for the *Los Angeles Times*, and he is an integral part of my daily coverage. I talk to him at least twice a day. I report his opinions and insights. He is the public face of the team, he sets the tone for each day's news, and he is the best source for the best material. If he's mad, my words scream. If he's funny, my words laugh. He is an important figure for journalists because he always generates news. But he can also be an impossible figure for journalists because he insists that such news make him look good. He will gladly share the story of a pregame spaghetti dinner with his players. But he will berate you for writing about the spaghetti stains on his collar. He will gladly supply inside information, as long as that information makes him or the Dodgers look good. He may be the most unassuming yet image-conscious figure in sports.

On this day, it's that inside information that I'm seeking. Lasorda has already held his pregame press meeting with the Dodger beat writers from five different newspapers, but I want something more. So I leave the serene field and dip into its sweaty bowels. I travel from the public Tommy Lasorda into the tiny office that houses the private one.

"Plaschke," he shouts brightly, seeing me at the door. "Get in here!"

When Tommy Lasorda summons you so cheerfully into his office, with that bony finger and that huge grin, it usually means just one thing.

He is alone. He wants the company. He needs the company.

Despite being constantly surrounded by backslapping sycophants, Lasorda often acts like a lonely orphan. He hates to be alone. He moans about being alone. He lives for an audience. When one audience grows weary of his stories, he searches for a new one.

"Plaschke," Lasorda shouts again. "Get in here and have a piece of pizza. Now!"

This has long been one of Lasorda's methods to ensure that he will never be alone. He fills his office with food. He is, in fact, the only manager in major league history to set up the postgame buffet in his office. Other teams feed their players in separate rooms, far away from the boss, giving them a private place to unwind. But not Lasorda, who uses food to draw the players to his quarters, where they can eat veal piccata next to piles of his soiled underwear. He's told the media he does this to foster teamwork. But he also does it so he will never have to do so much as dress by himself.

This morning I need only one bit of information—no time to eat, no time to hang out. Plus, I had just eaten a huge Sunday buffet at a nearby restaurant; no room for anything more. But Lasorda doesn't care.

"Here," he says, handing me a huge piece of pepperoni pie, dripping from a paper plate. "Eat this."

He's wearing white underwear with a wrinkled blue T-shirt covered with a sauce-splotched towel. He's sitting behind a cluttered desk that is nearly toppled by the six pizzas piled atop it. He's not giving me a choice.

"Pizza! Now!"

"Tommy, I'm stuffed," I say. "I can't eat it. I'll vomit, I swear. I just need to ask you one question. Can I ask you just one question?"

When dealing with Lasorda, you often have to fight outlandishness with outlandishness. And, yes, if he's going to try to force you to eat greasy pizza on a Sunday morning, you have to counter with the threat of vomit. Which doesn't work. It never works. Not even vomit.

"C'mon, sit down, take your time, eat this pizza . . . and I'll give you a scoop," he says.

"A scoop?" I ask.

"Yeah," he says, shaking his head as if disgusted by his own vulnerability. "You sit here with me and eat pizza until the start of the game, and I'll give you some inside information."

"Pass the pepperoni."

So I sit and eat my pizza while he slowly gets dressed. And then he starts talking. But, funny thing, he's not talking about baseball, he's talking about his feelings. For the next half hour, while lineup cards are being filled out and coaches are reminding him to hurry up and players are clanking toward the field in their cleats, Lasorda momentarily lets down his bluster and reveals himself.

Earlier that morning, he had breakfast with an old friend from his hometown of Norristown, Pennsylvania, so he talks about growing up. He says something about a stolen glove, and prison baseball, and oversize cleats. Then he's talking about pitching for the

Brooklyn Dodgers, and how he never won a game, and how it never seemed fair, and how, dammit, his parents never watched him pitch anyway. Soon I realize that this man who seems to have everything is talking as if he has nothing. This man who has nothing to prove is sounding like he has everything to prove.

What I suspected then has long since been confirmed. The real Tommy Lasorda is nothing like the national image that he works so diligently to protect. Fans think he is a giant, friendly, blustery baseball man. But behind that big smile burns an angry, endless fire, and beneath that loud laugh lives a quiet, continuous fight.

I've seen Tommy Lasorda be so kind and gentle to someone in need, it made me weep. I've also seen him be so surly to someone who is threatening him, it made me scream. He can be lovable, vengeful, unselfish, unkind, tender, and tough, all at the same time, all in the ten minutes it takes him to walk from the organ strains that fill Dodger Stadium to the salsa music that blares in the clubhouse below. I've seen him comfort and motivate a twenty-four-year-old journeyman who has just been demoted to the minor leagues. I've also seen him, on April Fools' Day, pretend to send a veteran to the minors, then laugh as the poor guy melted into a weepy puddle.

When Lasorda finishes talking in the dark clubhouse on this sunny Sunday—"Tommy, end the interview, they're starting to play the anthem!" shouts one of his coaches—it strikes me that he is very much like the stadium in which he sits. All those fans who love his nostalgic exterior—wouldn't they be interested in going deeper? And once they got there, wouldn't they appreciate him more?

Great Americans are like great ballparks, aren't they? To see them on the surface is to appreciate their style. But to navigate them from upper concourse to lower tunnel is to appreciate their substance.

Tommy Lasorda is a man of great personality, but he is also a man of great substance, and this book is about that substance. I realize that in writing it I may be asking too much of those baseball fans who really don't want to see anything deeper than a manicured outfield or a center-field fountain or an old guy pushing peanuts. But I also believe that once those fans see the underground pipes, they will better appreciate that the grass is so green.

I first began thinking of writing this book during that summer conversation in Dodger Stadium. That it has taken until now to finally put it down on paper has been, in fact, a blessing. Because over the past fifteen years, Lasorda has lived as much life as in his previous fifty years. He is the only sports hero who grows more interesting as he grows older. He is perhaps the only sports hero who retired and then became *more* famous.

Since that day in 1990, he's endured a lot. His only heart gave out and nearly killed him, forcing him into retirement. His first love, the Dodgers, abandoned him after retirement. His beloved game rewarded him, inducting him into the baseball Hall of Fame in 1997. His nation enlisted him to coach the U.S. Olympic team, a journey that resulted in a gold medal, the trip of his life.

Recently the Dodgers smartly brought him back into the fold as a vice president, and baseball returned him to the forefront with popular postseason commercials, and the world embraced him again as the World Baseball Classic's ambassador. Groups everywhere are once more begging for his appearance.

Tommy Lasorda today is by all accounts the most popular baseball figure in the world. But he is also perhaps the most complex. He is still the guy sitting alone in his underwear on a Sunday morning, using pizza to bribe someone to sit with him. He is still the guy surrounded by fans but fighting loneliness, the guy showered with accolades but fighting insecurity, the poor kid from a small Pennsylvania town who has something to prove—a complicated, shadow-filled, true American baseball hero.

Through it all, he has trusted in the goodness of a game that sometimes abandoned him. He still has faith in a sport where steroid-filled players slug too tightly wrapped balls. He still counts on the sanctity of three outs, nine innings, and 162 games as the only constants in a world where the body ages and the mind grows weary and where, after they have received his autograph, some people have the nerve to tell him that the national pastime has become a national joke.

Tommy Lasorda is baseball's last true believer.

Which I believe makes his journey one worth taking.

I LIVE FOR THIS!

1
...

I FOUGHT FOR THIS

Where is the concession stand?"

Tommy Lasorda marches through the dirt of a small city park on a cool fall Saturday in the San Fernando Valley. There are family members with him, but he is marching ahead of them. He takes long strides and his lips are pursed. He is only going to a girls' softball game, but he's still marching, because there will be people here who will stare at him and smile at him and surround him as if he were a triumphant returning general. He knows it. He plays to it.

He is marching like he once marched to the mound in a baggy Brooklyn Dodger uniform, a failed pitcher who always believed he was just one strike away. He's marching like he once marched to the mound in a too tight Los Angeles Dodger uniform, a manager carrying a giant chip, somebody always out to screw him, somebody always looking to send him from Hollywood back to where he's always afraid he belonged, the back alleys outside Philadelphia, turning him into just another sad-eyed, hook-nosed man driving a beer truck. He's marching like he marches across those same fields today as baseball's great living ambassador—nobody can touch him, nobody dares challenge him, a Hall of Famer who has earned every step of this march.

Only today, wearing a blue sweater, tan slacks, and brown suede shoes, the feared manager looks like everyone's favorite grandfather. And today that fits, because he is marching in to see his grandchild's softball game.

Her name is Emily Goldberg. She is the preteen second baseman on an all-star softball team. She calls him "Pop-pop." He loves that name. It feels like him. It even sounds like him. A left hook and a right jab. Pop. Pop. Even pushing eighty, he's the toughest of the tough guys.

He walks past swooning mothers and staring dads. He spots Emily standing on the field, a little girl with her grandmother's sweet face and her grandfather's sharp eyes. Lasorda's lips turn up in a weathered smile, and his arthritic fingers gently jab the air in a wave that glistens with a World Series ring. There are certain times when Lasorda's cartoonish exterior completely disappears, when the tough guy melts and the funny guy dissolves and all that is left is pure, unscripted emotion that can leave him looking stunned.

She is his only grandchild, born in the San Fernando Valley during the postseason of 1995. Lasorda drove to the hospital after a game and walked into the room while the doctor was giving Emily her first exam. He was so excited, he began shouting.

"Hey Doc, hey Doc, you a baseball fan?" he asked.

The doctor, wearing a stethoscope, could not hear him, so Lasorda shouted louder.

"Doc, I'm asking you. You a baseball fan?"

When the doctor realized what Lasorda was saying, he quietly answered "Yes" and returned to his examination. But Lasorda wasn't finished.

"OK, Doc. Then you must be a Dodger fan, right? Are you a Dodger fan?"

The doctor was preoccupied listening to Emily's heartbeat, so he couldn't hear Lasorda's bellows.

"I'm asking you, Doc. Are you a Dodger fan?"

When the doctor finally understood, he did not answer. He could not answer. He just shrugged. If only Lasorda knew that the first man to examine his most precious jewel was actually a San Francisco Giants fan.

As Emily grew, Lasorda's devotion grew with her, to the point where she is at the top of his speed dial. He calls her every day just to say hello. He will drive from his Fullerton home to see her, even if it's only to say good night, a ninety-minute trek for one kiss.

Some days their visits consist entirely of him watching her master the hula hoop. Other days he will fall asleep while sitting on the couch and she will crawl in by his side, neither needing words, both content to feel each other's breath.

As he settles into the stands to watch her play softball, the dialogue begins.

"Hey, Emmy!" he shouts in a voice that is smooth and reassuring.

"Hey, Pop-pop," she shouts back.

He stares at her, blinks, says nothing, as if rendered speechless by the sight of a Lasorda playing baseball again. Then he goes back to the business of being Tommy, a man in search of a concession stand, a man who must settle for a collection of confections on paper plates, snacks made by the moms.

"So, what have we here?" he says, staring down at some butterscotch cookies.

Whenever Lasorda goes somewhere new, the first thing he looks for is food. His twenty-year managerial career was defined by food. Pasta gave him his size, restaurants gave him his influence, dieting made him a national star, and regaining the lost weight made him a lovable human being. Each of his 1,599 victories was accompanied by food. Each of his two world championships ended in a celebration of food, which is not only his currency, it's his oxygen. In this case, he looks for the nearest person who would have such food, which would be a smiling mother. Sitting amid crushed Gatorade bottles and licorice wrappers, the mother opens a Tupperware container and deftly hands Lasorda a brown sugary square.

Mothers love Lasorda. They line up to hug him and brag about their husbands and ask for his blessing. They like him because he remembers their names and likes the color of their eyes, and isn't afraid to compliment them on their charm bracelets. They like him because they can hug him the way they used to hug their giant stuffed animals, two little arms around something large, cuddly, and soft. If they could, moms would take Lasorda home and prop him up on their bedroom shelf.

Lasorda knows that the way to anyone's heart—that of a player, a general manager, a sportswriter, or in this case one of Emily's friends—is through her mother. So he opens those arms wide.

"Have some coffee cake," says this mom.

"Mfmflflflfl," Lasorda says, filling his mouth.

Food crisis averted, Lasorda sits down to watch the only person in the world who can persuade him to drive for an hour and a half on a moment's notice just to watch her fall down while learning to skate.

"You've never seen anyone fall down like Emily," Lasorda says. "The thing is, you've never seen anyone get up like her either."

These are the stories he tells about his family. Stories of comebacks, stories of courage. This is how he defines not only himself but also those around him. Lasorda views life through the perspective of the fight. Even now. Especially now. At this stage of his life, when he has earned every creature comfort imaginable, it is a view that inspires him to keep punching, lest someone hit him first.

On this day, you would think that nobody is fighting anything. It's all little girls and colorful uniforms and laughs, right? Lasorda talks about Emily as if she were Ernie Banks or Albert Einstein. He brags about her hitting, her fielding, her spelling scores, just like any grandfather—only about ten decibels louder and in a voice that sounds remarkably like wooden wheels on a cobblestone road.

But then you look up and see a huge umpire crouched down behind home plate. So much for no fighting. As long as Lasorda is near an umpire, there is a chance for a fight.

"Hey, the umpire's in my way," he says, plopping down on a chipped wooden bleacher behind home plate after finishing his coffee cake. "That guy's so big, he'll block us from all angles."

You would think he's joking, but he's not. Years of arguing with umpires have left him eternally suspicious of anyone wearing dark blue and carrying balls in a fanny pack. Even if it's just some moonlighting history teacher standing behind the plate at a girls' softball game. Lasorda is perpetually wary of anyone besides him who would dare enforce the rules. To him, umpires have always represented how, with the simple waving of a hand or barking of a word, life can turn on you.

For all his public swagger, for all his youthful practical jokes, the only time Lasorda ever ended up in jail was because of an umpire.

It was in the Dominican Republic in the early 1970s, back when Lasorda spent every winter managing a team in the Caribbean, trying desperately to get noticed by a Dodger organization that already had a Hall of Fame manager named Walter Alston. His Dominican team was winning, 2–0. It was the bottom of the ninth, two out. The opposing hitter knocked a ball over the head of center fielder Von Joshua, into the darkness of deep center.

Joshua ran it down and threw it in. But one of the umpires called it a home run. He claimed that the original ball had gone over the fence and that Joshua had pulled a spare ball out of his pocket. Lasorda was so furious, he ran out of the cramped dugout onto the dying field. All around him, fans were singing and rattling noisemakers and pointing at him, jeering and cursing in Spanish. Lasorda ran up to the umpire and shouted, "You needle-nosed sonofa—"

He was ejected at "needle-nosed."

When the umpire threw him out, Lasorda decided he would go all the way out. He began carefully unbuttoning his shirt and gently taking it off. Then he threw it wildly into the stands. Next he bent over, untied his cleats, slipped out of them, and threw them over the outfield wall. Then he shrugged and, half naked, walked back into the small dugout and up the tunnel to the clubhouse.

"I was getting undressed after the game like everyone else," Lasorda remembers. "I was just doing it on the field."

Later, after he had showered—he was often the last guy to get dressed—Lasorda discovered a couple of strangers waiting for him in the clubhouse. They began speaking Spanish so quickly that Lasorda could barely comprehend. Only when he walked outside and saw the team bus driving away did he fully understand. They were the military police.

"My team was going home, but I was going somewhere else," he remembers.

A couple of hours later, he found himself behind the grimy bars of a Dominican jail, sharing a cell with a couple of vagrants and a woman who was madly screaming.

To quiet her down, "the soldiers came inside and hit her right in the face, knocked her cold. Scared the hell out of me."

Scared him clear to Sunday, apparently. The entire night of Tommy Lasorda's only night in jail, he stood in a corner and recited the Catholic Mass.

He was released the next day, with two explanations.

First, he had been arrested and charged with indecent exposure. "I told them, 'Because I had my shirt off in public, that was indecent exposure?'" Lasorda recalls. "I asked them, 'Don't you have boxing in this town?'"

Second, he was told that General Javier, the commanding presence in the small Dominican town, had bet on the other team to win the game. The umpire had to fix it in the final inning or face jail himself. That's why the double had become a phantom homer. And that's why Lasorda's argument never stood a chance. Lasorda heard this and shrugged. If anyone understood backroom justice, he did.

"The next day, my club's president warned me that everyone in the street was talking about my arrest," Lasorda remembers. "I told him, 'Good, because if they're talking about me, that means they're not talking about having a revolution.'"

Only Tommy Lasorda, it seems, could use the occasion of his arrest to take credit for saving a country. His time in jail, however, did have a profound effect on his life. No sports figure shows more respect for authority than Lasorda: he gives more free speeches before police and fire departments than even the smartest politicians.

"I see the pressure that these people operate under. I see what they're doing for our country," he says. "Believe me when I say that nobody has a better justice system than we do."

Today justice is blocking his view of his granddaughter, and he wants to change seats, but then he has another idea. This is also something he learned in the Dominican. He will stay in his seat and offer a bribe. He announces he will give the two softball umpires autographed balls, ensuring that they will not only try to stay out of his way, but perhaps also be kind to his beloved granddaughter.

"You catch more flies with honey than vinegar," he says with a wink. That has been one of his life mottoes: always be nice to the ones who threaten you the most; always keep your enemies close.

It's a simple theme for such a complex creature, but it's precisely how Lasorda began his baseball life. A career that would make him a celebrity on five continents and in five hundred cities, starting with five brothers and five straight miles.

In the early 1930s, on steamy summer mornings in Philadelphia, that's how far the sons of an Italian immigrant named Sabatino Lasorda would walk to play baseball. Not Little League or American Legion baseball. Not youth league or school or YMCA baseball. Just baseball. Just five boys from a cramped three-story row house in Norristown, Pennsylvania, which was then an aging industrial city about twenty miles from Philadelphia. Just five boys walking to an overgrown field known as Elmwood Park.

There was no scoreboard. There were no bleachers. There were no benches. There were no umpires. And, blessedly, there were no parents. There was just baseball.

Their opponents didn't come from a tryout but from a neighborhood, a family like the Lasordas, only with different accents. Lasorda and the other Italian kids would play the Irish kids. The winner of that game would play the Negro kids. The losers would wait on the playground. And on it would go, from jungle field to jungle gym to jungle field again, nobody keeping standings, nobody supplying snacks, nobody screaming anything about keeping your eye on the ball. Just boys and baseball.

One of the Lasorda boys didn't walk to get there. He ran. He was the one with the bushy black hair and the crooked nose and the fingers-on-the-chalkboard laugh. He was running today from the law that was his father's belt. He was always running from something.

Back at the house an hour earlier, ten-year-old Tommy Lasorda had been put in charge of cleaning the second floor, which had a bedroom and a bathroom. It wasn't that hard. But on mornings like this, with the sun shining and baseball calling, it was unbearable. Lasorda wanted to join his brothers immediately. He was the second oldest, the bold one, the fighter. Their team needed his spark. So he escaped his chores by using the hidden mop trick.

He grabbed the giant mop, a small bucket, and a few dirty rags and walked up the stairs to the second-floor hallway. But instead of cleaning and shining, he whacked the mop against the wall and rattled the bucket against the toilet. He made so much noise that his father, who drove a truck at a steel mill and understood the efficiency of noise, believed he was working.

Amid the echoing clatter, Lasorda stopped and quietly jimmied open the bathroom window. Then, before his father could notice the silence, he climbed out feet first, grabbed the drainpipe, shimmied down to the ground, and was gone, sprinting to the baseball game.

Several hours later, when the boys returned home, his father was waiting. Standing on the uncleaned second floor as his father removed his belt to begin a beating, Tommy made an announcement that would frame his life for the next fifty years.

"I'll take a one-minute beating for one day of baseball anytime," he said.

His brothers solemnly nodded and covered their ears.

The man doing the beating exuded the sort of tough love that the second-oldest son exhibits today. Sabatino Lasorda immigrated to the United States from the Italian region of Abruzzi. He never understood baseball. He barely understood English. He worked with his hands. His house was so rickety that when Sabatino died, his sons had to prop up the floor with pillars so it could hold the weight of his casket.

"But man, I tell you, my dad was rich," Lasorda says. "The things you hear me say today, that's my father talking."

His father would tell Tommy, "It doesn't cost you a nickel to be nice."

His father would say, "If you build a house and the foundation is off, everything you put on that house will be off. The foundation of life is love and respect."

Lasorda's first pep talks, when he managed minor league teams, came from his father, who preached, "If you have five guys on one rope, pulling together, they can pull half a town behind them. If they are pulling against each other, they go nowhere."

When Tommy didn't pull with his four brothers, he winced from his father's belt. Sometimes he winced even before he had a chance to pull. One day he was working in his family's backyard garden, where they grew vegetables—sometimes tomatoes would be their only dinner. His father wanted to water some plants, and so he handed Tommy a glass jug and asked him to fill it at a nearby spring. It was their last bottle. Tommy was reminded to be careful not to break it.

"Then all of a sudden my father hauls off and hits me," Lasorda recalls. "And I'm like, 'Why?'"

Sabatino Lasorda smiled and said, "What good would it do me to hit you *after* you break the bottle?"

Lasorda took a lesson from this incident. Later, as a manager, he would rarely rip his players after a mistake. There was no need. He had screamed at them so much about it beforehand, they already felt bad enough. In the 1980s, when second baseman Steve Sax inexplicably had trouble throwing the ball to first base, people wondered why Lasorda wasn't more critical of him. It all went back to his father. "What good would it do to criticize Saxie after the bad throw?" Lasorda says. "We had to figure out a way to get him to not make that throw in the first place."

When Lasorda was given an award on Ellis Island in 2006, he honored his father. "I thank God every day that my father didn't miss that boat," Lasorda said. "Of course, if he had missed it, I would probably be addressing you today as Pope Thomas the Twenty-sixth."

Because they had no spare time or money to travel, Lasorda's parents never got to watch him play. Not in the Norristown parks, not in the small-town southern minor leagues, not even in the major leagues. That is one reason why Lasorda, when he managed a team, made an effort to learn the name of every child of every player. And that is why he insisted that each of the kids call him "Uncle Tommy." Lasorda loved and respected his parents, but they were like most other working-class parents of their generation: life was hard, and children went out and played on their own.

Lasorda never had anyone in the stands cheering just for him. When he played in the major leagues, he wished his parents could see their second-floor runt running around the diamond. He prayed for those moments. But his playing career didn't last long enough. It was over before they could ever catch a glimpse. So he spent his managerial career making sure nobody else had the same experience. He acted more like a great-uncle than a great manager.

Jay Howell, a Dodger reliever from the 1988 world championship team, was once asked why he never criticized Lasorda for what some perceived as his overuse of the bullpen. Howell smiled and said, "How can you rip someone who your kids call Uncle Tommy?"

This approach also helped Lasorda with the sportswriters. Whenever he was introduced to anyone in a writer's family, he would act as if he were standing amid royalty. "So you're the parents of the best baseball writer in America," he would say as the writer scuffed the floor and blushed. "So you're the ones who raised this guy to win a Pulitzer." He did this with every writer, and then hoped the writer would remember this act of kindness when, later, he felt compelled to criticize Lasorda. Quite often, the writer held back. How can you take to task someone who, in front of the people you love, had made you feel like the most important person in the world?

Lasorda has little patience with the parents of today. On the softball field in front of Lasorda on this Sunday afternoon, a dad in a golf shirt and Sansabelt shorts is screaming at his nervous daughter as she attempts to pitch. The dad is saying the strangest thing. "Relax!" he shouts, again and again, each inflection filled with more tension. Lasorda cringes.

"The worst thing about youth baseball today is the parents," he announces, as those parents who are nearby uncomfortably listen. "Parents mess it all up. They put too much pressure on the kids. They try to live their dreams through the kids. More than in any other sport, every parent thinks they know baseball, so they think they can coach the kid from the stands, and that's wrong."

When watching Emily, Lasorda practices what he teaches. He doesn't say anything about the game. He doesn't pay attention to the score. He cheers her as she walks to the plate, cheers her as she swings the bat, keeps cheering no matter what happens. "Why can't everyone just cheer these kids for showing up? They have the rest of their lives to be yelled at by some coach."

Imagine, a guy who once set a record for using foul language in public having mellowed enough to cheer a strikeout.

"What's so funny about that?" Lasorda asks. "You act different in your home than you do at your place of work, right? Everybody does."

For the record, Lasorda has never cursed around his wife. He never curses around children. He rarely curses during speeches or public appearances that involve women. But everywhere else — around his players, his bosses, his buddies — he talks like the Norristown street urchin he once was. Lasorda curses like Picasso once painted, applying the most colorful words with broad brushstrokes of his tongue, using a single invective as an adjective, adverb, verb, and noun, all in the same sentence.

"I curse a lot?" he says. "What the hell do you mean by that?"

His profanity is rarely insulting, mostly harmless, and often hilarious, the equivalent of beating his chest and marking his territory. He cursed at players because it was often the only language they understood. He cursed at umpires because, in the heat of outrage, it was the only language he himself understood.

Then there was the time he cursed at Paul Olden, a local radio personality. That's when he set the bleep record. It is probably the most famous public display of profanity in sports history, which is like comparing it to the best car in Detroit or the tallest corn in Iowa.

Typical of Lasorda, he refuses to show any regret for the answer he offered the Los Angeles radio reporter on the afternoon of May 14, 1978. But, also typical of Lasorda, he rationalizes it in a way that crazily makes sense.

"If you think about it, nobody really heard me cursing, because everything was bleeped out," he says. "So what's the big deal?"

The question was asked after the Chicago Cubs' Dave Kingman hit three home runs — including the game-tying and game-winning homers — to beat the Dodgers in fifteen innings. The tape recording of Lasorda's answer has been replayed more than the fuzzy first words of moonwalker Neil Armstrong. Even when written on paper, it still steams.

"What is your opinion of Kingman's performance?" asked Olden.

"What is my opinion of Kingman's performance?" replied Lasorda. "What the BLEEP do you think is my opinion of it? I think it was BLEEPING BLEEP. Put that in, I don't give a BLEEP. Opinion of his performance? BLEEP, he beat us with three BLEEPING home runs! What the BLEEP do you mean, what is my opinion of his performance? How could you ask me a question like that, what is my opinion of his performance? BLEEP, he hit three home runs! BLEEP. I'm BLEEPING pissed off to lose that BLEEPING game. And you ask me my opinion of his performance? BLEEP. That's a tough question to ask me, isn't it? What is my opinion of his performance?"

For the record, that's a dozen bleeps, in several tenses and many conjugations. It was a tirade whose effect lasted the rest of Lasorda's managerial career, painting him as something a tad different from the funny fat guy, painting him as a competitor who was as quick with an arrow as with an embrace.

He hated the idea that everyone heard him explode. But he loved the idea that everyone knew he was capable of it.

"And still, Jo has never heard me curse," he said of his wife. "I mean, she heard the thing on the radio, but like I said, it was all bleeps."

Few may remember that another side of Lasorda was also revealed that day, after the tirade, when he asked Olden whether it was a tough question.

"Yes, it is," Olden said. "And you gave me an answer . . ."

"Well, I didn't give you a good answer, because I'm mad," Lasorda said.

In his own way, as quickly as he blew up, he was apologizing. That is how he always worked, with players as well as the media. He would scream at a player in the dugout, then hug him in his office after the game. Break them down and build them up. Show them how much he cared about winning, then show them how much he cared about them. Some of his players played hard because they wanted to avoid the scoldings. Others played hard because they couldn't wait for the hugs. Either way, they played.

On this fall day, in the fall of his life, the stakes are different. His granddaughter Emily's team scores two runs on a grounder that goes through two little sets of legs and rolls around the empty, crushed juice boxes in the right-field corner.

Immediately, five different parents scribble in their scoring books. Two of them shout, "OK, that's two to nothing."

Lasorda sighs again. "They shouldn't even keep score in Little League. I know you have to have a winner and loser, but why do you need a score? Why can't they just play? Nobody learns to appreciate the game anymore."

Yes, hearing Lasorda talk about the meaninglessness of a final score seems as likely as hearing him expound on the virtues of tofu.

But at the beginning of his life, it really wasn't about the score. It wasn't even about the game. It was about getting dressed for the game.

Start with the glove. When Lasorda was ten, he received his first glove, but it wasn't a gift. He stole it. It happened during a semi-pro game between the Moose Lodge and the Italian Club on a weed-choked field in Norristown.

During the game, the players broke into a brawl. Watching with friends from behind the backstop, Lasorda knew that this was their chance. When ballplayers fight, they drop their gloves. And when gloves are lying on the ground, well, why not take one?

The Moose and the Italians began throwing punches and chasing each other around the diamond. Lasorda hopped a fence, slipped through the melee, grabbed the first glove he saw, tucked it under his arm like a football, and ran the entire five miles home.

It wasn't until he arrived at his house that he made an interesting discovery: it was a right-handed glove. He was left-handed. What the hell, he would use it anyway.

The glove had a name written on it in primitive block letters: "Joe Burns." That was the name of the team's third baseman. While to-day's kids grow up with Rawlings or Nike, Lasorda grew up with Joe Burns.

Years later, somebody with the name "Joe Burns" stenciled above his shirt pocket was delivering beer to Tommy's brother Joe's res-taurant in Norristown. Lasorda happened to be there visiting, sampling what was cooking on the stove. He recognized the name on the pocket. He got chills. "Hey," he said to the beer man, "you're the guy whose glove I stole!"

Lasorda, being a local celebrity and former major leaguer, figured Joe Burns would gladly shake his hand. Instead Burns shook his fist.

"You son of a bitch," he shouted. "I was never the same without that glove."

Lasorda thought about it for a second. "Well, at least you didn't have to wear it on the wrong hand," he said.

This may explain why, at the height of his managerial career, Lasorda had tailors lined up outside the clubhouse to give him free suits. Clothiers all over the country would wait for the Dodgers to come to town so they could fit him with a freebie. Lasorda not only never apologized for this, he bragged about it, and people never understood.

Hear the glove story and understand. He wasn't being arrogant about his power. He was being thankful for his luck. You grow up wearing a stolen baseball glove on the wrong hand, then one day somebody wants to measure you for a free suit? God bless Tommy Lasorda's America.

Lasorda is constantly amazed by the strange truth that the more money you make, the more people want to give you things for free. Restaurant owners offer him free meals simply to sit at their tables.

America the beautiful indeed.

After stealing a glove, Lasorda soon figured out a way to steal some balls.

It was a summer night outside the town prison on Marshall Street. Lasorda and his friends gathered on a hill overlooking the maze of barred windows. It was not just any hill; it was the town cemetery. And it was not just any prison; inmates were allowed to play pickup baseball in the yard.

Lasorda and his gang came here to lean against the headstones and watch a little baseball and hope for a little luck. Down on the field, the real Murderers' Row played baseball, swinging from the ankles, swinging for the fences . . . And here it came, a long home run, hit out of the prison yard and sailing toward the cemetery. This was the moment Lasorda and his friends had waited for. The ball soared through the black sky and landed in a patch of flowers and bounced against a headstone and disappeared into the quiet. At which point Lasorda and his friends sprinted after it, hurdling Here Lies Uncle Ed, sprinting past Our Beloved Grandmother, dodging all the ghosts and grabbing the ball.

It was a lousy ball. It looked like it had been stitched in, well, the license-plate factory. Sagging leather, busted seams, broken bits of things that once were young and strong. The ball was sort of like the boys who chased it. But they didn't care. They wrapped it in black tape and tossed it in a bag and went back to wait for another one.

"You know what the best thing about them balls was?" Lasorda asks. "None of the prisoners ever came out to ask for them back."

Lasorda now had balls and a glove, but his young career was still missing another important piece. He had spent his elementary school years playing in old sneakers or work boots, which were fine as long as he didn't have to run. When he became a freshman at Rittenhouse High, his coach pulled him aside and told him that his game had a potentially fatal flaw: the shoes. He needed spikes. So Lasorda rushed home to his father. "I need spikes because I made the varsity team," he told him. And his father replied, "What's a varsity team?"

Sabatino Lasorda said no. He said he could not spend any portion of the family savings on the shoes. Tommy was furious. He screamed. He pounded his fist on the table. He went up to his tiny bedroom and cried. The next morning on the kitchen table Tommy saw a shoebox. In that box, with odd yellow laces and a giant leather tongue, were the spikes.

Lasorda was so excited he immediately tried them on. They were so big they swallowed his toes, his foot, and his ankle. They were the world's first high-tops. "Pop!" he wailed. "My feet swim in these things!"

His father shrugged. "The way your feet are growing, I'm not gonna buy you a new pair of shoes every year."

Thus it happened that the most media-savvy manager in baseball history had his first experience with newspapers when he had to stuff them in the toes of those spikes.

The last things Lasorda needed for his first baseball outfit were bats. They weren't going to come from a brawl or a prison yard, and his father certainly wasn't buying any wood that he couldn't burn. So Lasorda had to appeal to a higher power. He found the smartest kid on his neighborhood team—the kid who could read—and dictated a letter. It was a letter to the only person whom Lasorda could not sway with bluster or bravado, the only person who could truly motivate the motivator.

"Dear God," the letter read, "can you please send us $100 to buy some bats?" Lasorda's friend wrote "God" on the envelope and dropped the letter in a mailbox. The letter worked its way through the postal system and arrived on the desk of one of Pennsylvania's postmasters. Apparently feeling sorry for these poor batless creatures, he sent Lasorda a check for $20. Everyone was happy—except, of course, Lasorda. While the other kids on the team celebrated, he dictated another letter. "Dear God," this one read, "thanks for the money, but you should know, somebody in the post office stole $80 from you."

In the end, it took a divine act to make Lasorda look like a ballplayer. But he didn't care. He took the field with his glove on the wrong hand, with the wrong shoes flapping on his feet, with his address on the wrong side of town, and with baseballs he called "jailbirds." And look what happened.

"I showed 'em, didn't I?" he says today. "Didn't I?"

He says it twice, for emphasis, perhaps because he wonders why America doesn't show him more in return. He paid a high price for success—why won't anyone else? He was made in America, blessed by America, but today he's somewhat irritated by America. He bristles at America's lack of politeness, its indifference to loyalty, its increasing refusal to show gratitude.

All these kids rushing up to him for autographs here at the softball game—do they have any idea how lucky they are to have baseballs that weren't picked out of a graveyard? Do they know how lucky they are that their parents drove them here, and will cheer for them, and then will stand behind them while they get Lasorda's autograph?

Lasorda hates this, not only in kid ballplayers, but in real ballplayers, baseball's free agents who change teams for the money. When third baseman Adrian Beltre left the Los Angeles Dodgers after the 2004 season to sign for big money with the Seattle Mariners, Lasorda turned his back on him. Even though the move was legal. Even though the move was best for Beltre's family. Lasorda didn't care.

Lasorda can only remember how he brought Beltre to the big leagues, during his brief stint as a general manager in 1998. He can only remember how he backed Beltre in his early struggles, how he ripped critics who called for a trade, how he vowed that one day Beltre would be a star. Then, in 2004, Beltre did become a star, hitting 48 homers with 121 RBIs, and what happened? He immediately left town for Seattle.

No matter that Beltre's agent, Scott Boras, had difficulty just getting the Dodgers to return his calls. The way Lasorda figured it, Beltre should have stayed, accepted less money. And unlike all the politically correct Dodger spokesmen, Lasorda expressed his true feelings to everyone. "How could he leave us after all we did for him, I will never understand it," he said. "Where is the loyalty to the organization where you were raised? Where is the commitment?" Lasorda thought, "If I could work for nearly twenty consecutive one-year contracts, turning down several managerial offers to remain with the Dodgers out of loyalty, why couldn't Beltre do the same?"

Lasorda didn't think Beltre showed enough gratitude. He still doesn't think so. Although fans accept the fact that their favorite player will one day become another city's favorite player, Lasorda refuses to buy it. This is why, as a manager, he was rarely involved in player negotiations. This is why, throughout his life, the Dodgers have used him in nearly every capacity except those involving money. Lasorda is about loyalty, not money, and while that is a wonderful quality, it has little connection to baseball reality, which mandates that players follow the dollar signs as much as the steal signs. If he had negotiated with loyalty instead of guaranteed money, Lasorda would have run off the very players he was trying to keep.

His ideas about gratitude still work well in the real world. He has an actual rule about gratitude. It shows up today at the softball game, after a brave child walks over to Lasorda as he sits in the bleachers watching his granddaughter play second base. The child holds out one dusty ball, found in the dugout, and one bank pen from a mother's purse. "Mr. Lasorda," the child asks, "can I have your . . ."

And here it comes. Lasorda, as he always does, cuts off the child in midsentence with a question of his own.

"What do you say?" Lasorda says. "You want my autograph, what do you say?"

Only when the child says "please" does Lasorda sign the ball, setting off a stampede of children who have been cowering behind the bleachers. The line of autograph seekers blocks Lasorda's view of Emily even more than the large umpire did.

Yes, to Lasorda, the only p-word in the English language more important than "pasta" is "please." He will refuse a child, scold an adult, walk away from a crowd if people are not saying please.

"It's just the way I was brought up," he says. "Whenever an adult walked into the room, one of us kids had to get up so he could sit down. If I didn't tip my hat when I passed a church, my dad knocked it off."

So, then, does Lasorda always say please? It depends. When he is hurrying to order in a restaurant, he may forget. When he is asking his granddaughter to fetch him a Gatorade bottle, he always remembers.

Lasorda continues signing autographs for the children, their parents, and their grandparents, generations of fans bonded by one touchstone.

"I remember you in '88 . . . I remember you at the All-Star Game . . . I remember you doing Slim-Fast commercials."

Lasorda's face goes pale. "Slim-Fast commercials?" he shouts. "I don't do those anymore. I couldn't do those anymore. That diet had one problem—you couldn't eat! What good is a diet if you can't eat!"

Actually, Lasorda could eat while promoting the Slim-Fast diet drink back in 1988, and he did eat, one big meal a day with a couple of shakes. The problem, which he is loath to admit, is that the product sometimes sent him running to the toilet *after* he ate. So, yeah, between bathroom breaks he lost the weight. But the minute he hit his goal, he threw the stuff in the garbage, vowing never to drink it again.

To Lasorda, all is fair in love and war and sales. In front of him now, the game is ending and the girls are lining up to shake each other's tiny hands and Lasorda shakes his head again. This show of manners among combatants is almost as bad as the lack of manners among autograph seekers.

"I hate shaking hands with the opponent after a baseball game," Lasorda grumbles. "When the Dodgers did it against the Cardinals after the playoffs, I hated it. I would never do it. If I'm playing some team and I'm trying to knock them down and then we have to hug? No way."

What about sportsmanship? somebody wonders.

"It ain't about sportsmanship," he says. "It's about life."

And for Lasorda, from the beginning, life was one big punch. He began his career not shaking hands but swinging fists. He blames this on his four brothers. Isn't fighting always blamed on sibling rivalry? Lasorda once wanted a second helping of two-day-old bread. Bam! One cold night he wanted to sleep in the warmest spot in the house, the kitchen floor, near the stove. Bam!

"When you have to fight four brothers for everything, fighting with the rest of the world ain't so bad," Lasorda says.

Once he and his brothers pounded each other while standing in line for the bathroom. At the dinner table they fought over who would eat the first potato. It became so bad at home, Lasorda went to school one morning and began punching the first kid he spotted in the playground. When the kid asked why, Lasorda said, "Chances are, I'll be getting into a real fight in a couple of days, and I didn't want to be out of practice."

Lasorda was pretty good at dodging right-hand jabs. The left hook, however, gave him problems. He discovered this from his mother. Once he arrived home late from a movie in Philadelphia.

His mother asked him why he wasn't on time. He said the train ran out of gas. It took his mother all of five seconds to grab an iron with her left hand and fling it at him. The iron hit him in the side, pressed and starched him good. As with all important things in life, Lasorda's best fighting lessons came from home.

When he was fifteen, he engaged in his first fight for a team. That team was the Valley Forge Hotel. His position was starting bellhop. One night, three drunks began ridiculing his blue and gold suit. "Fighting for my hotel is like fighting for my country!" he screamed, and then he punched out two of the drunks and looked for more.

But the third drunk had a bandaged hand. He looked at Lasorda and said, "You wouldn't hit a cripple, would you?" Lasorda stood there for a second and thought, "Why not?" And he pounded him, too.

Though he hasn't punched anything tougher than a voting ballot in years, Lasorda looks at the world from behind two fists.

"Damn, I could fight him right now," Lasorda says when discussing one longtime enemy, an ESPN commentator named Skip Bayless. "You get me and him in a dark alley, only one of us is coming out, and it ain't him."

He loves to clench his arthritic left hand, on which he wears his giant Hall of Fame ring. He loves to pretend to be punching someone —an impolite fan, a bad driver in the next lane, anyone. "Boom!" he says of Bayless. "I'd get him right there under the chin."

One minute he is Rocky Marciano; the next minute, when Emily makes a lunging stop at second base in the softball game on this fall Sunday, he is Mary Poppins.

"Look at that! Look at that!" he shouts, kindly now. "Look at what happened! Isn't that something?"

He could say the same thing about the paradox that is his moods, going from fighting to fawning in the time it takes a little girl to catch a grounder. From his old fears to his new joy. From his past to his present.

When he cheers, it gives the nearby moms an opening to scoot next to him and compliment him on his granddaughter and chat.

"You want a scone?" asks one.

"Why not?" says Lasorda.

For the rest of the afternoon, he talks with the women about their kids, their food, their Dodger memories. By the time the afternoon ends, none of them knows the score, none of them has been following the action, but hanging out with Lasorda has made many of them feel that they've touched the heart of the game.

"He's something, isn't he?" asks one mom after rubbing Lasorda's shoulders.

When she leaves, Lasorda grins and points in her direction. "How old do you think she is? She claims she's forty. Man, what are they doing with forty-year-olds today!"

His love of mothers also comes from his love of his own mother. Carmella Lasorda was the perfect woman to raise this imperfect man. She always had something cooking on the stove, she always asked about Lasorda's games, and she was always there for a hug after Sabatino pulled off the belt.

In dealing with Emily, Lasorda is more like his mother than his father. He lets someone else be the tough guy. He wants the hugs. After hugging and kissing Emily, then directing her to some leftover bundt cake, Lasorda smiles.

"You wanna fix Little League baseball?" he asks.

His eyes narrow. He points a bony finger toward first base, where a middle-aged woman is consoling a teary-eyed third baseman. He points it toward the dugout, where a younger woman is kneeling in front of three giggling girls as they take turns painstakingly but properly gripping a bat.

"You wanna fix Little League baseball, let the moms coach."

2

. . .

I GAMBLED FOR THIS

Heads up!"

The football sails through an elegant living room into a mirrored foyer, pigskin flying past a Picasso knockoff, landing in a thump on the marble floor. Welcome to Las Vegas. Sin City. It is 10 A.M. on a November Sunday morning in an ornate two-bedroom suite on the top floor of the Venetian Hotel.

An old man is playing football in his checkered pajamas.

"What's wrong?" says a barefoot, bed-headed Tommy Lasorda. "It's Sunday. It's football day. Why can't I play football?"

The shiny floor is littered with wet towels. Rolling along a wood-carved back wall are a couple of ripe melons. Lasorda has an amazing ability to turn even a celebrity suite into his personal locker room. He picks up the football, spins it to show an autograph. It is an autograph not *from* Lasorda, but *to* Lasorda. It is from the Colorado State football team, the Rams. He stopped in Fort Collins on Saturday on his way to Las Vegas and spoke to the team. The players thanked him and gave him the autographed ball.

"You know why? You know why I was thanked?" he shouts, dodging a defensive line of throw pillows.

One can make a good guess. Anytime football and speeches are involved, Lasorda claims that his words are magic. He claims that, upon hearing those words, an Everyman becomes a Heisman. He is especially proud of his numerous speeches at the service academies, where he swears that he can turn a stiff plebe into a smooth player. So the guess here is that Colorado State um, er, won?

"You don't believe me, look it up!" Lasorda shouts. "I talked to them about heart! I talked to them about being blessed to be able to compete in this wonderful free country, nothing to stop them from success. If I could do it, so could they."

Someone laughs. Lasorda glares. He has an innate sense of distinguishing between when you are laughing *at* him and when you are laughing *with* him, and right now someone is laughing *at* him, and he's not thrilled. He bangs his fist on a coffee table, jostling a huge glass containing malted milk balls.

"You think I'm kidding?" He sends a chunk of the chocolate candy flying from the corner of his mouth. "Look it up! I'm telling you, they won!"

Las Vegas and Lasorda. Slot machines and a guy whose laugh sounds like the jingling of coins. Huge buffets and a guy who lives for them. You would think this city and Lasorda are a perfect match, but you would be wrong.

For instance, one of baseball's greatest gamblers doesn't gamble. He would always bet the Dodger fortunes, but never his own, because, well, the Dodgers could afford it. As a minor league manager, he once called for eleven suicide-squeeze bunts in a sixty-six-game season. Some teams didn't call one all summer. In makeshift minor league ballparks with lots of space behind home plate, he would also sometimes send a runner home from third on a foul pop-up. As a major league coach, Lasorda frequently attempted to score runners from second base on singles to left field. As a manager, he would start his runners so much, their necks grew sore from craning to see into the dugout. He was so aggressive, he once sent one of his slowest players, Joe Ferguson, from third base to home on a fly ball to a left fielder with one of the league's best arms, Ken Singleton. With a stadium full of fans in full groan, the throw hit a pebble and bounced over the head of the catcher and the plodding Ferguson scored. "When you force the action, you force things to happen, and you never know what will happen," says Lasorda.

Except when it comes to Las Vegas and gambling. Here Lasorda is positive about what will happen, so he does not bet.

"I work too hard for my money. I ain't just gonna give it away."

He works hard for his money, and even harder to keep his money. Lasorda may be baseball's only millionaire Hall of Famer who does not own a credit card. Not one.

"What do I need a credit card for?" he asks. "I'm lucky enough that if I need something big, somebody will buy it for me or give it to me."

For everything else, Lasorda uses cash. But he may also be baseball's only millionaire Hall of Famer who does not own a debit card. He has never used an ATM.

"I have no idea how to use one of those cards," he says. "And if I had one, my wife is afraid I'll lose it."

This is because three times in the past three years, Lasorda has lost his money clip, including his driver's license. Because he meets so many people, he is forever digging into his pocket for Dodger business cards or Hall of Fame business cards or a phony prayer card that features his face on the kneeling, hooded figure of Saint Thomas Aquinas. When he pulls out the cards, he sometimes pulls out the clip and drops it on the floor. And if he chooses that moment to start a story, the clip will lie there until somebody picks it up.

"Yeah, losing the driver's license is bad, but it doesn't stop me from driving," he says. "Any time I get stopped, it's usually by a policeman looking for an autograph. Anybody else, they don't need to see my license. They know who I am."

It's a startling thing to realize that, perhaps alone among sports celebrities, Lasorda's face is his ID card. Even in these times of heightened security, he is never searched and never questioned. Part of the reason is that, for more than thirty years, neither his face nor his voice nor his figure has ever really changed. He has had no plastic surgery. He has never gone on a diet that lasted more than a few months. He is like a walking Mount Rushmore, known by senior citizens as the loudmouth manager, known by kids as the home-spun salesman—known, it seems, by virtually everybody. Longtime companions cannot recall one public moment when Lasorda wasn't recognized. So who needs official identification? And because he doesn't have that, why would he ever get a credit card?

Tommy Lasorda has a simple idea for his banking needs. He goes to Jo. Every day his wife divides a stack of bills into different denom-inations and lays them out in a box like Monopoly money. Lasorda picks out what he wants and stuffs it into his pocket. And, of course, rarely does that pocket open.

"Hey, I buy meals now and then," Lasorda says.

When?

"Lemme think about that."

For Lasorda, it's somewhat of an appreciation of his past. It is a characteristic of his generation to be frugal. But Lasorda pinches it one penny further. He cannot forget those days when he broke into baseball using a stolen glove and stolen balls and shoes stuffed with newspaper. He cannot forget stepping onto a high school diamond feeling like you have to earn every pitch. He cannot bear to think of losing it all—or, worse yet, spending it all.

"Can you imagine a Hall of Famer who couldn't even play for his high school team?" Lasorda asks.

He's talking about the Tommy Lasorda of Norristown High in the mid-1940s. He wasn't his school's star pitcher. He wasn't one of its top two pitchers. He says his coach didn't like him. He says the other players didn't respect him. He was just another poor fool with a trick pitch and a mill future. His parents never attended any high school games. Sometimes his brothers didn't talk to him. So, he says, he motivated himself.

"One day I grabbed the coach, Harvey Fishburne. Then I grabbed two of the guys who played in front of me, Buddy Rider and Red Henning. I grab these three guys by our high school field and I tell them, 'You three guys are gonna buy a ticket to see me play.' And they all laugh, ha ha, real funny."

Lasorda is not laughing.

"Now it's ten years later, and I'm on the Dodgers, and we're playing in Philadelphia, and I hear two guys yelling at me from the bleachers."

Guess who? Yep, Buddy Rider and Red Henning.

"And then there was another guy yelling at me from above the dugout."

Naturally, Lasorda claims the guy was Harvey Fishburne.

Lasorda is famous for remembering the names and faces of everyone who ever snubbed him. He is famous for issuing constant reminders, sometimes years later, to those who never believed in him.

"All three guys yelling at me and waving at me and you know what I did?" Lasorda recalls. "I just grab the Brooklyn name on my shirt and pop it out at them, pop, pop, pop. That's all I had to do. They knew, and I knew."

What are the odds that all three childhood villains could have been in the same stadium for the same game during Lasorda's short stint with the Brooklyn Dodgers? In the revenge ride that screams through Tommy's World, anything is possible.

Buster Maynard, the New York Giants outfielder, is another guy who will live forever on this ride. Like most of the villains of Lasorda's past, you've probably never heard of him, but Lasorda will never forget him.

While attending a Phillies game against the New York Giants, a teenage Lasorda was standing outside the locker room scrounging for autographs. A Giants outfielder approached him. Lasorda made his request. The guy brushed past him, nearly knocking him over, refusing to sign.

Lasorda checked his program and confirmed that the guy's name was Buster Maynard.

"I committed that name to memory," Lasorda says.

Five years later, Lasorda was pitching in the minor leagues in Greenville, South Carolina, and who came up to the plate? A recently demoted Buster Maynard.

"I heard the name and I knew right away," Lasorda remembers.

You know what happens next. Even if you have known Lasorda for only ten minutes, you know what happens next.

First pitch, a fastball to the head. Maynard ducks. Second pitch, a fastball to the head. Maynard ducks. The old guy starts screaming at the young pitcher, who challenges him to come to the mound, so the old guy charges, and the kid stiffens, and they engage in a fist-fight that lands them both out of the game.

Afterward, Maynard sought out Lasorda.

"Who are you, and why do you hate me?" he asked.

"You were an asshole to me when I was a kid, and I never forgot it."

Today Lasorda gives that same speech to minor leaguers, warning them to be nice to everyone on their way up, because they don't want anyone knocking them on their ass on their way down. Revenge and respect are both a huge part of his game. They carried him from the start of his career, pushed him to his first World Series win in 1981, then crowned him in his defining moment in the 1988 postseason. That's when he won his final world championship, with a mediocre team, whipping two of baseball's greatest regular-season teams with several of baseball's greatest postseason speeches.

On this Sunday in Las Vegas, in the celebrity suite of the Venetian Hotel, Lasorda claims those kinds of words still work, because Colorado State won the previous night, whether anybody in the room believes him or not. So somebody rummages through a pile of chocolate-stained newspapers on a couch and looks for the score. And yeah, the previous night, in a football stadium down the street, Colorado State came back from a ten-point, third-quarter deficit to beat the University of Nevada, Las Vegas. And the Rams didn't just beat the UNLV Runnin' Rebels, they beat them on a 75-yard *punt return*. The final score was 31–27. And there it is, that same score, written in black marker all over the football that this pajama-clad man is tossing up and down.

"Welcome to Las Vegas," Lasorda shouts. "This is a heckuva town. We're going to have a heckuva day!"

Las Vegas indeed. What happens here stays here, right? Well, yes, except for those free hotel mints that Lasorda is shoveling into a plastic bag as he plops down on the couch and turns on the television and begins a day of football, food, and fist-waving.

There is a knock at the suite door. It is room service. Time for a midmorning snack. Piles of bagels and fruit and sweet rolls, giant pitchers of juice and water, all for three people.

"Why didn't anyone give me this free stuff when I didn't have any money?" Lasorda asks. "In this life, the only people who get free stuff are the ones who don't need it."

He still talks about the first time he made real money, working on the railroad during the summers he struggled on the high school baseball team. He was so desperate for the cash, he lied about his age. The lie was easy. The reason it was easy was sad. Lasorda used the birth certificate of another Tom Lasorda, his older brother who died of a respiratory illness when he was eighteen months old. After the infant died, the parents simply saved the first name for their next boy.

"So it was really a foolproof plan," Lasorda says.

Until about sixty years later, when Lasorda showed up at the Department of Motor Vehicles to renew his driver's license. Officials there told him that the age he listed on his application was not his real age. Somewhere in the depths of their files, it turns out, his brother's birthday was still listed.

"So here I am, standing there arguing with them about how I know my own birthday," Lasorda says. "But then, when they mention my brother's birthday, I'm like, oh yeah. I explained it to them that, back then, I had to do anything I could to survive."

He is surviving quite well at the moment, the mounds of breakfast food sitting in the middle of his suite. Lasorda stands up and inspects the plates as if peering into his wallet, appraising the value in every corner, handling and staring and shaking his head.

"It's all great except the water," he says. "Too much water. I don't want to waste the water."

So Lasorda, in a move surely never before seen by a room-service waiter, sends back the water.

"Maybe somebody else can use it," he says to the guy in the light brown suit.

It is a common thing in Lasorda's life, this generational, yet seemingly irrational, fear of waste, even of the most plentiful things. He is afraid he will end up the way he started, with nothing. So he doesn't throw anything away. He wraps everything up.

"I save everything, because you never know. What if one day I need it?"

It only figures that Lasorda's favorite food is hot dogs. When he was growing up, his mother used to cook a pot of hot dogs every Saturday night. In the Lasorda home, that qualified as their weekly gourmet meal. It was Tommy's job to run to the bakery and pick up day-old buns for the dogs, and though they were often stale, they never went uneaten.

One night while his mother was cooking his favorite dinner, a friend asked Lasorda if he wanted to go for a drive. On reaching his friend's house, Lasorda was told that they would be riding in a stolen car.

Lasorda thought about it for a moment. If he hung out with his friends, he would be breaking the law, but at least he would be considered cool. If he returned home, he would be labeled a chicken, but at least he could eat hot dogs.

"So I went home," Lasorda says.

The next day, he discovered that his friends had been caught and arrested, and to this day he believes his life had been saved by his love of hot dogs.

"Kind of makes you a little sentimental, don't it?" Lasorda says.

Lasorda's aversion to waste began with food but eventually spilled over onto the baseball field. He worked his starting pitchers to the point of exhaustion because he didn't want to waste pitching. Why bring in a reliever when the starter had twenty pitches left in that arm? He was tough, so why couldn't his pitchers be tough? He was hungry, so why couldn't they be hungry? Two greats, Fernando Valenzuela and Orel Hershiser, developed arm trouble while pitching for him, but they also earned World Series rings. It was a tradeoff both of them would have made again, and Lasorda knew it.

"Today," Lasorda says, "the pitchers are babied. They've lost their toughness. Their arms can handle it, but their heads can't."

On the Brooklyn Dodgers' 1955 world championship team, of which Lasorda was briefly a part, the pitching staff combined played forty-six complete games. On the 2006 Los Angeles Dodgers, the pitching staff combined for one complete game. Lasorda often talks about the time he pitched nineteen innings in one day. He wonders why others can barely pitch one-third that amount.

"I ask you, have our bodies changed all that much? You telling me Don Newcombe [seventeen complete games] had a lot more muscle in his arm than Brad Penny [no complete games]?"

One summer afternoon during the 2006 season, Lasorda spotted Penny in the Dodger clubhouse and began scolding him. Penny, who is six foot four and weighs about 250 pounds, was in his underwear. Lasorda was wearing a suit. But the way they talked, they both could have been in uniform on a mound. Just because the field has left Lasorda, doesn't mean he will ever leave the field.

"Hey, Penny, what's wrong with you? Why can't you last more than five innings? What happens to you out there?" Lasorda shouted. "You couldn't have pitched for me."

"Different era," Penny replied softly.

"Different era my ass! Same game. Same field. Same arms. What's different is your toughness. You guys aren't tough enough."

Lasorda's relationship with Penny is similar to his relationship with many current Dodgers. He acts not only as their loving grandfather but as their crotchety conscience. He can say things to players that a manager would never dare say. He can ask them questions that only the players have ever dared ask themselves.

Most of those questions are, as with Penny, about toughness. If a starting pitcher leaves a game in the fifth inning on consecutive starts, he can expect to see the old guy strolling past his locker with a sweet hug and stinging hyperbole.

Penny spent a year listening to Lasorda, then showed up at the start of the 2007 season as a reborn pitcher determined to work as many innings as possible, to show that toughness. Listening to his quotes early that season — "I have to keep my bullpen rested. I have to carry my team as far as I can" — was like listening to Lasorda himself.

"You think so?" Lasorda says, smiling.

Lasorda claims that the decrease in innings played by starters and relievers is directly related to the increase in the power of agents. "Agents want more money for all their pitchers, which means they have to divide up the innings, so they push to get their starters out of games earlier and make sure their relievers don't pitch too much." The lighter the workload, the more the players like it.

Tim Belcher, a gritty Dodger right-hander, once pitched nine innings on opening day. The next day, Belcher's agent called Lasorda to complain.

"I wish you were telling me this to my face," Lasorda said.

"Why?" said the agent.

"So I could drop you like a bad habit."

Once, when Lasorda was playing for the Kansas City Athletics, a trainer asked him why he never had his pitching arm rubbed down.

"Can you rub a win into it?" Lasorda asked him. "If not, then leave it alone."

Bam! There is a loud noise from the Venetian suite's plasma TV. Lasorda has bounced the football off the screen. Now he is yelling at it.

"Look at that!" He is pointing to a game between the Indianapolis Colts and the Miami Dolphins. "I mean, look at that!"

The funny thing is, he's looking at nothing. The play has ended, the players are back in a huddle, and Lasorda is screaming at the TV.

"This is why football doesn't deserve to be called the country's most popular game," he says. "Look at all that time between plays. Get a stopwatch and time how long between the end of the play and the next hike. Get a stopwatch. Do it!"

He is being rhetorical, but his assistant can never be sure, so he immediately rummages around the suite for a stopwatch.

"Football is also worse because only a certain kind of guy can play football. He has to be huge, just like in basketball, not a normal person. Baseball is the best sport because it is all about normal-size people."

Baseball is about normal people indeed. Look at the guy who is talking, the Hall of Famer who couldn't get off the bench on his high school team. Lasorda was forced to find another way to get noticed, so he talked his way onto a *Norristown Times Herald* recreation league team. It was a glorified neighborhood crew that fielded only the best players. Lasorda didn't have to be nice to a teacher or a coach; he could just play. The third-string high schooler became one of the star pitchers, but the kids went mostly unnoticed.

One day they figured out a way to make somebody watch. They were scheduled to play against the rich, savvy, well-equipped Connie Mack All-Stars. The cool kids. The best kids. Lasorda thought this would be his big chance. If he could impress the Connie Mack folks, he might be picked for their traveling team. Then he could show his curveball to the world.

The night before the big test, he slept on his cold second-floor bed with a blanket wrapped around his throwing arm. He beat the All-Stars, 4–1. It was enough to impress their coaches, who invited him to an official Connie Mack tryout.

"It was the answer to my dreams," Lasorda says. "Problem was, I didn't have an answer for how in the hell I was going to get there."

The tryout was to be held on a field forty-five miles from his house. His father was working. His mother didn't have a car. The only available method of transportation was a laundry truck that had finished the day's deliveries. The only licensed driver was a neighborhood coach who had never before driven a laundry truck.

Lasorda climbed in the back with some scattered smelly clothes. The coach got into the front with sweaty hands. For the next hour, as the truck careered down a potholed highway, Lasorda bounced around as if in a dryer.

Suddenly he heard sirens and knew the truck was being pulled over. He heard a police radio. Someone opened the back, and Lasorda saw the coach and two policemen staring at him.

"This boy has one chance at a baseball future, and that chance is right now," said the coach. "Please, Officer, if you let us go to the tryout, I'll drive this directly to jail."

The cops relented. By the time the truck pulled up at the field and Lasorda hopped out, he felt so queasy he threw his first three pitches over the catcher's head. But he struck out the next batter. And the next. And the next. And the three after that. The streak of six consecutive strikeouts was not just a sign of Lasorda's immediate future;

it would also become a metaphor for his life. Just when he's down, whether it be at the disillusioning end of his pro playing career, the controversial end of his scouting days, or the near-deadly end of his managing days, he seems to find a way to strike out those next six hitters.

"I get that from my dad," he says. "I always have."

Sabatino Lasorda and his son never played catch. Sabatino Lasorda never knew how to say "catch" in English. Sabatino Lasorda didn't teach his son to be a ballplayer, but he taught him to be a man.

"I still hear him in my voice today."

It was Lasorda's father who showed him how a poor man could survive with a good story. Sabatino would spend hours preaching to his young neighbors at a local social club.

"I remember him sitting in the middle of a big group, talking in broken English, making everyone laugh and cry and think, just because he told a good story," Lasorda says. "You look at me today, I'm my father."

Besides the beatings, Lasorda's father also stoked him with inspiration, which Lasorda would later instill in his teams.

"My father said it doesn't cost you a nickel to be nice, it doesn't cost you anything to smile," he says. "That's me, and that's what I tried to pass along to everyone else."

Lasorda's father also talked about having the right foundation, a speech that Lasorda would repeat word for word to his struggling teams.

"My father would say that if you build a house and the foundation is off, everything you put on it will be off," Lasorda remembers. "That foundation has to be love and respect. If you have love and respect, you have the foundation of life."

And every time Lasorda talks about being the luckiest man in the world, well, that also comes from his father, who said it every day despite living at the poverty line.

"He said he was lucky because when he came from Italy, he had nothing, and now he had a wife and five sons and a car, and who could ask for more?"

Lasorda began his baseball career in much the same way. All he had were the six hitters he'd retired when he tried out for the Connie Mack team. Those hitters led to a brief Connie Mack career, which led, in 1945, to a visit from a Philadelphia Phillies scout named Jocko Collins. It was wartime and the teams were desperate for players—otherwise Collins would not have shown up. If Lasorda hadn't had his trick pitch working on the one day that Collins scouted him in Baltimore, maybe none of this would have happened.

"What's the difference?" Lasorda says. "The thing is, it happened."

Collins offered him a $100 signing bonus. But Lasorda made him wait. He spent most of the evening mulling it over with his parents before taking the money and signing the contract. Collins was relieved. Lasorda remembers that night not for getting his first real job, but for using his first psychological ploy.

"It's like I told Collins later," Lasorda says. "I said, 'If you had just held out a little longer, I'd have paid *you.*'"

At the ornate doorway of the Venetian suite, the waiter in the light brown suit is waiting for Lasorda to acknowledge receiving the complimentary snacks.

He says his name is Ken and he is from Vietnam. He says he came to the United States on a boat. He says that when he arrived, one of the few Americans whose photograph he recognized was Tommy Lasorda. That would explain why his hands are shaking.

"Here, add twenty percent on top of the charge, for your tip," Lasorda says. Then he reaches into a manila envelope that rarely leaves his side. "And take this autographed picture—under one condition."

"Anything for you. Anything!" the waiter says.

"Don't go putting it in a cheap frame."

Lasorda was a $100 bonus baby for the Philadelphia Phillies, on his way to Delaware for spring training in 1945. He spent that first spring following around the great Jimmy Foxx. He never talked to him, he just watched him. He watched Foxx take extra practice. He watched him spend extra time with reporters. He became pretty good at watching, which was a good thing, because his first manager said Lasorda would never do anything else.

The manager's name was Pappy Lehman, and the team was Class D, in Concord, North Carolina, the lowest Phillies farm club. Lehman immediately told Lasorda that his ability was "limited."

"When all those guys come out of the service, you won't be playing professional baseball anymore."

Imagine being told you are one of the worst players on a low-level team during the least talented time in baseball history. Lasorda took the news with a shrug. It is the same shrug with which he would deliver similar news to countless players over the next half century. For him, criticism was so common, it was nothing more than a challenge, whether receiving it or delivering it.

"Well, then, let me play as much as I can before those guys get back," Lasorda said.

Oh, he played all right, as only Lasorda could play. In his first pro game, against a team from Landis, North Carolina, Lasorda threw what he thought was a perfect curveball that was hit on the ground for an easy final out. Except his shortstop watched the ball skip through his legs and into left field, allowing the winning run to score.

Afterward, in the clubhouse, Lasorda approached the shortstop with his hand outstretched. Surprised by the display of sportsmanship, the shortstop stood up to shake his hand. At which point Lasorda pulled back the hand and planted it in the shortstop's face. The players tumbled to the floor and began slugging each other until a couple of older players pulled them apart.

The bloody and dazed shortstop plopped down in front of his locker. Was this pitcher so desperate that he would fight a teammate over an error?

The desperate pitcher was grabbed by his manager and pulled outside.

"As long as you're here, you've got to remember one thing," Pappy Lehman said into Lasorda's ear. "If you want your teammates to play hard behind you, you've got to stand hard behind them."

Pappy shoved Lasorda back into the clubhouse to face those teammates, who could only shake their heads at the surly little Philadelphia kid. Lasorda never forgot the looks on their faces, and he never forgot Lehman's lesson. Throughout his Dodger career, the man who began with punches became famous for his hugs. As a manager, Lasorda never tore into his players in public. He fawned over their children, joked with their wives, remembered the names of entire families, insisted that everyone refer to him as an uncle or brother or grandfather.

"I can still hear Pappy's words today," Lasorda says. "Everyone thought I was just being nice to my players for the sake of the media. I was being nice to them for the sake of winning."

Only once did Lasorda not publicly stand behind one of his players, and it haunts him still.

It was the spring of 1991. Dodger pitching hero Fernando Valenzuela had come off a 13–13 season during which he pitched a no-hitter. He was thirty years old, and the fans loved him. But his body looked older, his screwball looked tired, and the Dodgers didn't want to be stuck paying a salary in excess of $2 million a year.

So, that spring, one day before they would be required to guarantee his entire salary for the season, the Dodgers cut Valenzuela. And soon thereafter, Valenzuela filed a grievance for unfair labor practices.

All of which meant that Lasorda was dragged into a courtroom to sit across from Valenzuela and testify about his pitching ability. For the first time in his life, Lasorda was forced to denigrate a member of his baseball family. And, it turns out, he didn't mean a word of it.

"Here's a guy who had pitched his heart out for me," Lasorda remembers. "But I had to stay loyal to my organization. And they wanted to save money by releasing him. So I had to say what they wanted me to say."

Fifteen years later, Lasorda is still remorseful.

"I had to lie for them and tell them Fernando could no longer pitch and was not in our plans," he says. "Neither was true."

Valenzuela was so angry at Lasorda, he didn't speak to him for more than a decade. Valenzuela was so angry at the Dodgers, he wouldn't set foot inside Dodger Stadium during that time, even though he lived right down the street.

Only recently, when the Dodgers agreed to hire Valenzuela as one of their Spanish-language broadcasters, did the former great pitcher and his formerly loved manager meet.

"We didn't talk about what happened. We just said hello and moved on," Lasorda says. "But I will never forget that. It was the only time I had ever publicly hurt one of my players, and it will hurt me forever."

At the beginning of his career, Lasorda couldn't afford to alienate anyone, particularly those catching balls behind him. He needed all the help he could get. He was such a struggling pitcher that first year, he played sixty games at first base. Then the season ended and he began playing for Uncle Sam, having been drafted into the army in October 1945. In typical Lasorda fashion, he spent his entire two years of service pitching for teams on various bases in the South. By the time the army discharged him, in the spring of 1947, he was also making $200 a week pitching for a mill team in Camden, South Carolina.

The Phillies offered him a minor league contract for the 1947 season. But it was for only $200 a month. So, in one of the best sales jobs in this salesman's life, Lasorda asked the Phillies if he could skip that summer and rejoin the organization the following year. The reason? Lasorda told the team he had suffered a nervous breakdown in the army. He informed the Phillies that he needed the summer to recuperate from the rigors of active duty. In fact, he just needed that bigger Camden paycheck.

The Phillies agreed. Lasorda earned enough money that summer to buy his family home new beds, new paint, and a new heater, the kind that could actually heat all three floors. For the Norristown fighter, the end justified the means. It always did.

"There are three kinds of people in life," Lasorda is saying as he hops off the cushy Venetian couch. "People who make it happen, people who watch it happen, and people who wonder what happened."

Walking over to a window to stare down at the sunny Las Vegas Strip, Lasorda tugs on his pajamas and sighs like a king staring down at his subjects.

"That's why I do all these speeches," he says. "Because I like to make things happen."

He laughs. "There's another reason I do all these speeches," he says. "Because of the money."

Tonight he is speaking for a corporation that is raising funds for a private school. Besides his speaking fee, he will receive first-class airfare and stay in the penthouse suite.

"I have to fly first class, because what if the plane goes down? If the paper says that a Hall of Fame manager died while sitting in coach, what does that do for my reputation?"

He speaks at approximately two hundred functions a year, and when he says it is for the money, he means that in two ways. He likes the money for himself, and he likes the money because it enables him to do many other speeches for free.

Lasorda has never charged a church. He has never charged a legitimate charity. He has never charged a public school. He would never charge the military. He doesn't charge for his autograph. Part of this involves the size of his heart, certainly, a heart that remembers when nobody would speak to his sandlot teams or sign autographs for them. But part of this also involves the size of his shrewdness.

Remember what he likes to say: You catch more flies with honey than with vinegar. By making all the free appearances, he keeps his reputation sweet for the big-money speeches. And for the people paying, it will be worth it. Tonight's banquet will sell out. The school will raise thousands of dollars. All for thirty minutes of a speech that comes completely off the top of Lasorda's head, a speech he has already given fifty times this year.

"I try to help people—is that wrong?" Lasorda says. "I try to help them make money."

From a corner table, Lasorda's cell phone rings. It is not a rich man's ring. It is not a $10,000-per-speech ring. It is the sound of a calliope. An honest-to-ballpark calliope.

"Don't know how it got there, don't know how to get it off," Lasorda says, shaking his head, and you believe him. Just when you start thinking Lasorda is little more than an aging entrepreneur, baseball happens. Just when you begin examining Lasorda's shadows, a stream of delightful light shines in.

And the voice-mail greeting? "Hi, this is Tommy Lasorda. Please leave a message, and remember, if you don't pull for the Dodgers, you may not get into heaven."

But please be careful when you leave your message. Lasorda's understanding of cell-phone technology is spotty. On this Sunday, he begins dialing a friend's number but instead pushes the voice-mail buttons and ends up listening to a recorded message from his friend that he thinks is live.

"I'm talking to you, man. Answer me, answer me!" he screams into the cell phone.

When he finally realizes his mistake, he tosses the phone onto his cluttered desk with a grunt.

"That's why I never fool with this thing," Lasorda says, laughing at himself. "That's why, when my assistant says I have eighty-one messages, I tell him to write them down. I'm too old to change."

In fact, in the decade that he has owned a cell phone, he has changed its number only once, when the Associated Press accidentally released it. But even then, he changed it for just a couple of months, then changed it back again. "I was having trouble remembering the new number," he says, laughing again at the exaggeration of his life.

And he hasn't changed the number of his home phone in decades. Every English-speaking person in the world has that number. Because Lasorda is fluent in Spanish, many Spanish speakers have it as well. He doesn't care. For a guy who hates to be alone, a prank phone call isn't always such a bad thing. He has received several serial prank calls, yet refuses to press charges.

"Hey, if they want to talk to me that bad, aw, what the hell."

His cell phone is never turned off, it is never away from his side, and he has his assistant check his messages so he can return all his calls.

"I'm a guy who loves his country, loves his game, and loves to help people," he says. "If somebody wants me, I'm here."

The phone rings again. He recognizes the number on the caller

ID and answers. It is Whitey Ford, the Hall of Famer who pitched for the Yankees in the glory days of the fifties and sixties. He is asking Lasorda about an upcoming speaking engagement in the Midwest. Lasorda loves to be wanted, but he prefers his admirers to be one-Hall-of-Famer guys.

"Hey, Whitey, what are you doing, stealing my territory?" he says, only half kidding.

Revenge and respect. The themes surface often in Lasorda's life, from the frivolous to the, well, Phanatical. The themes are what led Lasorda not only to win two world championships but to set the major league record for beating up mascots.

One rampage started with the green Phillie Phanatic mascot. The incident occurred before a Dodger game in Philadelphia. Steve Sax, the Dodger second baseman, sneaked into Lasorda's Veterans Stadium office and grabbed one of his extra jerseys. He then ran outside and slipped it to the Phillie Phanatic, a fat, fuzzy, green creature with a long snout. Just before the first pitch, the Phanatic paraded in front of the Dodger dugout, laid the jersey flat on the ground, got into his trademark scooter, and drove it over the jersey.

The crowd roared. So did Lasorda, only he wasn't cheering.

"Give me back my shirt!" he shouted at the Phanatic, who shook his head, put his scooter in reverse, and calmly drove over the jersey again. With the jeers becoming louder, Lasorda jumped out of the dugout, pulled the Phanatic off the scooter, and threw him to the ground. Everyone was laughing. Everyone but Lasorda.

"Little jerk," Lasorda recalls.

Despite his sense of humor, Lasorda has always understood the difference between having fun with the game and disrespecting the game. Players have fun with the game. Mascots disrespect the game. Players have paid the dues necessary to squirt water on the fans and set fire to each other's shoes. Mascots don't even belong on the field. The players are the show. The mascots try to steal that show. Despite all the odd promotions and stunts attempted by the Dodgers, they remain one of baseball's few teams without a mascot, and that is not a coincidence. Fans will tell you that for many years the Dodgers had a living, breathing, laughing mascot. His name was Tommy Lasorda.

Once, he grew irritated by the pounding feet of Youppie, the Montreal Expos' furry mascot, who was dancing on the dugout roof. Lasorda reached up, pulled him down, and pounded him to the dugout steps.

"That thing was nuts," Lasorda recalls.

Finally there was the San Diego Chicken, who crushed Lasorda's cap during one of his routines, only to have Lasorda grapple him into a headlock.

"Crush my hat now, you little donkey," he told the Chicken.

The Venetian suite's doorbell rings. More food. This time it's a late lunch, three hours after the snack: huge platters of hamburgers and chicken fingers and french fries and saucer-size onion rings.

This is Lasorda's prespeech meal. He sits and eats for an hour, then shuffles drowsily over to the couch.

"I'm not full," he says. "My arms are just tired."

He remains on the couch for the rest of the afternoon, dozing sporadically in his pajamas. This is the extent of his Las Vegas experience. Watching football in his pajamas, eating, dozing, eating some more, dozing.

Anyone who wonders how the aging Lasorda can maintain such a rigorous travel and speaking schedule should check the video. As he shows on this Sunday afternoon, he has the ability to sleep whenever, wherever. Television cameras have caught him nodding off in the dugout. Players have caught him in deep slumber in his office.

Once, when he was spotted sleeping during a game, it turns out he was sick, but he'd refused the Dodger trainer's advice to go home. Another time, he snoozed after participating in a pregame long-distance swim for charity. He doesn't sleep because he is slacking; he sleeps because he works too hard.

A sportswriter, staring through binoculars in the press box during one World Series game in St. Louis, saw Lasorda dozing in the stands while sitting next to the baseball commissioner Bud Selig. The sportswriter called Lasorda's cell phone to awaken him before the TV cameras caught him. Thank goodness for that calliope, or he might still be snoozing.

Lasorda is defensive about his penchant for instant-anywhere sleep. He thinks it gives people the wrong idea: people perceive it as a weakness, when it is actually a strength.

"Sure, I sleep, so what?" he says. "I work hard. I work harder than anyone. So sometimes I sleep to get through it all. Write that I sleep—but write about how hard I work to earn that sleep."

When he awakens on this Sunday afternoon in Las Vegas, he will get into the shower and dress for his speech. He will not do what everyone expects a spotlight lover to do. He will not go downstairs to the crowded casino and gamble.

He doesn't gamble in places like Las Vegas because of places like Schenectady, New York, the home of the lowly minor league club where he was sent by the Phillies after rejoining them in the spring of 1948. He had miraculously survived his nervous breakdown, but he was about to have a real one.

"I couldn't spell the name of the city, I couldn't pronounce it, so I told my parents I was pitching somewhere near Albany," he says.

His good news that summer was that he struck out twenty-five batters in one game. Unfortunately, it was a fifteen-inning game against a team called the Amsterdam Rug Makers. He was such a mediocre pitcher with such a dim future, he became the target of gamblers, who offered him $100 to fix games. Wrong guy. After one loss, he chased one of them out of the stadium.

At the end of the year, his record was 9 wins and 12 losses, and he had pitched only a couple of truly good games. But lucky for him, they were both against the Dodgers' farm club in Three Rivers, Quebec. The Phillies refused to protect his contract when the season ended, so Brooklyn drafted him, paying $4,000 to the Phillies and paying Lasorda $300 a month. It was the winter after the 1948 season, and the first chapter in one of the most enduring and most compatible marriages in baseball history was being written.

Well, not quite.

"Hell, I figured if they paid four thousand to get me, they could afford to pay me more than three hundred a month," Lasorda recalls. "So I wouldn't sign. I wanted more money."

Fifty years later, after spending a day in Las Vegas without having to dip into his pocket, Lasorda strolls down a Venetian Hotel hallway with a security guard and a song.

"Fly me to the moon . . ." he croons as he heads to the elevator, singing the song made famous by his late friend Frank Sinatra. Lasorda often sings when he's walking. The sound is horrible, but his smile is so big, nobody asks him to stop.

"Am I a lucky man or what?" he says as he exits the elevator in the bowels of the hotel, where he can walk without being mobbed by the Las Vegas Middle American demographic that admires him so much. "I get to motivate people tonight! I get to make money for people tonight! Me! Just me! Is this a great country or what?"

He stops the security guard when they reach the hotel kitchen. The mostly Latino employees surround him and applaud. He gives them a pep talk in Spanish. They're laughing, and it is apparent that the talk includes a challenge to ask for a raise.

He eventually steps into a ballroom filled with tuxedos and evening gowns. Presiding over an auction, he will raise $10,000 in ten minutes. Posing for photographs with guests for more than an hour, he will persuade people to spend more money.

Tommy Lasorda, from Hall of Fame manager to human slot machine, a man with more bells and whistles than the entire floor of the Caesars Palace casino, the only man who can come to Las Vegas and consistently make money. Who needs blackjack and craps when you can sell revenge and respect?

"Hey, this private school got a football team?" Lasorda asks. "Maybe I should come back later and speak to the football team."

3
· · ·

I TRAINED FOR THIS

sit right there!"

The chair is not marked. There is no sign on it. There is nothing spectacular about it. It is just one of eight blue chairs circling a round blue table in the corner of a plain dining room in Vero Beach, Florida.

But don't touch it. Don't move it. Don't brush it. Don't even think about sitting in it.

For thirty years, this chair has belonged to Tommy Lasorda. He plopped down in it when he became Dodger manager in 1977 and hasn't left it since. While dozens of players and coaches housed in the Dodgers' spring training facility use the dining room only for breakfast and perhaps an occasional dinner, Lasorda uses it every day, for every meal, from February 15 to April 1.

Surrounding this simple throne is a simple place known as Dodgertown. Spread over 450 acres, shielded from the public by thick trees, accessible only through small gates manned by aging guards, Dodgertown serves as the annual birthplace of Dodger seasons and dreams.

For more than sixty years, from Brooklyn to Los Angeles, Dodgers have flocked here every winter and early spring to train. They play on six unmarked fields, some with no dugouts. They travel on golf carts or bikes along narrow blacktopped streets and sidewalks. Some of them sleep in hotel-style rooms across from the dining hall, which borders tennis courts and a swimming pool.

It is the perfect kingdom for a ruler like Lasorda, because it is all about baseball, and all about the Dodgers. There is no advertising anywhere. There is no paved place for fans to park. The streets—like Koufax Way and Campanella Drive—are named after Dodgers. The walls in the buildings are lined with photos of old Dodgers. One waiting area even contains seats from Dodger Stadium.

And the secrets here all belong to the Dodgers. There is a fully stocked bar with pool tables and card tables down the hall from the dining room, but it is unmarked, to discourage visitors. Lasorda can often be found here, howling at the television set or challenging someone to beat him in poker, but his words disappear amid the crickets chirping in the outside darkness. What happens in Dodgertown stays in Dodgertown. And when Lasorda settled on a single dining room chair, that chair, like the rest of this place, became stuck in time.

"I guess I sat down and never got back up," he says.

It is a spring morning, breakfast time, and the elderly waitresses have put his name on a placard reading, "Reserved for Tommy Lasorda." Although the dining room is a buffet, the waitresses appear out of nowhere and insist on bringing your drinks and busing your tray. And although it is essentially a cafeteria, the tables are laid with freshly pressed white tablecloths and the napkins are as thick as towels. Steaming buffet trays sit behind a thin wall, but the dining room forever smells of fresh flowers and newly cut grass. This makes it the favorite stop of visiting scouts and writers during exhibition season. Everyone wants to spend thirty minutes going back thirty years and eating lunch in the middle of what feels like a baseball diamond.

This morning, Tommy must make what has been one of his most important decisions in thirty years. It is not about a lineup. It is not about pulling his pitcher. It is about whom he will dine with.

If he doesn't ask, you can't sit. If he's not in the room yet, you can't sit. In every sense of the word, a throne.

When Lasorda was a manager—unlike most managers, who hang

out only with their coaches or with celebrities — he would invite a couple of minor leaguers to sit with him for dinner. He would then produce a telephone, with a cord attached to a plug near his table, and ask the players to call their mothers and tell them they were having dinner with Tommy Lasorda. The players would dial nervously, mumble into the phone, then hand the receiver to Lasorda, who would soothe the stunned, often crying mom and say to her that she had produced a future MVP. It was not only a sweet gesture but a smart one. It gave Lasorda great credibility with the distrustful young stars. When they reached the major leagues, those kids would remember that phone call. If a teammate asked them to join in a mutiny against their manager, which sometimes happened, they would also remember that phone call.

"I recall sitting next to Pee Wee Reese in this dining room, then writing home and telling my mother all about it," Lasorda says. "If I could do it, why couldn't my players do the same thing?"

Sadly, even in this age of cell phones, Lasorda can't do the phone trick anymore. Many of the young kids have barely heard of him, and they don't think it's cool to phone their mothers in front of him. He's not as cool anymore. And, more important to the kids, he's not considered as vital to their careers.

Now he calls over a minor league slugger, Cory Dunlap, as the player is picking up a piece of fruit and walking out the door. Dunlap veers right, as if trying to avoid Lasorda's eyes. He doesn't look at the legend. Like most Dodger kids these days, he doesn't want to hear one of those infamous pep talks. He doesn't think Lasorda can help his career. He doesn't think Lasorda has any more juice. He takes two steps past the table when Lasorda turns and shouts to him. Dunlap stops and sighs. He is stuck. He walks over and shakes Lasorda's hand and stares at the ground and listens.

"My report on you is that you are a major league prospect, Cory," Lasorda says. "But it's not just gonna happen."

"Yes, sir," says Dunlap, staring into space.

"There are three types of people in this world!" shouts Lasorda. "Those who make it happen, those who watch it happen, and those who wonder what the hell happened! Who are you? Who are you!"

"I'll make it happen, sir," says Dunlap, yawning.

Lasorda speaks so loudly, you would think the rest of the patrons would be staring at him. None of them are. He says these things so much, they are like the soft-rock music coming out of the ceiling or the hushed queries of the aging waitresses. They are background noise.

"I see a lot of me in you," Lasorda shouts. "I see a lot of me in you!"

"Yes, sir," says Dunlap, who then slips away.

The kids here know that they must listen to Lasorda. But, being kids, they don't always agree to like it. They don't understand Lasorda's history. They don't always get his jokes. Their older managers and instructors watch the interactions and shake their heads the way you would shake your head at a spoiled child. These kids just have no idea.

Lasorda smiles as if he's just managed another victory, and now it's time for him to fill his table.

"Charley Steiner, come over here!"

"Me?" says Steiner, one of the Dodger broadcasters, obviously honored.

"Ralph, you with me?"

"I'm right here," says Ralph Avila, the Dodgers' Latin American guru.

In addition to Steiner and Avila, Lasorda will invite a couple of front-office secretaries and a couple of Latino broadcasters. They are a diverse group, speaking different languages and talking about their various jobs, having only one thing in common.

They are good listeners. To be more precise, they are Lasorda listeners. There is a difference. A good listener is usually someone who nods a lot and offers his own thoughts after the speaker is finished. A Lasorda listener is one who nods a lot, period. A Lasorda listener does not offer thoughts of his own. A Lasorda listener does not try to match Tommy's stories with their own stories, except if those stories are about Lasorda.

A Lasorda listener knows not only when to laugh but how to laugh. Whenever Lasorda is looking at you while telling a funny story, you laugh. When he's not looking at you, you should wait until the punch line, then you should laugh, with huge heaves and big tears and a loss of bodily control. That way, he knows you're listening, and you'll be invited back to his table.

For a guy who never had security as a player, the laughter became his security as a manager. More than the wins, more than the Hall of Fame ring, the laughter is proof to Lasorda that he will always be wanted. He connects with current players by walking through the clubhouse telling funny old stories. "Lemme tell you about Jesse Orosco and my promise to God . . ." He connected with past players by telling jokes to cut the tension. When you saw Lasorda standing behind second base with his arm around a struggling player, chances are he was telling him a joke. The player would laugh, meaning the player would listen, meaning Lasorda could then yell at him for a baserunning blunder. To Lasorda, laughter was like that spoonful of sugar that helped his medicine go down.

Of course, when the jokes get old, it takes a true Lasorda listener to rise to the occasion. The greatest Lasorda listeners in Dodger history were Kirk Gibson and Orel Hershiser. The secret of success of the 1988 world championship team wasn't how those two stars played on the field, it was how they hung out in Lasorda's office. Some players would wince at having to hear a story for the seventeenth time and immediately stand up and grab a bat and claim they have to take extra batting practice. Gibson and Hershiser were smarter than that. They would sit on couches and nod their heads, and when they wanted the story to end, they would put an arm around Lasorda and gently escort him to the field while he was talking.

Jaded outsiders were astonished at the patience Gibson and Hershiser showed. "Hey, Tommy," Gibson would shout to Lasorda outside the batting cage, "tell me about dinner last night." And Tommy would tell a story about eating too much or paying too little, the same story everyone had heard before, yet Gibson would lead the team in laughter. Hershiser would do the same thing in front of the pitching staff: "Hey, Tommy, tell me about the time you hit that guy who wouldn't give you his autograph!" Everyone around him would groan. Hershiser would shrug. Lasorda would beam.

Through this ability to listen to Lasorda talk about himself, Gibson and Hershiser helped connect their young and cynical teammates to the old and corny manager. Players who thought Lasorda was full of himself realized that if their two best teammates could listen to the boss, they could too. Gibson and Hershiser understood that to get to Lasorda's gleaming wisdom, sometimes you had to wade through the musty stories.

The bits of straw Lasorda would often spin into gold. He would recount the tale about once trying to pitch for the Brooklyn Dodgers with a bleeding gash in his leg. Gibson would listen and smile, and then, in August one season, in a game against the Montreal Expos, he found himself standing on second base in the bottom of the ninth inning of a tie game. When Joe Hesketh's pitch scooted under the catcher Nelson Santovenia's glove and rolled to the backstop, Gibson raced to third. But instead of stopping, as any other baserunner would do in that situation, he kept going. With Lasorda in the dugout screaming with glee, Gibson rounded third and raced home, diving past a shaken Hesketh for the winning run. Gibson not only scored with hustle, he scored with smarts: he later revealed that he knew Hesketh might be afraid to block the plate because he'd suffered a broken leg in a previous season. By living this Lasorda gospel, Gibson and Hershiser weren't just baseball players, they were village storytellers carrying on a tradition.

On this spring morning at Dodgertown, Lasorda is talking about one of those corny Vero Beach moments involving Dusty Baker, who was not a good Lasorda listener. On April Fools' Day in 1976, Lasorda was playing his usual joke on another poor Dodger soul.

"So I call Dusty into my office and tell him, 'I got bad news for you. I've just traded you to Cleveland for Boog Powell,'" Lasorda says. "And Dusty starts crying. He says, 'Boog Powell? How can you trade me for an old guy like that?' So I turn to the p.r. guy and say, 'We need to make an announcement. What day is it?' And he says, 'It's April first.' And Dusty goes crazy, gets the joke, wants to kill me."

Even though this makes them a bit uncomfortable, the Lasorda listeners laugh, which encourages Lasorda to continue talking about April Fools' jokes. There was the time he told star hitter Pedro Guerrero that he had been traded, which made Guerrero so mad that he phoned the general manager, Al Campanis, and cursed him out. Then there was the time Lasorda put a camera in the closet of his Vero Beach office and secretly filmed a couple of young guys who were fooled into thinking they would be traded.

"Those were the good old days. We had a lot of fun with the players," Lasorda says between bites of tomato slices and sweet rolls.

Not all the Lasorda listeners think such pranks are fun. They are veterans of a game where a trade can end your marriage or ruin your career. They are clearly uncomfortable listening to him joke about somebody's future. But this is Dodgertown, this is Lasorda's table, this is his throne, and this laughter is his nectar.

They know it wasn't always like this for him in Vero Beach. They know that if anybody deserves an audience here, it is a guy who, nearly fifty years ago, had a hard time getting in the door.

Lasorda first arrived in 1948. The struggling young Dodger pitcher had just been purchased from the Philadelphia Phillies. He'd flown to Vero Beach from Norristown, which was like trying to get to heaven from the corner of a damp basement. The flight required seven stops before it finally landed, at 10 P.M. Lasorda walked across the airfield to the camp, where he encountered an angry night watchman, who took one look at the squat man with the bulldog face and messy shock of black hair and gave him his official Dodger welcome.

"Why are you here so late?" the guy yelled at Lasorda. "Why couldn't you get here early like everyone else?"

So Lasorda's first experience as a Dodger began with rejection, and it continued the next day when he awoke in his crowded barracks and walked to the dining room and saw a line of nearly seven hundred players snaking around the facility. This was Dodgertown in its glory years, the biggest baseball school in the world, with enough players to fill two dozen minor league teams.

The players all wore different-colored uniforms. They responded only to their numbers. They would go from field to field, from bunting drills to running drills to batting practice, coaches shouting out numbers and colors in military fashion. Lasorda had just left the service, and he wasn't ready to return. Nobody knew Lasorda's name, and he was tired of nobody knowing his name. This wasn't a baseball team, it was one giant faceless army. And so on his first night of spring training, he made his first official Dodger pronouncement.

He asked to be traded.

He found the Dodgers' farm director, Fresco Thompson, a kindly veteran official who had seen it all, in the players' lounge. He begged to be sent to a team where he would feel like a person instead of a number. He begged to be sent to a place where he'd have a chance.

"Son, you've been here one day," said a laughing Thompson. "Stick around."

Lasorda realized he might be stuck. The thought horrified him. Thus far, he had spent his life squeezing through loopholes, from stolen prison balls to army transfers. He thought that if he could get out of Norristown, he surely could get out of Dodgertown. So he tried a different strategy. He asked Thompson for a raise, hoping that the mere gall of such a request would hasten his departure.

"Son," said Thompson, still laughing, "you want more money, go out on those fields and earn it."

Thompson would not listen to his pleading. Lasorda was stuck, and he knew it. So he tried the next best thing: burning his way out of Vero Beach. He went fishing in the nearby Atlantic Ocean on one of his first days off, bringing everything but sunscreen. His starchy body was burned so badly he could hardly walk. The next day, he wrapped his entire body in gauze and covered himself with three shirts and tried to pitch in a spring training game. Maybe if he threw well enough, he thought, the Dodgers would want to trade his eccentric soul to a team where he might have a chance to pitch in the major leagues.

Bad idea, worse execution. Unfortunately for Lasorda, he pitched too well—five shutout innings—and the Dodgers promoted him from Class D to Class A, to a team in Pueblo, Colorado. Not only were the Dodgers not trading him, they were sending him to a place he never knew existed. And if he was going to have to stay with the Dodgers, he wanted to live near Norristown or some other familiar place. The Dodgers had a team in Greenville, South Carolina, where he had enjoyed success as a mill pitcher and had come to know a number of people. He asked to be transferred there. Thompson threw up his hands, shook his head, and agreed.

It had happened again. Lasorda had banged on a door until it opened. A pitcher who began training camp as an anonymous number ended it by picking his own assignment.

Thus, in a maneuver that became typical of his managerial career, Lasorda began his Dodger life by surrounding himself with friends. It was a habit he could never break. Part of the reason he never left the Dodgers is the reason he wanted to leave them in the first place: he does not like strangers. He is not comfortable in an environment where he is an unknown. He needs those Lasorda listeners.

"Hey, Tommy," says one of them on this spring morning, looking at him shaking his right hand after taking a bite of cantaloupe. "What's wrong with your finger?"

"It's the stinking thumb," Lasorda says, rubbing it.

A week before, Lasorda had noticed some gum on the bottom of his shoe and angrily grabbed the nearest piece of metal, a coat hanger, and started scraping it off. He scraped so hard, he banged his thumb on the heel of the shoe, and now it is twisted and hurting.

For anyone else, a sore right thumb might not be cause for concern. Pitchers can ice it and work. Batters can take it and work. Not so for Lasorda, for whom the right thumb is his most important, irreplaceable appendage. No athletic figure in the world shakes more hands. No celebrity is more approachable, and so more likely to be touching thumbs with hundreds of people a day. Lasorda shakes so many hands that when he takes his granddaughter Emily to Disneyland, his daughter Laura has to constantly spray his hand with disinfectant. Lasorda shakes so many hands that a sore right thumb is like a lost limb.

"I gotta get this fixed," Lasorda says, shaking the thumb, standing up, spotting the stately-looking Dr. Frank Jobe eating his breakfast. "Hey, Doc, let's meet later in your office."

Only Lasorda would enlist a renowned baseball surgeon to treat a thumb injured in an accident caused by a coat hanger scraping gum. And only Lasorda would consider that "office" to be a stool in the darkened Dodgertown bar, where they meet briefly before beginning their day.

"We need to get this x-rayed," Dr. Jobe says.

"For what?" asks Lasorda. "Can't you just put something on it?"

"No, we just need to check it out."

"I don't have time to check it out," says Lasorda. "How am I going to get around all those people?"

In Lasorda's world, a Vero Beach day when he cannot shake hands is like a Vero Beach day of spitting rain.

"People see me shaking with my other hand, they think something's wrong with me," he says. "I need it fixed now."

Dr. Jobe smiles. He knows the thumb is not going to get fixed in a dark bar. But, knowing Lasorda, he'll eventually forget about the pain. Shake enough hands, get enough laughs, and Lasorda always forgets the pain. Attacking life like he attacks gum on his shoe with a coat hanger, Lasorda is used to the pain.

His fight to be transferred from that tiny speck in Colorado to a South Carolina town for his first Dodger minor league job? It resulted in playing for a manager he soon hated. It was in Greenville, in 1948 and 1949, that Lasorda learned what kind of manager he did *not* want to be. That would be a manager like Clay Bryant.

Bryant was a tough, stoical man who treated his players like cattle. With every bark, with every stare, he reminded them that they weren't human—they were cogs, little parts of a giant Dodger machine that could easily spit them out. Lasorda, who had used every bit of guile to advance to this point, did not enjoy being treated like a machine. Everything his first minor league manager did, Lasorda later did the opposite.

Bryant did not allow his players to talk to anyone in the stands before or during a game. When Lasorda became manager, his teams practically camped out in the stands. His players were permitted to visit their relatives and friends wherever they sat, furthering the notion of the Dodgers as family.

After a game, if his team lost, Bryant refused to allow the players to shower or dress until he himself had showered. This meant they sometimes had to sit in front of their lockers for nearly an hour. When Lasorda became manager, he would fume in his office after a loss, but he refused to let that anger seep into the clubhouse, creating an atmosphere where it was difficult to tell who won.

When Bryant took a pitcher out of the game, he did so in stony silence. When Lasorda took a pitcher out, he always patted him on the back, even while sometimes cursing inside.

Lasorda saw how Bryant's coldness affected his Greenville team. He saw how fear of the manager turned to passive at-bats, resulting in strikeouts. He saw how anxiety over Bryant's moods prevented players from stealing bases or trying out a new pitch. He realized that a baseball team needed light to grow. He would go home to the tiny room he rented and sit on his bed and vow that one day he would do things differently. One day he would be that light.

"I remember seeing Bryant in a hotel lobby and he wouldn't even say hello to me," Lasorda recalls. "I never thought about managing until then. And all of a sudden I thought, 'You know, if I'm ever going to be a manager, I'm going to be just the opposite of Clay Bryant.'"

On one occasion, Lasorda broke Bryant's rule against fraternization with the fans. In true Lasorda serendipitous fashion, this infraction would change the rest of his life.

In the middle of a midsummer game, he spotted a handsome-looking young woman in the stands. Bryant was coaching third base. When his back was turned, Lasorda made his move, shouting up into the stands, asking for the girl's name.

"Joan Miller," replied the girl's friend.

Lasorda then asked if this girl would go out with him.

Joan Miller shook her head.

Lasorda met her in the parking lot after the game, and she shook her head again. He asked if he could phone her at home, and she kept shaking her head. Finally he was able to coax her into giving up her work phone number.

Twenty times in the next three days, Lasorda called that number. Twenty times, the operator told him that Joan Miller was not there.

"Then I realized—the operator was Joan Miller."

Lasorda had rarely been on a real date. He was a high school jock who never had time for girls. Then he graduated and became just another low-paid minor league pitcher with a crooked nose. He was looking for someone who didn't care that he wasn't successful or famous or conventionally attractive.

Eventually she relented and met him for lunch. The following winter, Lasorda and Joan Miller—whom he called Jo—became engaged, during a break in the winter league in Panama. Then Lasorda threw a wild pitch. By the following spring, he had saved $200 for the wedding, and stashed the cash in his Vero Beach bunk. But when he returned to his room after one workout, he discovered that the money had been stolen.

Thus began his first serious negotiation with the Dodger management. He bothered general manager Branch Rickey, already known as one of baseball's great minds, for a $500 loan in order to get married. Lasorda knew that Rickey thought marriage was good for the ERA and the batting average, and sure enough, Rickey agreed. The money was given to Lasorda by Buzzie Bavasi, who was then the general manager of the triple-A farm team in Montreal.

It was Lasorda's first sign of faith and family from the Dodgers, and one that would become the hallmark of his tenure with the organization.

A year later, Bavasi called Lasorda into his office and asked him to sign a paper indicating that he had paid back the $500.

"But I didn't pay it back," Lasorda told Bavasi.

"Your marriage is on us," said Bavasi.

Ever since then, on Lasorda and Jo's wedding anniversary, April 14, Bavasi has sent Jo flowers and a card with two simple words: "I'm sorry."

"Yeah, he thinks he's real funny," says Lasorda with a grin. "I was going to pay back that five hundred, but after fifty-six years, with compounded interest, it would be about fifty-eight thousand bucks, so forget it!"

Lasorda is telling this story after breakfast as he swaggers around Dodgertown, in slacks and a golf shirt, four hours before a game, a couple of Lasorda listeners in tow. Everyone is laughing, but suddenly Lasorda gets serious. He looks around at the players in their crisp white uniforms, filling every green corner. He waves to the rows of fans straining against the yellow ropes that separate them from their heroes. In one area of the complex kids struggle to hit curveballs in a batting cage, their curses drowning out their thwacks. In another area a couple of aging pitchers try to throw a baseball through a small string square, sweat rolling down their faces in the morning Florida sun.

Everywhere Lasorda looks, somebody smiles at him. Every time he talks, somebody laughs. If he indeed wants to die on a baseball field, as he has often joked, then that baseball field would be here, the home of eternal hope, the bastion of baseball's last true believer. Lasorda rarely gets misty, but when he looks around at what surely must be his idea of heaven, his eyes become teary.

In the past sixty years, Vero Beach has grown into a bustling central-Florida coastal retreat. Where there was once just one bridge leading down to the ocean, now there are several. Where there were once only a few restaurants, now there are hundreds, surrounded by dozens of new hotels, ringed by wide and busy streets. Rich people live on islands off the coast. Tourists shop in tony boutiques. But in the middle of it all, Dodgertown remains unchanged, from the bicycles to the elderly telephone operators to Holman Stadium, which provides no shade for fans or players, just bleachers and benches in a field in the sun. A haven from progress, an oasis from change, sort of like Lasorda himself.

"Fifty-eight years ago, I was trying to get out of this place," he says, shaking his head. "Thank God I'm still here."

Lasorda has played or worked on every inch of this place. Even when he was manager, he would start his day at 8 A.M. to pitch batting practice, once throwing for nine hours of practice on a dare.

"And my arm was fine, perfectly fine," he says. "You see these wimps today, they can't go five innings in a game. Man, I once went nine hours in one day."

He would show up early to spring training games, one of the only Dodgers who loved the fact that Holman Stadium had no dugouts. He didn't mind the beating sun as long as he was also exposed to the adoring fans.

"What's wrong with people being able to see the players?" he asks. "Ain't that what they pay to see?"

After a game ended, Lasorda would hold up to three hours of ex-tra practice for the young players, a session known as Lasorda University. The youngsters would be exhausted, but they didn't dare miss a class, which featured Professor Lasorda talking about everything from squeeze bunts to curveballs to the dangers of squeezing curves in strange cities. It was quite a sight—a chubby, aging man on a mound shouting invectives and inspiration at smooth-cheeked kids standing sixty feet away. That the Dodgers had five consecutive Rookie of the Year Award winners in the mid-1990s was a direct result of the work of Lasorda University, where classes sometimes ran so late, he would order the stadium lights lit, just before the players collapsed.

"I told all the guys, if you enroll in Lasorda University, your tuition will be perspiration, determination, and inspiration," Lasorda says. "And if you are lucky enough to graduate, you'll make more money than a professor at Harvard or Yale."

Although many great players have passed through it's sweaty halls, Lasorda University's valedictorian is surely Mike Piazza. He is the future Hall of Fame catcher who might never have played major league baseball without the support of one of his father Vince's best friends. It has often been written that Lasorda is Piazza's godfather, but that's not technically true. Lasorda uses that term for all the children of close friends who have received his support. And never has he supported someone so fiercely against such deep skepticism.

In the late 1980s, Mike Piazza was considered little more than a rich kid from Philadelphia who thought that being Lasorda's batboy would qualify him to play professional baseball. He worked hard, but nobody believed in him. He had a great swing, but everyone thought it was manufactured through countless private lessons and therefore probably temporary. He was just another first baseman stuck in a Florida community college when Lasorda approached the Dodgers' scouting department with the request for a favor.

"I said, 'This is my godson. Could you please just draft him somewhere, make him feel good, give him one tryout, that's it?'"

So Piazza was drafted by the Dodgers in the sixty-second round, the last battered box of cereal on the shelf, a cosmetic pick that the kid could put on his résumé when he began his career in something else.

The Dodgers never called him. When Lasorda asked about it, the scouts said they didn't want to sign someone who was even a remote relative of a club employee.

"I thought, 'The heck with this,'" Lasorda says. "I called the kid and told him to get on a plane and come to California. He was going to have a tryout if I had to do it personally."

When Piazza showed up at Dodger Stadium, the coaches didn't want to upset Lasorda, so they gave him a quick tryout. With Lasorda standing in the outfield so he wouldn't be a distraction behind the plate, the kid hit the ball all over the park. The scouting department thanked him, bid him farewell, then told Lasorda the Dodgers still wouldn't sign him.

"They said he didn't hit well enough for a first baseman," Lasorda recalls. "So I told them, 'Would you sign him if he was a catcher?' They said yes. So I told them he was also a catcher."

Thus, with an irony not lost on Lasorda, the Dodgers signed a player who would become the best hitting catcher in the franchise's history, though they had no idea he wasn't a catcher.

Next Lasorda secretly shipped Piazza off to the Dodgers' camp in the Dominican Republic, where he spent the winter as the only non–Spanish speaker in the camp. He slept on a hard bunk and understood only a few of the instructions, but somehow he learned to catch. When he arrived at Vero Beach for the first time in the late 1980s, Mike Piazza was ready to enter Lasorda University.

After classes had ended for the day, Lasorda would often organize games of two-on-two basketball at a nearby court. The games were usually little more than thirty-minute boxing matches, with Lasorda and coach Mark Cresse—"the Bruise Brothers"—pounding on whoever was foolish enough to challenge them. One of those players was a Dodger executive named Tommy Hawkins, formerly a forward on the Los Angeles Lakers. Hawkins says that in his day, the NBA was never this physical. Lasorda would punch him a couple of times in the ribs and the game would be over. It got so rough once that the Bruise Brothers played wearing shin guards.

Can you imagine Joe Torre or Sparky Anderson ending his spring training day playing basketball? Can you imagine any manager who would ever need to play basketball? Lasorda was tired, but he needed it. He needed to show that he was the toughest guy both in and out of the dugout. For his motivation to work on the field, he felt he had to have credibility with the players off the field. And to him, credibility meant showing no weakness, ever, even when you are a five-foot-ten runt being posted up by a six-foot-five ex-pro.

Only after he finished his pickup game would Lasorda return to his room, to quickly shower and change for dinner, where his table and his admirers were waiting. Often, the people sitting around him at dinner were different from the ones who hung around him during the day. Being a Lasorda listener can be tough. There is only so much motivation one person can take.

"Then, after dinner, when I go back to my room, that's where it would get crazy," Lasorda recalls.

If that dining room chair is his throne, then room 112 is his castle, tucked in a corner next to the Dodgertown entrance, behind a huge palm tree. Just another hotel room, like it was just another dining room chair.

But for thirty springs, he has never slept anywhere else. His highly paid players eventually drifted off campus and rented apartments in the Vero Beach area, but Lasorda never left room 112. Even when decent restaurants and stores finally arrived in this Midwest-by-the-sea town, Lasorda never left room 112.

"Why would I go anywhere else?" he asks. "I've got everything I want right here."

The room is a mini-suite, the kind you would find at any discount chain hotel. There is a couch and a TV in one room, a bed and a dresser in the other room. The place is spotless, but not because Lasorda is a clean-freak. It's spotless because Lasorda is never there. He stays in Dodgertown because it is the one place in the world where he's guaranteed never to be alone. He is a one-minute walk from the guard at the front gate. He is a five-minute walk from the dining room. He is a ten-minute walk from the field.

Fifty-eight years in Vero Beach, and only once has Lasorda actually been to the beach. "I keep hearing about this undertow," he says. "Last thing I need is to get caught in an undertow." He is Vero Beach's most famous winter resident, yet never has he shopped there, or seen a movie there, or spent any money there. To an increasingly cynical generation of baseball folks, Dodgertown is merely a workplace. For Lasorda, it has always been a home.

The players soon learned that Lasorda would never leave that room. So they tortured him in it. Room 112 may have been empty during the day, but it was a busy ground zero for practical jokes at night.

Once, perhaps mocking the longtime Dodger tradition of wearing green caps on St. Patrick's Day, someone sneaked inside and painted everything green. Another time, someone entered his room and took all the furniture. Then there was the time the players thought Lasorda was being too cozy with the media, and they filled the room with five tons of newspapers.

Once, in the middle of the night, there was a knock on Lasorda's door. It was the night watchman and Walter O'Malley, the team's owner. They accused Lasorda of stealing the wheels of O'Malley's golf cart. Lasorda vigorously protested, until the wheels were discovered under his bed. Of course, Lasorda hadn't put them there and never discovered who had.

"The guys played a lot of jokes on me, but it was fine because it meant they weren't scared of me," Lasorda says. "And if they weren't scared of me, that meant they weren't scared to be aggressive on the bases or take chances at the plate. They weren't scared to be great."

If Lasorda had been scared, he wouldn't have taken that wild truck ride to that Connie Mack tryout in Philadelphia. He figured the same applied to his players. He wanted them taking chances. You couldn't succeed unless you weren't afraid to fail, and nothing spoke of boldness like painting the manager's underwear green.

The greatest of these practical jokes occurred, not coincidentally, in the season before his first world championship. Lasorda awoke one morning and found that his door was stuck. He tried to call for help, but the phone wouldn't work. He tried the door again, but it wouldn't budge.

"I couldn't get out and I couldn't tell anybody I couldn't get out.

I nearly threw a chair through the window." Lasorda is still vexed about it today.

After waiting for several hours, he was finally discovered missing when he didn't show up at the team bus. It turns out, someone had stripped his phone and tied a rope from his outside doorknob to the trunk of that giant palm tree outside.

Lasorda was certain the culprit was Jay Johnstone, who later became a World Series hero. He retaliated by nailing Johnstone's dress shoes to his locker. This started a practical-joke feud that reached its peak when, during the national anthem of a spring game in Orlando, Lasorda discovered his dress pants flying from the flagpole. By the middle of the game, the pants had been replaced with the glove of Mickey Hatcher, another future World Series hero.

"Talent, you either got it or you don't," Lasorda says. "But desire, that is something you can make up your mind about. Those practical jokes came from desire. I knew those players had it, and I used them because of it."

It is no coincidence that both Johnstone and Hatcher were great Dodger players off the bench. That is the kind of job—entering a game in the late innings with the pressure high and the body cold—that requires the sort of desire Lasorda loved.

The desire in Lasorda was first recognized by Al Campanis. In the spring of 1950, Campanis was just another scout, and Lasorda was just another pitcher for the Dodgers' triple-A farm team in Montreal. Campanis had seen Lasorda fighting and heard him shouting. He had watched him throw under batters' chins and behind their backs and—just to scare them—over their heads. He saw Lasorda fearlessly throw slow curveballs on full counts, knowing that the batter would either hit a home run or strike out, daring beyond reason but tough beyond explanation.

On a bus ride from Miami that spring—Lasorda remembers the exact trip, the exact moment—Campanis plopped down next to him and said, "Son, if I'm ever in a position to hire you, you're going to work for me one day."

Lasorda laughed and nudged Campanis and changed the subject to food.

"At the time, I had no idea this guy would ever be general manager of the Dodgers," says Lasorda. "And this guy had no idea that, when the time came, I would still be somebody he wanted to hire. It was just spring training talk. Who'd have thought?"

Who'd have thought, indeed, that Campanis would eventually be the Dodger general manager who would give Lasorda his first and only big-league managing job. And who would have thought that Lasorda would later try to keep Campanis in his job when the general manager made racially offensive comments on a national TV news show. Back then, they were just two guys who realized they might one day need each other.

In the spring of 1950, when he made his debut against big-league hitters, Lasorda was the one needing all the help. It was in Miami, a game against the Cincinnati Redlegs, in the fourth inning. Lasorda had been waiting and working for years for this moment. There were only a couple of thousand fans in the stands, but it felt like the first game of a World Series. And it looked like the end of a career.

He walked the first batter. He walked the second batter. He walked the third batter. He walked the fourth batter.

"Right there on the mound I started crying," Lasorda remembers. "In my mind, everything I worked for was finished."

Burt Shotton, the Dodger manager, met him on the mound to take him out of the game. Lasorda remembers the walk to the dugout as the longest of his life. "I never thought I'd see a major league mound again."

A couple of weeks later, Lasorda had to deal with a different sort of weight. He was now playing for Walter Alston, the Montreal boss who later became Lasorda's predecessor as Dodger manager.

Like Lasorda, Alston was a failed major league player—one at-bat, one strikeout, one error. Like Lasorda, Alston believed that the best managers weren't afraid to be close to players.

"Alston was the opposite of Clay Bryant. He taught me that you could be a player's friend and still earn his respect," says Lasorda.

Alston wouldn't broadcast his friendliness the way Lasorda did; he was much quieter, more reserved. But his methods were the same, as he would challenge his players to beat him in everything from pool to poker. He was open, accommodating, and he would even let his pitchers talk him out of pulling them from games.

You would think that 1950 in Montreal would be the beginning of a lifelong closeness between the young player and the manager he emulated. But no. It was the beginning of a lifelong chill.

"He never liked me," Lasorda says. "I have no idea why. But it is one of the greatest disappointments of my life that Walter Alston never liked me."

That first season in Montreal, Lasorda went 9–4, which is enough to like. Except, well, that first season Lasorda was better known for the practical jokes he would play on Alston.

"Hey, he wanted to be one of the guys, so I made him one of the guys," Lasorda says.

There was the time that Lasorda and Don Hoak spent most of a train ride cheating Alston in hearts. When the manager finally figured out what was going on, he was so angry he ripped the cards in half and stormed away. Lasorda also irked Alston during a batting practice on a hot day in Syracuse, when the manager was pitching a half-hour session. Every few minutes, Lasorda, who was shagging balls in right field, would push back the minute hand of the giant clock on the outfield fence. Alston kept looking at the clock and shaking his head. After forty-five minutes, he walked into the dugout, exhausted.

"He told everyone it was the longest half hour of his life," Lasorda recalls. "When he found out what happened, he chased me around for a week."

Lasorda was never sure that Alston valued him. Maybe Alston saw Lasorda as a threat. Maybe Alston saw Lasorda as only a journeyman. However Alston saw him, Lasorda never forgot those looks.

On this March afternoon a half century later, he is walking through Dodgertown intent on never giving anyone those looks. He goes behind one of the batting cages and starts shouting inspiration at some of the Dodger veterans. It might be the only time someone will shout at them all season — nobody tries to verbally motivate millionaires anymore. They're not used to it. Some of them wince. Many of them don't listen. But they all hear him.

"José, show some enthusiasm!" he shouts to José Cruz Jr., a journeyman who is trudging sullenly across the grass, carrying his bats over his shoulder like a kid walking to school with his backpack. "C'mon, José, smile. Make it look like you're happy!"

Cruz looks up briefly and smiles and keeps walking. Actually, he starts jogging. He doesn't want to attract the attention Lasorda brings. He sort of waves and cocks his head toward Lasorda and then he's gone, past Lasorda and behind the batting cage. He throws down his bats and then picks one up and flexes it, facing away from Lasorda, then swings it powerfully enough that nobody would dare approach him.

It is instantly clear that this guy is not going to last the season here—his heart is not in it. You know, because Lasorda knows. He has always had an uncanny ability to perceive a player's weaknesses and make lighthearted chatter that exposes those weaknesses. He can tell by the way a player walks in front of him. He can tell by the way a player talks to him—or if a player even bothers to talk to him.

Lasorda will later shake his head in disgust over the lack of enthusiasm shown by Cruz. "That guy, what's wrong with him? He has the best job in the world!" And then, as often happens with Lasorda's words, they become reality. On August 3, batting .233 with 17 RBIs, the Dodgers' opening-day left fielder is released.

Next up, J. D. Drew, the sluggish outfielder walking toward Lasorda with his head down.

"My man, J. D.! My kind of guy!" Lasorda shouts.

Drew keeps looking down, then looks away, as if spotting a friend—anything to avoid eye contact. Lasorda is relentless, staring, stalking Drew, walking toward him with his hands waving. Drew finally stops, looks up, almost scared, meets him eye to eye.

"Hey, Tommy," Drew says softly.

Now Lasorda has him, and they both know it, and Lasorda starts shouting.

"J. D., J. D., when I look at you, I see a lot of me!" Lasorda says. "My man J. D. Drew!"

While Lasorda's greeting of Cruz was actually a warning, his greeting of Drew is actually a challenge. Although Lasorda wouldn't admit it, this is his most effective method of individual motivation. He finds a player's weakest trait, then repeatedly compliments him on that trait until the player begins believing it is a strength.

The best example of this was Orel Hershiser, a thin, bespectacled, nerdy pitcher who showed up on the Dodger Stadium mound in 1983 at age twenty-four. In his first eight innings for Lasorda, Hershiser walked six and struck out five and had a 3.38 ERA. He wasn't fooling anyone. More important, he wasn't scaring anyone. One day before Hershiser's second season, Lasorda called the odd guy into his office.

"You know what I'm going to start calling you?" Lasorda said. "I'm going to call you 'Bulldog.'"

He couldn't have been any more outrageous if he had nicknamed Fernando Valenzuela "Skinny," or catcher Mike Scioscia "Speedy."

Hershiser's thin frame recoiled on the hard chair in front of Lasorda's desk.

"Bulldog?" he said.

"Bulldog!" said Lasorda. "Because that is how you are going to pitch from now on. You are going to go out there and be a bulldog!"

When the nickname reached the clubhouse, it was met with loud snickers. At first, players called him Bulldog strictly as a joke, yet the more Hershiser heard it, the more he believed it. Whenever a batter reached base against him, he would squint and fidget with his glasses and actually get tougher. Whenever he allowed runs to score, instead of slinking off the mound, he would storm off. Though he still looked like a shushing librarian, Hershiser suddenly believed he was a growling animal. And his statistics proved it. By the end of his first full season, he had a 2.66 ERA. Four years later, he put away his pocket protector long enough to break one of the toughest records in sports, throwing 59 consecutive scoreless innings. He finished that 1988 season as the Cy Young Award winner and the winning pitcher in the clinching Game 5 of the World Series.

He was still a nerd, but he was now also a bulldog. Hershiser remains Lasorda's finest creation. On this spring morning, Lasorda is trying to duplicate that with Drew.

He knows the Dodger right fielder often babies himself. He knows that Drew will rarely play when in pain. He knows that Drew is absolutely nothing like himself. But that doesn't stop him from making comparisons.

"J.D., I'm serious, I love the way you go about your business, I love how hard you play, I love your passion!" Lasorda says.

"Um, thanks, Tommy," Drew says, shrugging and walking away.

Because Lasorda doesn't spend much time in the Dodger clubhouse—even at his age, he hates to be seen as a threat to the current manager—he was unable to keep working on Drew. And by the end of the 2006 season, Drew was again plagued by the criticism that he just didn't play hard enough or long enough. When Drew decided to use a clause in his contract to leave the Dodgers in the winter after the season, there wasn't a wet eye in the house.

"You're gonna be a great one for a long time here!" Lasorda shouts to Drew, who steps into the batting cage without acknowledging the words.

At around noon, Lasorda leaves the batting cage and stalks back toward the dining room to pick up a box lunch for today's trip to Port St. Lucie for a spring training game against the New York Mets. He is almost skipping. It is not just because of excitement, but also out of necessity. Any time he is not exhorting players here, he is hustling to the next meal or the next assignment. It's not that he doesn't like jabbering with fans; he just doesn't like being surrounded and shoved and suffocated by them. With Vero Beach's wide sidewalks and easy access, that can happen as quickly and heavily as an afternoon rainstorm. Because this is three thousand miles from Dodger Stadium, many fans here have never seen the Dodgers in person. Many of them have never seen Lasorda. So they hustle more than the players.

"Tommy, Tommy, stop a second, let's get a picture!" shouts a fan, jumping on the sidewalk and throwing his arm around Lasorda.

"Make it fast," Lasorda says under his breath, spying a dozen other fans who are jogging to join them.

"Hey, Tommy, we posed for this same photo when I was ten years old," says the fan, whipping out an old Polaroid. "Now that I'm thirty, look at the difference!"

Lasorda glances at the photos and frowns. "Well, seems like I've gotten better-looking and you haven't!" Lasorda is joking but not joking, accommodating but irritated.

Then, just like that, he is gone, striding with an ungainly step but steady direction between the diamonds, with Ralph on one side of him and an assistant on the other. It's time to climb into the car and drive the forty-five minutes to Port St. Lucie.

The assistant is behind the wheel; Avila is sitting in the front passenger seat; a Dodger executive, Acey Kohrogi, is in the back with Lasorda, who is sitting behind Avila. No matter where he is going, no matter who else is in the car, if Lasorda isn't driving, he always sits in the back seat, on the right. He sits there because, from that vantage point, it's easier to tell a story that can be heard by everyone. He's also there because it is the easiest spot to quietly take a nap. At age seventy-nine, Lasorda is still in such constant motion that he often falls asleep the minute he sits down anywhere other than a restaurant.

But right now he's in the mood to tell a story. Which means that Avila, his longtime friend who has heard all of them twice, will probably fall asleep. But everyone else in the car listens. It is a story about what happened after Lasorda walked four batters in a row in his spring training major league debut.

"So, you know, my biggest problem as a pitcher was my wildness," Lasorda says. "I thought I could strike everybody out. Instead, I kept walking everybody."

He tells the story of how his former teammate Preacher Roe made him realize that his aggressiveness on the mound was foolishness. After that bad first game, Roe came to Lasorda with a question: "What if the batter gets a base hit, takes three steps out of the batter's box, and dies?"

"The ball is thrown in from the outfield and first base is tagged and the guy is out," Lasorda answered.

"Right. So, now tell me, what if that same batter is walked, takes three steps out of the box, and dies?" Roe asked.

"They bring in a pinch runner for the guy and put him on first base," Lasorda said.

"That's right," Roe said, "and that proves my point. There is no defense against a walk. Even death is not a defense against a walk."

Lasorda said that story finally made him understand. Later, as a manager, he told it to his own players. But when he was a pitcher, it could help him only so much. Even when he threw the ball over the plate, it was often hit, and so despite the fact that he won twelve and fourteen games in his next two years with the Dodgers, he was not considered a top prospect. Before the 1953 season, unable to break a big league rotation that included Preacher Roe, Carl Erskine, Clem Labine, and Russ Meyer, he was sold to the St. Louis Browns for $50,000.

"I was heartbroken to leave an organization that was so much like a family," he says. "I was also stunned. Somebody wanted to pay fifty thousand dollars? For me!"

Suddenly the story stops. Amid the central Florida dreariness, Lasorda sees a shortcut and shouts, "Turn left here!" He points to a narrow road cutting through a swamp. "I'm telling you, turn left here, it's a lot faster."

The car turns left, and Lasorda spends the next ten minutes complimenting himself. "You guys didn't know that, did you?" he says. "All these years coming to Vero Beach and you didn't know this road? A great shortcut!"

Just because his games have ended doesn't mean Lasorda's love of competition has ended. It's just that the stakes are different now. Instead of victories, he competes over who can show up for dinner first. Instead of bragging about championships, he brags about shortcuts.

"You can go faster, you know," Avila tells the driver.

The high swamp grass is already whipping along on both sides of the car.

"You can go faster because you've got the Free Pass with you," says Acey Kohrogi, and Lasorda howls.

That's him. Lasorda is the Free Pass. Put him in a car and you are assured of never getting a speeding ticket. How can any government employee punish a guy who spends so much time talking about the flag? Put him in a car and you can park anywhere, anytime, although it usually takes an attendant a few moments to peer past the driver's seat and spot Lasorda in the back.

This is what happens when the car pulls up to the field in Port St. Lucie. The Dodgers are a big draw here among the transplanted New Yorkers, so traffic is slow, cars are everywhere, workers are posting "Lot Full" signs.

"Just go," says Kohrogi. "Just remember the Free Pass!"

The car pulls up alongside a scowling senior-citizen attendant, the kind who treats a spring training park as his personal fiefdom, and tourists as trespassers.

"You can't park here!" the attendant shouts, sticking his head inside the car, where Lasorda is waving furiously at him from the back. "You can't . . . Hey, wait a minute, is that who I think it is?"

Lasorda says, "Thank you, thank you. We'll find a spot!" and within seconds the car shoots past attendants and guards and pulls up next to the stadium.

In this case, the Free Pass needs only to smile. Sometimes it takes a handshake or an autograph. At most it requires an autographed ball. The only rule Lasorda has for such balls are: he must sign them to a particular person, and that person must have a name. It is not because he wants to know each of his fans personally. It is because he doesn't want anyone selling his autographed balls on eBay. If Lasorda won't sell his autograph, he doesn't want anyone else selling it either. And if the autograph is personalized, it is generally worthless.

Such a ball is needed a short time later, when Lasorda is walking through the stadium's media lounge looking for lunch. "Tell you what," he announces to one of the workers, beginning a common Lasorda transaction. "I'll give you an autographed ball for some soup." A ball is produced, Lasorda quickly signs it, and soon he is slurping down beef-and-barley. There are many advantages to being inducted into the Hall of Fame, but perhaps none is more helpful to Lasorda than the ability to sign a baseball that instantly becomes legal tender, ensuring that he will never have to take out his wallet again. He makes sure he has constant access to balls and a Sharpie pen for just this purpose. He signs them "Tom Lasorda, HOF 8-3-97," signifying his date of induction.

Notice anything else unusual about that signature? Everyone calls him Tommy, yet he signs his name "Tom." This is also how he introduces himself and answers the phone. When asked for an explanation, he says simply, "That's my name, Tom Lasorda." It's as if he allows the rest of the world to call him Tommy because it's good business, but keeps his personal life separate by calling himself Tom. The fans can get close, but not too close. The players can hug him, but they may never really know him. The only thing that's certain is that for a former pitcher who never won a major league game, he signs an inordinate number of autographs.

Not that Lasorda didn't come close to a win. In fact, for about three hours, he was actually part of the St. Louis Browns' starting rotation. It was 1953, a couple of months after he had been sold to St. Louis. He was traveling east with the Browns after they finished spring training in San Bernardino, California. Just before the trip, Lasorda had been informed that he was in the opening-day rotation. He was staring out at the desert and marveling at his good fortune when the train stopped in Phoenix and Bill Veeck, the Browns' owner, asked to see him.

"I knew it couldn't be good," Lasorda recalls. "But I'm thinking, 'What are they gonna do, throw me off the train in the middle of nowhere?'"

In its way, it was just as bad. Veeck told Lasorda that because of the team's mounting debt, he couldn't afford the $50,000 it had cost to buy him. He was sending Lasorda back to the Dodgers. Just like that, Lasorda had been dropped from a big-league mound into a maddening purgatory and passed back and forth like a bruised piece of fruit. Everybody admired him, but nobody wanted him. Because he had already missed spring training with the Dodgers, he couldn't start the season in Brooklyn, so he went back to Montreal, where he'd had his best season ever, winning twenty games and being named the International League's left-handed pitcher of the year.

The following spring, Walter Alston became the Dodger manager, and Lasorda was given another chance to retire a spring training major league hitter, and this time he did it: Yankee Stadium, in one of the final exhibition games before the start of the season, against one batter named Yogi Berra. One curveball, one grounder, end of inning.

"I knew I had finally arrived," says Lasorda.

Nevertheless, he would be departing again. He was quickly shipped back to Montreal, just before the start of that 1954 season. When he asked for an explanation, he was told that he needed to become more consistent. When he reminded general manager Buzzie Bavasi that he had just put in four triple-A seasons of consistency, Bavasi told him to keep trying. Lasorda was so upset, for his second time as a Dodger, he quit the Dodgers.

Bavasi, smiling strangely, told Lasorda that he could help him. Bavasi picked up the phone and called a friend who ran a Brooklyn brewery. After a few minutes of conversation, Bavasi turned to Lasorda and said, "Congratulations, I got you a job paying a hundred and twenty-five dollars a week. You want it?"

It was Lasorda's turn to smile strangely. He would make $9,000 pitching for six months in Montreal; he would make $6,500 working all year long at a brewery.

"I was no math whiz, but I figured I'd be better off staying with the Dodgers," Lasorda says. "Hearing about the brewery made me realize how lucky I was. I ask Buzzie when I should show up in Montreal."

After that incident, Lasorda never made an issue of money again. He never hired an agent. He never engaged in anything more than one day of negotiations. Until the final years of his managerial career, he never signed anything more than a one-year contract.

"After each season, I would walk into Peter O'Malley's office," Lasorda recalls (Peter, Walter O'Malley's son, took over as president of the club in 1970). "He would have a number written down and he'd say, 'Well, we think this would be a good salary for next year,' and I would look at it and say fine. I loved being a Dodger. They wanted me to keep being a Dodger. It was easy."

Even when the Atlanta Braves and the New York Yankees pursued him in the early 1990s, it wasn't about the money. Lasorda was happy to be wanted, and he was thrilled that people knew he was wanted, but he never insisted on more money. He always remembered that baseball was better than the brewery.

"What does the luckiest man on earth need more money for?" he asks.

So he stayed with Montreal in 1954, won fourteen games in the first half of the season, and was recalled for his major league debut in early August. It was against the Cincinnati Reds, at Brooklyn's Ebbets Field, in the ninth inning. Lasorda retired the first two batters and was seemingly out of the inning when Gus Bell hit a routine grounder to Gil Hodges at first base. In what Lasorda considers a trademark of his pitching career, bad luck ensued. The great-fielding Hodges booted the ball, allowing the runner to take first base, with the mighty Ted Kluszewski coming to the plate.

"The guy had already hit three homers," Lasorda recalls. "No way in hell was he going to hit another one."

Because he had walked all four batters in that spring training debut, Lasorda did not want to unintentionally walk Kluszewski. But because first base was occupied, Alston would not want to intentionally walk him. So Lasorda came up with a plan. He would intentionally balk, forcing Bell to second base, leaving first base open so he could intentionally walk Kluszewski. The man who would later scold his pitchers for not being tough enough admits that in his first big-league appearance, he backed off.

"I looked at home plate and threw to first base, an obvious balk," Lasorda recalls. "But the umpire doesn't call it. So I do it again, and again, and again. And the guy won't call a balk!"

Six times in his major league debut Lasorda attempted to balk. And six times umpire Bill Stewart ignored it. Finally Lasorda held his breath and pitched to Kluszewski, and the big guy with the cut-off sleeves and bulging biceps bounced the ball in front of the plate, leading to the third out.

Walking off the field, Lasorda almost became the first player in history to argue with an umpire for *not* ruling against him. But the umpire spoke first, Stewart telling Lasorda, "You didn't know it, kid, but you were balking like hell out there. I know it's your first big-league game, so I was giving you a break, but be careful next time, OK?"

Lasorda didn't know what to say. It didn't matter. For the rest of the 1954 season, nobody really listened to him anyway. He didn't pitch again. Alston didn't think Lasorda was worth the trouble. Lasorda thought Alston was holding a grudge from the Montreal days. At one point, Lasorda was ordered to sit in the dugout instead of the bullpen because he was more valuable to the team as a cheerleader. This upset Lasorda, and it led to a shouting match with Alston, which brought to the surface feelings that haunted Lasorda for the rest of his career.

Just as he hated that Alston thought him a better cheerleader than a pitcher, Lasorda hates it that some people think he was a better motivator than a game manager. He hears it all the time. When he entered the Hall of Fame with managerial statistics equal to those of other managers who were not in the Hall—former St. Louis and Boston manager Billy Southworth also won four pennants and two world championships and is not in Cooperstown—some critics complained.

He was elected because he was an ambassador, they said. He was elected not for his lineup cards but for his pep talks. The credit for his first world championship went to the likes of Steve Yeager, Ron Cey, and Pedro Guerrero. His second title was attributed to Kirk Gibson and Orel Hershiser. Lasorda's managerial skills have always been smothered by his people skills, and it has burned him. You talk about how he motivated the 1988 championship club, and he will show you how he pulled winning games out of mediocre players. Talk about his cheers, and he will talk about his division titles. The doubts and dismissive comments that began with Alston followed Lasorda all the way to Cooperstown, where he felt he had to convince America that he was entering the Hall of Fame as a manager, not an entertainer. In his speech he made sure everyone knew that he had earned the honor in the dugout and not on the podium, with two world titles and 1,599 wins and not just with his smile.

"You wanna see something that's more impressive than anything in Cooperstown?" asks Ralph Avila as he watches Lasorda slurp down his soup in the Port St. Lucie media cafeteria. "Look at this piece of paper."

From his wallet Avila produces a wrinkled scrap bearing elegant handwriting that reads, "Aug. 9, 1998, 9:15 P.M., Pro Player Stadium.

Tom Lasorda doesn't want to eat any more, he is full." And underneath the proclamation is Lasorda's signature.

"I've kept this for seven years," Avila says, "because I thought nobody would believe it."

Lasorda shakes his head and frowns with the knowledge that even Cooperstown can't save someone from his own reputation.

Lasorda enters the stadium area about a half hour before the first pitch, and ushers point him toward his seat. The place is half full, several thousand fans, but enough for Lasorda, who decides to step out of the stands and walk across the diamond.

Yes, they all see him. And yes, they are all shouting, "Tommy! Brooklyn! USA! Hey, Tommy!"

He walks up into the stands, and someone hands him a ball to autograph, and someone else hands him a ham sandwich, and around him everyone smiles and cheers. This is the Tommy they love, embracing his fans and his food. This is his role, this is his own bright spotlight, and he will bask in it until the end.

"Funny thing about baseball," he says between cheers and bites. "I thought, when I stopped managing, people would forget me. But they remember me even more today. How does that happen? I mean, how does that happen?"

4
. . .

I BOUNCED AROUND FOR THIS

Have some breakfast!"

On a February morning in a small house in Fullerton, California, the cluttered kitchen suddenly shakes. It is not an earthquake. It is not a sonic boom. It is a McDonald's bag filled with Sausage McMuffins dropped on the kitchen counter. It is Tommy Lasorda's breakfast. This being the Dodgers' Winter Caravan Day, Lasorda needs his strength.

"You accuse me of never buying you a meal, but look here, I bought us these McMuffins," Lasorda says, digging in. "Man, these are good eatin'."

Lasorda loves McDonald's. He has ordered a limousine to go to a McDonald's drive-through. He once attempted to purchase a whole McDonald's restaurant while he was in the drive-through. "Turns out, man, those things are expensive," he says. Surprisingly, Lasorda has never owned a restaurant, although he once lent his name to three Italian restaurants, only to see his investment suffer when one of the places was discovered to have rats.

The McMuffins disappear, and Lasorda is ready to join the caravan, which is a good thing, because all across Los Angeles children are waiting. In the course of eight hours, Lasorda and several Dodger players and officials will barnstorm throughout southern California, stopping at an elementary school, a high school, an inner-city baseball academy, and an aquarium. When he was manager, Lasorda would take half the team along on these tours, the players joining him out of both loyalty and duty. These days, only a handful of Dodger major leaguers live in the area, so the tour is lucky to feature one star. Today the biggest name is the local-born Nomar Garciaparra, who has been with the team for only one season. That means the real star will be Lasorda.

"Eat that last one, Dad," says his wife, Jo, pointing to the last greasy lump. "Did you take your pills? Do you have directions?"

Lasorda eats standing up, which is a good thing, because his small house is so stocked with boxes and magazines and memorabilia there aren't many places to sit. For more than forty years, the Lasorda empire has been run from a modest stucco home that is more cozy than castle. Some of Lasorda's closest friends have never seen the place. It is an hour's drive from Dodger Stadium and a world away from his Hollywood image.

Sitting modestly in a nondescript middle-class neighborhood, the house has two small front windows and a decoratively barred screen over the front door. It is so unlike the home of a king, new UPS drivers are apt to be confused. They show up bearing a package with the Lasorda name and think maybe it's a mistake.

Just as confusing are the expensive cars in the driveway, easily the nicest cars on the street. Tommy would move them into the garage, but there is no room, the garage being full of large storage boxes and more memorabilia and a giant washer and dryer, the same kind you find in a baseball clubhouse.

"There's a lot of legends about the stuff I have in this garage," says Lasorda. "I can't confirm or deny any of it."

Inside, the house has a sliver of a kitchen, a small dining room, and a back den that was added on, built by some of his players. In that den there is a big-screen TV that dwarfs a couple of comfortable chairs. "Somebody once asked if we were ever going to get a house to go with that TV," Lasorda says. The den is where he and

Jo watch movies on Lifetime together. This is where they sit in their pajamas each evening and share their days. This, they say, is all they need.

The Lasordas have lived in this house since moving to California in the mid-1960s, when Lasorda was working on a scout's low salary. Jo made good friends, including neighbors with whom the Lasordas still share Thanksgiving and Christmas. Jo found plumbers and electricians and handymen. Jo discovered the rarest of commodities for baseball wives, the feeling of security. When Lasorda became manager and embraced Hollywood and began making good money, the woman who supported him through all the lean years had but one request: she did not want to move. Ever. So they stayed.

"We would come home from having dinner in Beverly Hills with Frank Sinatra or the Gregory Pecks and Jo would smile and say, 'Now you're coming back to reality. So go take the trash out.'"

Lasorda would take out the trash, but he hardly lifted a finger otherwise. Until recently, he could proudly say he has never washed a dish, cleaned a table, laundered a shirt, or made a bed.

"Lemme tell you a story about that. I was playing in Puerto Rico, and Jo complained that one of my teammates was helping his wife do the dishes, and so I asked her, 'How many ballgames have you been to? Do you ever see me on the mound with the bases loaded, nobody out, and that fourth hitter staring me in the face? Do I ever ask you to get him out? I don't ask you to pitch, you don't ask me to do the dishes.'"

Lasorda often follows this story with another one about Jo: "In an interview, she was once asked if she ever considered divorce. She answered, 'Divorce, no. Murder, yes.'"

When you consider Lasorda's pitching career, it was probably less messy for Jo to do the dishes herself. As hard as Lasorda tried, he pitched the way he fought—too aggressively, with blood everywhere. Lasorda's first major league start was in 1955 with the Brooklyn Dodgers, one of the greatest teams ever, a roster boasting future Hall of Famers Jackie Robinson, Roy Campanella, Duke Snider, and Pee Wee Reese. This was the first Brooklyn team to win a world championship. This was also the perfect team on which Lasorda could get that first big-league start, because the Dodgers had such a commanding win-loss record that even a junk-throwing lefty couldn't mess it up.

With the team leading in the standings by double-digit games, Lasorda took the mound against the St. Louis Cardinals. He wanted to show his nemesis, Alston, that he was more than just a mouth. He was eager to show he could be a big part of a team that he knew would win a championship. Alas, he did neither.

He walked the first batter, Wally Moon. He bounced his next pitch past Campanella to the backstop, moving Moon to second. He stepped off the mound. He wiped the sweat from his nose. Oh, no, he was thinking. Not again. Please, not again.

He stared down the next batter, Bill Virdon. He growled at him. He shook his head at him. It didn't matter. He couldn't fight his way through this. He walked Virdon. This brought up the great Stan Musial, and now Lasorda's head was back in Norristown.

He was a third-string pitcher again. He wasn't good enough again. Forget his fastball, forget his curveball. Lasorda would have to trick his way out of this jam. So he threw, of all things, a knuckle ball. Campanella couldn't catch it. The ball bounced to the backstop, and now the runners were on second and third.

A Hall of Famer at the plate, two runners in scoring position on two walks and two wild pitches, and Lasorda's mind continued to spin. He had worked all of his life for this? He had fought from Cuba to Greenville for the right to do this? Embarrass himself in his first big chance? Show Alston that he was right? That Tommy Lasorda was a better heckler than a pitcher? Life was so unfair. Those trick pitches worked in the minor leagues. Why not now? Why didn't I get the big arm that could blow hitters away? Why didn't I get the great legs that could push me toward a strikeout? Why was my body not as strong as my heart? It was so unfair.

"Then," Lasorda remembers, "I threw the greatest curveball of my career."

And in the greatest out of his career, he quite unbelievably whiffed the Man, striking out the swinging Musial.

If only the story ended here. But the stories of Lasorda's playing career never ended here. They never ended in a strikeout. They never ended in triumph. As with many great sports motivators, all Lasorda's playing stories ended in misery.

With Ken Boyer at the plate, Lasorda threw another wild pitch —his third of the inning—and Moon raced toward home. Lasorda ran in from the mound and blocked the plate like a catcher—except he forgot he wasn't wearing shin guards. Moon slid toward the plate and sliced up Lasorda's leg. The kneecap was cut open. Blood dripped from his knee into his sock. Lasorda finished the inning, hobbled to the dugout, and tried to hide the gaping wound.

But Pee Wee Reese saw it. And Jackie Robinson, who grew sick at the sight of blood, smelled it. And Alston, looking for any excuse to rid himself of Lasorda, immediately ordered Clem Labine to take over on the mound. Lasorda protested until a team doctor warned him that he would be risking his future ability to walk if he returned to action. This only made Lasorda protest more, until finally his teammates Don Newcombe and Russ Meyer grabbed him by the arms and dragged him screaming into the dugout.

"I was twenty-seven years old. I had been working my entire life for that moment. I knew how precious it might be," Lasorda recalls. "And then it was gone. Forever."

He was right. That was his only start that season, his only start for the Dodgers, and one of only six starts in a career during which he was 0–4 with a 6.48 ERA.

"Now you see why I wanted to go back to that mound?" he says. "Being able to walk right for the rest of my life didn't really matter. Being able to pitch for the Dodgers did."

On this February morning, his legs are hurting again. This time it's his left hip. It's so sore, he winces with every step. Yet he refuses to see a doctor. He'd had his knees replaced several years ago, and he dreads any talk of a hip replacement, saying, "I ain't going to no hospital, not again, no way. I can take the pain."

So he winces some more and hobbles out the front door of his Fullerton home, and the cool morning breeze hits his face, and his mood instantly changes.

"I love these caravans. I love being with the people," he says. "Isn't it a beautiful day? God bless America!"

When driving with Lasorda, the first thing you want to do is salute. Not because he sounds like a statesman, but because his Cadillac looks like it belongs to a president. From the back passenger window an American flag flaps. It flies above the roof, shadowing the side of the car, whipping furiously in the 65 mph draft, a decoration far more distracting than anything one would find on a tricked-out Escalade. Some drivers swerve to avoid it. Others slow down to stare at it. Every time Lasorda's car is washed, the workers get rid of it. Every time, Lasorda just finds another flag.

"Everywhere I go, I want everyone to know I'm American," Lasorda says, and there is little doubt of that.

The second thing you want to do when riding with Lasorda is cover your ears. His car has satellite radio, and the station is constantly tuned to forties music, and Lasorda insists on singing each song at the top of his lungs, even when he has no idea of the words. "Baby face . . . you've got the cutest little baby face . . . Da-da-na-na-da-da baby face."

The car mercifully comes to a halt at the caravan's first stop, Ocean View Elementary in Whittier, about twenty minutes from Lasorda's house. Lasorda has arrived before the busload of players and officials. No matter where he goes, he seemingly arrives before everyone else. There are rows of children sitting in folding chairs in a playground. He hobbles out of the car and they barely notice him. But as he gets closer to the group, the adults start to buzz, and soon they are surrounding him.

"Tommy, you are the ambassador of baseball!" says one.

"See what they say about me?" Lasorda replies to the bystanders.

In that one statement, from a science teacher at 10 A.M. on a winter morning, the equation of Lasorda's life is once again clear. Lasorda needs his fans as much as they need him. He still glows at the platitudes heaped upon him, still shrugs as if he can't believe it, still listens to every word, even though his hearing is dimmed.

"Dod-gers, Dod-gers, Dod-gers," chant the children.

The team bus arrives, and the players and officials walk slowly toward the cheering children. But first each of them stops to greet

Lasorda. For Dodger employees of all kinds, it is like kissing the ring of a pope. If you see Lasorda, you stop and shake his hand or pat his back, anything to acknowledge him. To ignore him is akin to blasphemy. The younger players follow the lead of Garciaparra, who hugs Lasorda like a grandfather. And if they wonder why such affection is required, they need only to listen to the crowd. Once again, even in a group that includes one of the most popular short-stops in the game, the biggest cheers are reserved for Lasorda.

"The Dodgers are here to show you what you need to do to do the right things in life," shouts Lasorda. "You go to school to get a good education. As you grow older, education is something that no-body can take away from you."

It is a routine speech met by bored glances from kids who don't really connect. Then Lasorda pauses. He can read an audience the way he once read a scoreboard. He knows when he is trailing. He knows how to make a comeback. Out of nowhere, he shouts, "The unsung heroes are the teachers. So how about a nice round of ap-plause for your teachers!"

Not only do the kids cheer, but the teachers cheer too. Everyone is rocking in their folding chairs, the playground is alive again, and Lasorda takes another big swing.

"When you're hungry, your mother feeds you! When you're sick, your mother takes care of you! When you need clothes, your mother and father buy you clothes! You can't give them any money for any of this, can you? No! You have to show them love and respect. That's what you owe your parents. Love and respect. Let's hear you say it!"

Together the kids begin chanting, "Love and respect, love and re-spect!"

Now Lasorda makes sure this crowd will never forget his voice, even though, moments earlier, many of them didn't know his name.

"OK, everybody, hold your head back now and do something for me! Say, 'I loooove the Dodgers!' Say it!"

Together, heads back, everyone says it, laughing and giggling and shouting as Lasorda adds one more footnote.

"And the Dodgers love you!" he says, and he steps back from the microphone into the lineup of mere mortal players and officials.

As with all of his speeches, he had none of this planned. He didn't know what he would say, or how he would say it, until he actually said it. He makes speeches like he once managed, from his heart— this is a guy who once ordered newfangled laptop computers banned from the dugout because they confused him. On this day, though, he is also speaking from the depths of resilience, because he's speaking in great pain.

It's that hip. It's hurting him. The elementary school speeches end, and the Dodger entourage heads back to the street, and it would be so much easier if Lasorda continued the caravan in his Cadillac. But at the last minute he insists on riding with the rest of the Dodgers in the bus. His assistant will drive his car. Even now, more than a decade after his last managerial appearance, Lasorda likes to be there for the players, hanging with them in close quarters, listening to them if they need advice. He struggles to climb up the three steps to the bus, and he curses when he squeezes into the front-row seat.

"Gawd, this leg is killing me," he says.

But he is there, close to his team, even if that team is a hastily assembled group of guys in the middle of winter. He has tried to stay close to his teams ever since one of his managers refused to stay close to him. It was later that 1955 season, and Lasorda had rushed back from a knee injury and allowed the Pittsburgh Pirates to hit a couple of homers while pitching with a bad leg and sore arm. After that game, he sat for more than an hour in front of his locker, waiting for Walter Alston to applaud him for trying, waiting for Alston just to recognize him for showing up. But Alston never came near him. Only one player, Pee Wee Reese, approached Lasorda, and that was only to ask him why he fought so hard to pitch so soon.

"You weren't ready," said Reese.

"You wouldn't understand," said Lasorda.

Lasorda vowed to never again allow a beaten player to sit alone. This is another reason why he always had the team's postgame buffet in his office, and why he was always one of the last to leave the stadium, sometimes walking back to the Dodgers' hotel if he missed the team bus.

"I know what it feels like to be alone in defeat, so I promised myself that nobody I managed would ever know that same feeling," he says.

His collapse against Pittsburgh was the beginning of the end of Lasorda's Dodger playing career. Soon thereafter, he was summoned to Buzzie Bavasi's office, where the boss asked Lasorda an unusual question: "Tommy, we need to cut someone. If you were the general manager of this team, who would you cut?"

Lasorda looked around the room and came up with an answer. It is an answer that he will never apologize for giving. It was an answer that haunts him to this day.

"I told them, if I was in charge, I would cut that Sandy Koufax kid," Lasorda remembers.

That Sandy Koufax kid, of course, was the rookie version of the guy who would become one of the best left-handed pitchers in baseball history. Imagine Lasorda, known as one of the best talent evaluators in baseball history, trying to persuade the Dodgers to cut Koufax.

"But it wasn't about baseball," Lasorda says. "It was about survival."

The Dodgers were not fooled. Koufax stayed, and Lasorda was cut, and he angrily finished the season in the minor leagues. He might have quit again — how many times would that be? — if it were not for a visit from his father, who blew up when Lasorda began complaining while they were waiting for room service.

"I drive a truck in a quarry and you're getting room service, and you're complaining?" Sabatino Lasorda asked. "Shut up!"

Lasorda did shut up, finished the season, and watched his former teammates win a world championship and vote him a half share of the playoff money. Partly because of his father's pep talk, Lasorda used that money to send his father back to Italy in the off-season. Love and respect — he showed it long before he ever convinced children to shout it.

The next spring, Lasorda's Dodger voice was finally silenced. He was quietly sold to the Kansas City Athletics, where he could pitch once more. The Dodgers thought they were doing him a favor. Lasorda didn't see it that way.

"The Dodgers had helped me start my life, helped me get married, taken care of me when I had kids. They were there for me at every step, even if sometimes I stumbled. I knew I would have to get back to the Dodgers."

Thus began a sabbatical that has since become the fodder for a piece of Dodger trivia. Although Tommy Lasorda often says he has spent every year since 1949 with the Dodgers, you must subtract one year.

"I don't even count that year," Lasorda says, except there is one big reason it belongs.

After only half a season in Kansas City, in 1956, he was traded to the New York Yankees, who promptly sent him to their minor league team in Denver, where Lasorda met the man who would shape his managerial style more than any other boss.

His name was Ralph Houk. From Lasorda's first game in Denver, Houk rolled out a blueprint that Lasorda would follow for the rest of his career. On that midsummer night in high altitude, Lasorda took the mound with a curveball that was not stronger than science. In the thin air, it wouldn't dip. It wouldn't dart. It wouldn't fool anybody. Lasorda quickly allowed five runs, which quickly brought Houk to the mound.

Here it came, another lecture from a disappointed manager. Lasorda had heard it before. Another weathered man coming to the mound to lecture him on the obvious. Lasorda shrugged and handed Houk the ball and started toward the dugout when Houk grabbed him gently by the shirt.

"Hang in there," Houk told him. "I like what I've seen so far."

Lasorda shook his head in amazement. What? His manager liked what he saw? Five runs in his first appearance and his manager was patting him on the back? He thought of Walter Alston, who wouldn't come near him after a bad game. He thought of Clay Bryant, who, after a losing game, would make him wait for an hour before he could take a shower. Perhaps nowhere had he pitched as poorly as he just pitched here in Denver, and yet his manager was embracing him.

Houk later explained that he understood Lasorda wasn't used to the mile-high air. He understood that the poor kid must have been tired after driving all night from Kansas City. That Lasorda may have been thinking about the problems of moving his family. Houk was giving him a break. He was treating him like a human being.

"When I came off the mound that day, I would have killed for Ralph Houk," Lasorda remembers. "On a day when I should have been incredibly embarrassed, I was incredibly fired up."

It was Houk who taught Lasorda the phrase that has become one of his mantras.

"Ralph taught me that if you treat players like human beings, they will try to play like Superman," Lasorda says. "He taught me how a pat on the shoulder can be just as important as a kick in the butt."

Houk also knew when to be tough. He is the only person who ever asked Lasorda to start a fight — as if Lasorda needed to be asked. It was during the American Association playoffs against the Omaha Cardinals, and Lasorda responded by throwing an errant baseball at the pitcher's head. This provoked a brawl that inspired the Denver club to win the series. Lasorda was both applauded and fined, and the next spring he was sold back to the Dodgers for good.

"I fought my way into the organization, and I fought my way back," he says.

Through the cool afternoon and the thick Los Angeles traffic, the Dodger caravan bus heads toward St. John Bosco High, where Garciaparra went to school and played baseball. Lasorda is fighting again, this time with that hip pain.

"If you were me, you couldn't take this!" he shouts from his bus seat. "This is hurting every inch of me, but I ain't taking nothing, no Advil, nothing. The players couldn't take this. Nobody could take this!"

The pain is worse on the rattling bus, but Lasorda will stay, just as he plans on staying with the team throughout spring training, which will begin in a couple of weeks. His role there is largely ceremonial, but he treats it like he's still the boss. Every day he puts on the uniform. Every day he hangs out behind the batting cages. And even if his morning workouts leave him needing a nap, at every home game he will sit with the team by the bench, sometimes snoozing between innings.

"I hate to leave these guys," he says.

The Dodgers will be leaving the Vero Beach fans in a couple of years, moving to Arizona, a relocation that surprisingly causes Lasorda to simply shrug. Vero is his favorite place in the world, it's his kingdom, but it's no longer attractive to his bosses because of its dwindling fan base, and Lasorda will always back his bosses.

"I think we should leave Vero Beach. We just don't get the fans anymore," he says, ever the loyal employee. "We'll do better in Arizona."

As the bus rolls toward St. John Bosco, it becomes apparent that the school is a long drive from Whittier, where Garciaparra grew up. Lasorda can't believe that someone would travel for thirty minutes to go to school. He stands up in his seat and begins doing one of his favorite things in the world, shouting insults to the back of a bus.

"Hey, Nomar, you went so far from home. Did John Bosco pay you to go to high school?"

"We'll talk about that later!" says Garciaparra, laughing.

"Did Arn Tellem represent you at John Bosco?" Lasorda shouts, mentioning the name of Garciaparra's agent.

"Yeah," shouts Ned Colletti, the Dodgers' general manager, who is sitting behind Lasorda. "Nomar held out for longer recess and no homework!"

Everyone on the bus is laughing now as the bus creaks its way up to St. John Bosco. Lasorda has done it again, turning a dull trip into an amusement park ride, causing one Dodger marketing employee to stop at his seat as she leaves the bus.

"Oh, Tommy," she says, shaking her head at the wonder of it all.

The star of this stop is the returning hero Garciaparra. But again, when Lasorda steps in front of the several hundred cheering boys assembled in the playground, he gets all the ooohhs.

"You're all fortunate enough to be living in the greatest country of the world, the United States of America," he says to bursts of applause. "Dream! Dreams become reality. When I was fifteen, sixteen years old, I used to dream I was pitching for the New York Yankees. Then my mother would shake me and say, 'Wake up, Tommy, it's time to go to school!' And I would cry. Why didn't she leave me alone? Why did she take me from that dream? Then one day, when we played the Yankees, I took the long walk up to the pitcher's mound and said, 'I've been here many times in my dreams.'"

One of the students asks him about regrets. "My one regret is never going to college," he tells them. "I signed to play baseball out of high school and never had a chance to attend college, and I regret that to this day."

Yet talk to him privately and he scoffs at the notion that he could have been accepted by a college. "Man, I wasn't the best student in high school."

A student asks Lasorda about the rival Los Angeles Angels.

"The only angels are up in heaven, and they're all ex-Dodgers!" he shouts, and the crowd roars.

The angels line is one that he uses often to tweak the Anaheim-based team, which changed it's name to the Los Angeles Angels in hopes of stealing market share from the Dodgers. Yet there is another funny aspect to Lasorda's ridiculing the name.

He actually once pitched for the Los Angeles Angels, which used to be a triple-A farm club of the Dodgers. That was where Lasorda was assigned after he was traded back from the Yankees in the spring of 1957. He spent a season as an Angel, then returned to the Dodgers' farm club in Montreal in 1958. Yes, it was his seventh year there, perhaps a record for any one player in any one minor league city. The Montreal fans were so enamored of him, they held a Tom Lasorda Day and gave him a new car.

If only he had used it to drive out of town. Because he would become the only player in history to *return* to a minor league city after being honored with a special day there. He pitched in Montreal again in 1959 and the first part of the 1960 season before he wore out his welcome with too many fights and too much controversy.

When he was released, he was given a letter written by Dodger general manager Buzzie Bavasi, essentially banning him from the organization for life because he was a troublemaker.

"I was stunned. It was like my whole world had collapsed," Lasorda recalls. "I didn't know what to do."

He phoned Bavasi and pleaded with him to explain his reasoning, begged to be allowed to return as a coach or an instructor. Bavasi said that Lasorda's bosses in Montreal had complained that he was undermining their decisions. Lasorda disputed the facts, then begged for one last thing. He begged Bavasi to read a letter he had written earlier to then–scouting director Al Campanis. In the letter, Lasorda professed his undying love for the Dodgers and his willingness to do anything for the organization. Bavasi dug up the letter and was impressed. Thus the most important Dodger Blue "speech" of Lasorda's career ended up being his first one. In July 1960, he was rehired by the team to work for Campanis as a scout.

"My love for the Dodgers had once again saved my career with the Dodgers," Lasorda says. "And the fun was just beginning."

The fun is also just beginning as the players file back on the bus, all of them heading toward the rear, leaving Lasorda in the front seat, traditionally reserved for managers. Lasorda also has to sit there because people tend to jump on the bus to shake his hand before it leaves. At this stop, it is a local Catholic bishop who boards the bus, to say goodbye to Lasorda, who always knows where to find the highest-ranking clergy. Then a policeman climbs aboard, to say he wishes he were like Lasorda, who also knows where to find the highest-ranking cop.

Just as the players are settling in behind him, Lasorda gazes out at a parking lot filled with late-model cars, and he howls, "Imagine all these kids with all these cars, and I walked six miles to school. I remember a guy coming to our house selling encyclopedias, and my father says, 'We're not buying an encyclopedia. My sons can walk to school like everyone else.'"

Half an hour later, the bus pulls into the Major League Baseball Urban Youth Academy, a sparkling new facility amid the boarded-up businesses and cluttered streets of Compton, south of Los Angeles. The academy was built to bring baseball back to the inner city, which has long since abandoned the sport. It was built to embody what Lasorda says in his speeches about dreaming big. It is the perfect place for the former manager to again stand up for the underappreciated and the barely noticed.

Which is something he begins doing as soon as the bus grinds to a halt and the doors wheeze open and the entourage saunters warily toward a picnic area filled with box lunches. A Dodger marketing hotshot starts shouting: "Everybody wait until the players get their lunches! Everybody let the players get their lunches first!" This is where Lasorda intervenes.

The hotshot is pandering and playing favorites, and even though it is only box lunches, Lasorda will not stand for it. In this case, "everybody" includes Lasorda's main constituency, the Dodger front-office workers who have carefully planned the day's activities. They are all women, and they are being marginalized, and Lasorda has to speak up.

"Wait a minute," he says. "These people have worked every bit as hard as the players. They are every bit as important. Let them eat!"

The hotshot quivers behind mirrored sunglasses as the grinning women parade past him for their food, thus revealing yet another secret of Lasorda's success. His Dodger managing empire stood for twenty years amid the shifting winds of failure and discontent because of the strength of the hidden foundation of folks like these. It wasn't the stars who kept Lasorda in business, it was the role players and clubhouse guys and low-level employees, whom Lasorda coddled and embraced and eventually owned. If any player grew angry with Lasorda—even the biggest of players—he would be surrounded by so many people who were undyingly loyal to the manager, his voice would be silenced.

"I would tell my players," Lasorda says, "we play hard not just for ourselves but for all those unsung heroes upstairs who make these games happen every night, from secretaries to janitors, the real heart of the Dodgers."

And, in turn, whether it be washing his car or getting him tickets or stifling criticism of him, those people would forever pay him back.

It worked the same way with newspaper writers, as evidenced

here at the Urban Youth Academy when Lasorda spots a local columnist and asks about her.

"She loves you, Tommy," says an assistant.

"Why on earth does she love me?"

"A long time ago, you did something nice for someone in her family, and she's never forgotten it," the assistant says.

"Oh," says Lasorda, who has heard that story a million times. "Of course."

And, sure enough, the writer approaches and treats Lasorda like a favorite grandfather. This is not unusual. Even the most hard-bitten journalists who cover Lasorda will not casually criticize him, if only because he was once nice to their visiting mother, or he signed an autograph for their sick cousin, or he spoke at their church for free. If someone was going to rip Lasorda, it would have to be about something big, something worth losing his favor and the favor of all those players who would see him snub you in the clubhouse. Sometimes, as when he decided not to intentionally walk the St. Louis Cardinals' Jack Clark in the 1985 playoffs, and Clark went on to hit a pennant-winning homer, the criticism was worth the risk. Most times, it was not.

Lasorda's cell phone rings. Yeah, the calliope. It's an old friend inquiring about an invitation for Lasorda to appear at a function in New York—on the same night he is supposed to be attending a bull-riding event with his wife and granddaughter. Lasorda will put family above even his closest friends. But he will agonize over it. And when it's a really close friend, he will be physically unable to tell him no. That's what his assistant is for.

Lasorda says, "Can you call him back and tell him I'm too upset to talk, but I have to miss the event?"

"Upset, like, mad?" his assistant asks. "Or just upset, like, sad?"

"What are you talking about?" Lasorda shouts. "Just say I'm upset—as in, I'm upset!"

The assistant walks away with Lasorda's cell phone, shaking his head. Lasorda smiles. He hates delivering bad news so much that, when he managed, he eventually stopped going to the mound to change pitchers. He would walk out to give a lift to a struggling but proud pitcher. The pitcher might argue his case, and Lasorda would either allow him to remain in the game or pull him out and feel like a bad guy. And Lasorda hates feeling like a bad guy.

"So if I sent out the pitching coach, if the player argued, the coach would just shrug and point to me," Lasorda says. "There would be no scene. There would be no arguing. And by the time the player reached the dugout, maybe he wasn't so mad at me anymore."

His assistant, who does everything for Lasorda, including buttoning his shirts when his arthritic fingers won't work, is like that pitching coach. Today he walks away and makes the call and delivers the bad news, and Lasorda wipes his brow, relieved.

By now, the kids from the community begin to file into the academy. The shiny walls and spotless locker rooms do not match their torn shorts and stained shirts and sad eyes. Lasorda does not notice this, though, because he has to visit the bathroom. And, as usual, he finds himself in a most unlikely spot when this need arises. He is standing in the girls' softball locker room. It is a compact but clean room with rows of red lockers that seem vacant. Lasorda was brought here on a quick academy tour by its director, Darrell Miller.

"How many girls play softball here?" he asks.

"We're still growing. It's still just twenty-five," says Miller.

"Is that all?" says Lasorda. "Well, at my age you can never pass up a bathroom, so I'm going to use the one in here."

"But Tommy . . ." says Miller.

"Hey," Lasorda says, "did I ever tell you about the time I helped the U.S. women's softball team win a gold medal?"

The man has an anecdote for everywhere, even a women's bathroom. He proceeds to talk about how, during the 2000 Olympics in Sydney, Australia, he was summoned to speak to the team after it had lost its first three games.

"The coaches said, 'We want you to really blister them,'" recalls Lasorda. "I told them, 'I will not use that kind of language around women.' And they repeated, 'Let them have it.' So, well, I did."

Lasorda launched into a lengthy tirade: the women were embarrassing their country and themselves. He reportedly stopped short of calling them murderous traitors, but not by much.

"I called them every name in the book," Lasorda remembers. "They gave me permission to curse in front of women, so I did. I gave them everything I had. And what did they do?"

They won five consecutive games and an Olympic championship, a feat that nearly matched the men's baseball championship, which Lasorda guided. Although coaches do not receive Olympic medals, Lasorda now jokingly claims he should have gotten two.

"If you ask me, I helped two teams win medals that day."

He hobbles out of the girls' bathroom and into a nearby room for a quick rest before meeting the neighborhood kids. On the table is a phone. The phone rings. Without hesitation, Lasorda answers. He loves doing this, answering calls that are not meant for him, hoping that the person on the other end will, at the very least, faint from the excitement of talking to him.

"Your name is Martha?" he says into the receiver. "You want to know if your kid has practice today? OK, Martha, I'll check." He pauses and checks. "No, Martha, the kids aren't doing anything tonight. We're giving them a day off. Hope everything goes well for you and your son. Bye."

The woman on the phone didn't recognize his voice. She was talking to a baseball Hall of Famer and never knew it. Lasorda laughs uncomfortably, then walks outside to face groups of Compton kids who aren't laughing. They look weary, distant. They clearly don't know much about Lasorda. This doesn't bother him, however, it just makes him work harder.

"I know what it is to be your age, but you don't know what it is to be my age," Lasorda tells them. "So listen!"

He notices that many of them are dressed in mismatched and worn clothing. He shakes his head.

"When I was growing up, my shoes were so thin I could step on a coin and tell you whether it was heads or tails," he says.

The kids seem to perk up and listen.

When Lasorda spots a girl sucking her thumb and staring into space, he gets her attention by talking about the Louisiana girl who used a glove signed by Lasorda, which inspired her to become one of the state's first female baseball players. That girl is now coaching college softball and has become a good friend of Lasorda's.

"Believe you can achieve anything you want!" he screams for the third time today, coaxing the thumb out of the girl's mouth. "You must believe. You must believe!"

Lasorda pauses and scans the crowd. "What do you want to be? What do you want to be?"

One child shouts out, "A football player!"

Wrong answer.

"Football? Football?" Lasorda looks incredulous. "You're talking to the wrong people, son! Go down the street and talk to the football people."

He is only partly serious. But when another boy says he has never seen a Dodgers game, Lasorda becomes dead serious.

"You've never seen the Dodgers play? You don't go to Dodger Stadium? Why not? Every little kid wants to see the Dodgers."

The child looks down and shakes his head. It seems obvious that he lives in a household that cannot afford baseball tickets. This would be the perfect opportunity for Lasorda to treat him, and he is preparing to do just that when—

"GAWD ALMIGHTY!" Lasorda screams. "GOOD GAWD ALMIGHTY!"

Walking through the crowd of kids sitting at picnic tables, Lasorda has just stepped over a boy's giant sneaker and landed awkwardly on that left hip, and the pain has shaken his entire body, sending him staggering toward five wide-eyed girls.

"GAWD, IT HURTS!" He teeters toward the girls as the kids stare in shock. "GAWD ALMIGHTY."

Then, just as quickly, he is quiet and walking normally. He leans down and pats the back of one of the girls. He asks another about her homework. He turns to the child without Dodger tickets and says, "Son, I'm telling you, you *will* see the Dodgers one day."

Even in these occasional unsteady moments, he is doing what he does best, what he will do forever. He is managing.

"See what happens when you get old?" he says, laughing, and everyone starts laughing with him.

"Hey," shouts Ned Colletti, the general manager. "I know some of you want to be football players or baseball players, but do any of you want to be leg surgeons?"

Everyone laughs again, and that is how Lasorda will leave them, laughing and waving and thankful for the memory.

He hobbles back on the bus, saying, "Stinking leg."

And to think that Lasorda used to be one of the strongest men on these streets. The Compton area had been part of his territory as a Dodger scout. And man, could Lasorda scout. His skills as a talent evaluator, combined with his power of persuasion, turned simple scouting assignments into the stuff of legend.

Lasorda once brought a prospect to a Dodger intersquad scrimmage where he himself was the pitcher. Lasorda threw the prospect fat fastballs that the kid could hit out of the park. The prospect was signed.

Lasorda once pounced on the bleachers rumor that a certain prospect's father had been overheard talking about giving his son an injection. "Gosh, guys, do you really want to sign someone who already has a bad arm?" Lasorda said, never bothering to explain that the prospect's father was a doctor who was talking about a flu shot.

"You did what you had to do," Lasorda recalls. "I thought scouting was no different than playing, you know?"

In this South Los Angeles area in the early 1960s, Lasorda attended the funeral of a prospective player's grandfather, even though he had met the man only once. Lasorda was late for the funeral, so he wound up sitting in the last empty chair, on the altar, behind the preacher. Lasorda was the only white person in the church, so the preacher figured he was important, and surprisingly summoned him to the pulpit.

"We have a dignitary here today with us," said the preacher, who then turned and whispered to Lasorda, "What did you say your name was again?"

"Nobody knew me," Lasorda recalls. "But I knew this was my big chance to land this player."

Instead of admitting that he barely knew the deceased, Lasorda sung the grandfather's virtues, whipping the crowd into a frenzy, referring to the grandson as cut from the same mold. The grandson listened and admired and, sure enough, a day later, he—the outfielder Willie Crawford—became a Dodger.

"That ain't even my best scouting story," Lasorda says.

There was the time that Lasorda was trying to get to his Dodger Stadium office during a game. The guard at the front gate didn't know him or recognize him, and Lasorda didn't have a pass, so he was prohibited from entering.

"First thing I did was tell this guy, 'If I can't get in the parking lot, man, I'm going to clean up the place with you,'" Lasorda recalls. "Then I asked him if we could make some sort of deal."

The guard had a buddy who played baseball and was willing to deal. If Lasorda was truly a scout, then he would evaluate his buddy. In exchange, he would be allowed into the parking lot.

"So I ask him, 'Where's this player?'"

A couple of days later, Lasorda drove to a nearby field and watched him play. And soon thereafter, Tommy Hutton became a Dodger. He is forever known to Lasorda not as a first baseman, but as a parking lot 12 player.

"And that still ain't my best scouting story."

His best scouting story, it turns out, is his first. The target was Dick Krotz, a high school third baseman from Allentown, Pennsylvania. Lasorda, who began his Dodger scouting career in Pennsylvania, followed around the slugger for weeks. In what would be his closing move, he invited Krotz and his family to see the Dodgers play in Philadelphia. But the game was canceled because of a hurricane. So Tommy and Jo had to drive to the Krotzes' house to close the deal.

"I told Jo, 'No matter what, if you see me crying, don't say anything,'" Lasorda recalls.

Sure enough, after a long night of dinner and verbal dancing, at 3 A.M. in the Krotzes' living room Lasorda started crying. In the end, he directed his sales pitch to the person most of his sale pitches would be directed to—a mother. He was imploring Dick's mother, Florence, to look at him. "I said, 'Florence, do I look like the type that would lie to you? Right now I feel like a priest who asks people if they want their souls saved. Shouldn't those people be asking him? I'm asking you to join the greatest organization in baseball, but shouldn't you be begging me to join us? I would be leading your son around like a father. Look at me! You need me!'"

At this point, Lasorda began bawling, wailing, streaming tears. Only when the mother agreed to sign did he finally stop.

"Of course, the kid met a girl in the minor leagues and quit baseball to be with her," Lasorda says. "But that's another story."

By the time Lasorda finishes spinning the tale, the Dodger bus has pulled up at the next stop, the Long Beach Aquarium, the only spot on the caravan to which the public has been invited. This explains the huge lines that snake around the fish tanks. This is an autograph session, so no speeches are planned. This makes it the perfect time for Lasorda to give a speech.

"On behalf of the entire Dodger organization—Long Beach, we love you!" he shouts to the four hundred people waiting in the autograph line. "You are great fans. Keep coming! Get your tickets now! Let's sign some autographs!"

Lasorda will not sign every autograph. Sitting at a table next to several Dodgers, Lasorda is the only one who will not autograph a bat. People have stood in line with their bats for hours, but he will not sign them. One man has a 1988 championship bat with everyone's signature on it but Lasorda's, yet Lasorda still will not sign it. This is a strange quirk for one of the only living sports celebrities who never charges for autographs. Lasorda shrugs. "I don't sign stuff that gets sold on the Internet," he says.

What about balls? he is asked. What about gloves? What about ticket stubs? What about all the other autographed stuff that fills eBay like old boxes fill his garage?

"I just know that bats go for big money," he says. "And I'm not signing anything that goes for big money."

But as long as somebody gives him a name, he signs everything else—shirts and caps and cards—while carrying on a running commentary with the fans. As long as you say please, it is worth it to ask for Lasorda's autograph, because you never know what he's going to say when he signs it.

"Do you love Uncle Tommy?" he asks a small child wearing giant glasses. "Say you love Uncle Tommy!"

Any time a male Dodger fan shows up with an attractive woman, Lasorda's response is always the same: "You better never let her get an eye exam, buddy, or you're finished!"

Sitting next to him at this ninety-minute session is the newest

Dodger, Juan Pierre. The fans don't know him, and few are talking to him, so Lasorda decides to introduce him.

"Everybody, this is one of the greatest players on our team, Juan Pierre. If you don't like Juan Pierre, you don't like Christmas!"

Pierre laughs, but he will remember this comment. Lasorda will walk into the clubhouse on a June afternoon looking for a buddy, and Pierre will be there for him. That's how it has always worked for a man who continually catches more flies with honey.

"You know the great thing about getting old?" Lasorda says to another fan. "This means you don't die young."

By late in the session, he indeed begins to look old. During a lull in the autograph parade, he tilts his head back and falls asleep. Fans look bemused. Officials look worried.

"That's it, folks, Mr. Lasorda has to go home now," somebody announces, and with that, Lasorda rises slowly to his feet and hobbles back through the aquarium's kitchen.

"Gawd, my leg hurts," he keeps saying.

On the way to his car, he passes a group of Mexican kitchen workers. He stops and gives them a pep talk in Spanish, something about if they don't start moving faster, he will tie a horse around them.

Then he slows to secretly give an autograph to an aquarium employee, despite the fact that aquarium employees are forbidden to ask for autographs.

"What's your nephew's name?" he whispers, signing a napkin, handing it to a bystander who will later hand it to the employee.

Then he is finally in his car, moaning softly but waving steadily to the fans that crowd the doors as the Cadillac pulls away, American flag flapping in the evening breeze.

"This gets harder and harder," he says, settling into his seat with a sigh. "But this is what I do, right? This is who I am."

5

. . .

I HUNGERED FOR THIS

W hat's going on in there?"

Tommy Lasorda is walking by the offices on the fifth floor of Dodger Stadium when he passes a meeting room with its doors closed and Venetian blinds shut. He stops, leans down, and peeks through the blinds. He spots some business folks through the cracks. He waves to them.

"Oh, OK, it's a marketing meeting," he says, walking away. "No big deal. Just wondering."

As the club's most universally respected active employee, Lasorda should never have to worry that he's being excluded from Dodger brainstorming sessions. But he does, because that's who he is, always fighting to keep what nobody believed he could ever obtain. Even on this winter day when he is being paid just to be Tommy Lasorda—he will answer some mail, then have lunch in a blighted downtown neighborhood while mentoring some young office workers—he still worries about protecting his place here, and quite a place it is.

His office overlooks left field, with a wonderful view of palm trees and rolling hills beyond the outfield parking lot. Nestled in the parkland of Chavez Ravine, just above downtown Los Angeles, Dodger

Stadium is considered one of the crown jewels of ballparks. In this manner, Lasorda's office is the throne room.

It's the first office on the right as you enter the executive suite. It's big enough to house a desk, two chairs, and the memories of a man who has become larger than life. On his walls are photos of that life, dozens of them, many in cheap frames, many in simple black and white, but all of them meaningful. The photos crowd every inch of wall space, seemingly cutting the room in half while opening Lasorda's life. There are pictures of Frank Sinatra and Ronald Reagan and Don Rickles and the scout who signed Lasorda and the parents who raised him. There are also a few photos of Lasorda, but the walls are clearly decorated in the manner of a church elder decorating the altar. It's all about worshiping a high power. It's Lasorda's version of stained glass.

"Your office is supposed to be about who you are, right?" Lasorda asks. "Well, I'm a collection of a lot of people. You want to know me, you look at these walls."

He shows his gratitude on the wall facing the door. At the top of the wall is a certificate, a blessing from Pope John XXIII. Underneath it is an autographed photo of Mother Teresa, which raises a question: Mother Teresa signed autographs? And if so, did she also refuse to sign bats?

"Oh, c'mon," says Lasorda. "Can't you just appreciate the damn picture?"

Underneath Mother Teresa is another nun, in a traditional white habit, and you want to make a joke about Sally Field, but Lasorda interrupts again.

"That's Sister Immaculata, my seventh-grade teacher, the only one who believed in me."

At the bottom of the wall is a picture of Cardinal Roger Mahoney, the archbishop of Los Angeles, and just as you're wondering whether this old manager's den could be any more religious, Lasorda points to a stack of prayer cards on the corner of his cluttered desk. On one side is a prayer, and on the other is a traditional drawing of a penitent monk who blessed the prayer. Underneath the monk it says "St. Thomas." Above the name, the face of the monk looks amazingly like Lasorda's own face. Turns out, it is.

"I'm telling you, if I never became a manager, that would be me, right there on that card," Lasorda says, laughing.

He did become a Dodger manager, in the summer of 1965, when he was promoted from scout to the boss of a team on baseball's lowest level, the rookie league. At a meeting with Dodger executives, he was asked to lead their team in Pocatello, Idaho, where the season is only sixty games long.

Although he had never formally applied to be a manager, it all made sense. He had gotten the most out of his ordinary ability as a player—could he apply the same methods to inspire better players to greatness? He had used all sorts of motivational tools in all sorts of living rooms to sign players—would the same tools work in a clubhouse?

The Dodgers had also seen some flashes of managerial potential a couple of years earlier, when Lasorda was working as an instructor in spring training. The club needed someone to briefly manage the team's Class A minor league campers during intrasquad scrimmages. Lasorda didn't just manage them, he brainwashed them, convincing the players that the team's triple-A campers had been badmouthing them, and then challenging the triple-A campers to play his single-A team.

"So we take the field with these low-level kids against the triple-A guys, and all my guys are screaming and pointing and fired up, and nobody can understand it," Lasorda recalls. "We beat the heck out of them, and we win sixteen straight spring games. Maybe my bosses get the idea that I can do this someday."

That day arrived in the summer of 1965, a great time, the perfect promotion, but with one catch. After the promotion meeting, Buzzie Bavasi grabbed Lasorda as he left the room.

"Tommy, no more fights," Bavasi said.

"No more fights?" It seemed to Lasorda that someone had just asked him to stop breathing.

"You heard me, no more fights. You're a manager now, and the fighting has to stop."

"OK, OK," said Lasorda. "It will stop, I promise."

Is it any surprise that within moments of the start of his first game in his first season as a manager, Tommy Lasorda broke that promise? Pocatello was playing at Idaho Falls. In the top of the first inning, Pocatello loaded the bases with none out when a foul ball was hit to Lasorda in the third-base coaching box. Lasorda picked it up and rolled it into the Idaho Falls dugout.

"What are you doing?" shouted Fred Koenig, the Idaho Falls manager.

"The ball is scuffed. I'm putting it out of play."

"You can't do that," shouted Koenig.

Lasorda had barely buttoned up his uniform on his first day on the job and already his managerial credibility was being tested. This may seem like a small thing, but to Lasorda it was huge. Fred Koenig wasn't just an opposing manager, he was everyone who had challenged Lasorda at every step from Norristown to Pocatello. Lasorda needed to shut him up, and fast.

"You don't tell me what I can do," Lasorda yelled into the dugout. "I'll do whatever I want to do."

Koenig, a large man, jumped off the bench and raced to challenge Lasorda, who threw one punch and knocked him down. This brought the entire Idaho Falls team out of the dugout in their manager's defense. This led to Lasorda's first official motivational speech as a manager in the Dodger organization. It was short but impassioned.

"Everybody get out here and fight!"

It took forty minutes and several policemen to stop the brawl, which included another Lasorda teaching moment, when one of his black players, Leon Everitt, began screaming, "One of my own kind hit me!"

Lasorda, fearing that his players were fighting each other, screamed back, "Which one hit you?"

Everitt looked over at the opposing bench and replied, "A brother hit me! One of their black players hit me!"

Now Lasorda was really mad. "From now on, Leon, your own kind are the guys in Dodger uniforms. The other kind are the guys in the other uniforms. Of course that guy hit you. Now hit him back!"

Lasorda's refusal to make racial and ethnic distinctions was good for the colorblind Dodger organization and earned him the respect of players of all backgrounds for the rest of his career. He had the street smarts to communicate with inner-city kids like Reggie Smith. He spoke the language of the rural players from the Dominican Republic like Pedro Guerrero. It was on his watch that the Dodgers once started a game with minorities manning all nine positions. What he preached to Everitt that day, he preached to the entire organization from then on.

After Pocatello's brawl with Idaho Falls ended, a cop was stationed in each dugout for the rest of the game. Lasorda's team had a police escort when it left town, the cops following the Pocatello bus all the way to the city line.

"The bad thing about that was, they wouldn't let us stop and get something to eat," Lasorda recalls.

The players arrived home at 4 A.M. Five hours later, Lasorda's phone was ringing. It was, of course, Buzzie Bavasi. Lasorda was exhausted, but he grabbed the receiver with the fear that this could be his last conversation as a Dodger manager.

"Tommy, you promised me," the general manager said.

Lasorda thought for a second, then mounted his defense.

"I was attacked by a big guy coming out of the dugout. Would it have made you feel better if the guy killed me and I was laying in my casket and you could say to my wife, 'Well, at least he didn't start any fights.'"

Lasorda stopped and listened, hoping, praying for the sound of laughter. Finally it came. Bavasi chuckled, but only briefly.

"OK, so was anybody hurt?"

"No way," Lasorda said. "We've got some good fighters on that team."

"OK," Bavasi said. "Just don't do it again."

Lasorda's minor league managing career had officially begun. It would last eight seasons, taking him from Pocatello to Ogden, Utah, to Spokane, Washington, to Albuquerque, New Mexico. He was part-time traveling salesman, part-time foster father, full-time baseball teacher, doing what he loved the most with the kinds of kids who would listen to him the most. Every summer he was given a six-month run before a captive audience for a variety show that few people saw. The minor leagues were the best place for Lasorda to hone the role of Tommy. They were among the happiest days of his life, so happy that when the Dodgers asked him to become a big-league coach after the 1972 season, he initially balked.

More than anything, Lasorda loved being a mentor to his players, an amazing seventy-five of whom eventually advanced to the majors. His own father never got to watch him play, so he knew what it was like to compete alone, and he made sure his players never had that feeling. Those players included the future big-league stars Steve Garvey, Bill Russell, Davey Lopes, Ron Cey, Steve Yeager, Bill Buckner, and Charlie Hough. They came to Lasorda from different backgrounds, but they all left with several things in common. Lasorda got to know them all like sons. And they all obeyed him like a father.

Why else would such young elite athletes agree to drop to their knees on command and shout, "I loooooove the Dodgers"?

That was Lasorda's mantra, the first thing he taught them from his first days in Pocatello. He convinced them that their chances of making it to the big leagues would increase if they would fall to their knees and answer a few questions.

"Who do you love?" Lasorda would shout.

"I looooove the Dodgers," they would reply.

"Where do you expect to get your mail one day?" Lasorda would shout.

"Dodger Stadium," they would reply.

"Who is going to sign your checks?"

"The Dodgers!"

These were some of baseball's most sophisticated prospects, guys who would rather strike out than show emotion. Yet there they were, throughout their minor league careers, showing their allegiance at Lasorda's every whim. This allegiance continued when they reached the majors. Joe Garagiola, a former player who became a baseball announcer, was stunned when the players dropped to their knees in Joe Ferguson's back yard during a big-league party. He drove off to find a camera, and returned to film it. Members of the San Francisco Giants' farm teams were also astonished when the Dodgers dropped to their knees behind the batting cage before games. Lasorda loved to hold such "prayer services" in front of the rival Giants, who would walk away jealous.

"It was all about getting these guys to visualize the major leagues," Lasorda remembers. "What better way to visualize it than to shout about it?"

Sitting in his Dodger Stadium office on this winter day nearly forty years later, Lasorda is still visualizing. Only this time he is visualizing his death. He may be the only executive in history with his tombstone leaning against his desk. It is metal, with an engraving of his face over the words "Tommy Lasorda, 1927–33. Dodger Stadium was his address but every ballpark was his home." It also contains the engraving of a heart. The heart appears to be bleeding blue blood.

"What?" says Lasorda when asked about the headstone. "What's wrong with it?"

When somebody mentions that it might be considered strange to work every day in the company of your own gravestone, Lasorda shrugs. "I don't have anywhere else to put it. And what the hell," he says, "it's not killing me, is it? As long as it doesn't kill me, it can stay."

That's the theme of many of the knickknacks in his office. On the edge of his desk sits a bag of broken sugar cookies. Next to that is a trophy labeled "Worst Male Voice." And next to that is a child's View-Master toy, filled with photos of, well, who else?

"Lemme look at that again," Lasorda says, holding the plastic red View-Master to his eye while clicking to the best pictures of himself. "Hey, I like this little toy."

The area between the photo-filled walls is part museum, part storage closet, part playroom. All around are piles of photos and ignored Post-it Notes and letters, some of which he even reads.

"Whoa, look at this one. This one looks official," he shouts, summoning his assistant to read a thick white missive that has fallen from a large envelope.

"It's about your pension," says the assistant.

"Pension?" says Lasorda.

"Yeah. It says you have to make a decision on the distribution of your major league pension."

Lasorda pauses.

"I've been getting a pension?"

Only in the depths of his office is it obvious that Lasorda is bliss-fully unaware of any world outside the diamond. He signs thank-you notes for people he doesn't remember meeting; he signs con-tracts to receive checks that he will never see; he occasionally drops everything to look at his wall and recognize an old friend.

"Look at Al Campanis over there," he says, pointing to an auto-graphed photo of his old boss. "Heckuva guy. Heckuva friend. They hung an innocent man."

Before expounding on this, he is back to his letters, signing and stacking and sighing, and somebody asks, "Where is your com-puter?"

"Computer? Computer?"

Lasorda does not own a computer. He has never had an e-mail address. He has never gone on the Internet. "I don't even know what the Internet is," he says.

Lasorda is perhaps the country's only blogger who doesn't know how to *turn on* a computer. His blog on the Dodger Web site is writ-ten by an aide.

Lasorda had a computer once. He talked about it during a speech he gave to AT&T's computer division. He claimed he was the first manager ever to use a computer in the dugout.

"We fed it all the information on every player in the National League," he remembers. "Then, when I got into a jam, I would ask the computer what I should do. Invariably it would say, 'Fire the manager.' So I got it out of there."

It isn't that Lasorda is technophobic. It's that he loves people too much to waste time talking to a blank screen.

"Let me ask you a question. How much time do you spend on the computer?" he asks a visitor. "I bet you're going to say 'Too much.' Everybody says 'Too much.' That's why I can't start. Because I've seen people who can't stop."

The only high-tech items in Lasorda's office are the two teddy bears behind his desk. When you push one of the bears' bellies— which Lasorda does often—the bear sings "God Bless America." The other bear, which wears an Uncle Sam hat, sat in the dugout next to

Lasorda at the 2000 Olympics. Every time the United States scored a run, Lasorda would push a button and the bear would shout, "America, home of the free and the brave," then play part of the *1812 Overture,* then conclude with "USA Number One."

By the end of the Olympics, the players wanted to strangle that bear. To this day, Lasorda embraces it. Which pretty much sums up the difference between the modern ballplayer and this Stone Age manager.

"What is wrong with a bear singing patriotic songs?" Lasorda asks. "You tell me, what is wrong with that?"

It is nearing noon. Lasorda puts down the bears, sits up at his desk, and says, "Round up the kids. Let's have lunch!"

Today he will take the club's young front-office personnel to lunch at an aging downtown Chinese restaurant called Paul's Kitchen. He will tell stories and toss barbs and make them feel they are part of the old-fashioned Dodger tradition.

Forty years ago, from his first days as a minor league manager, he made his mark by doing the same thing, only on a smaller budget. With shared lunches and shared jokes, Lasorda embraced his young players, turning them into the sort of loyal major leaguers who would win him a World Series. He literally embraced them, becoming one of baseball's first managers at any level to hug players after home runs, a tradition he continued throughout his career.

"A lot of these kids were away from home for the first time, and their parents weren't there to see those home runs, so they could use a hug," he recalls.

He invented the phrase "Big Dodger in the Sky" so his players would have something outside themselves to believe in. He would stand over his players when they called home to recount their exploits, which fostered a sense of gratitude.

He would call his players' hometown newspapers, to make sure their friends could see and share in their success. Actually, he made calls to all but one player's hometown paper.

Bobby Valentine, who joined Lasorda at Ogden as a first-round draft pick in 1968, would show him daily stories about his progress in his hometown paper in Stamford, Connecticut. Sometimes the stories would read, "Valentine didn't get a hit but made a great throw from the outfield." Other times they would read, "Valentine struck out but had three great swings." It turned out, Valentine was writing and filing those stories himself. Lasorda fell in love immediately.

"Everybody always asks for my favorite player," Lasorda says. "That's like asking a father to name his favorite child. But I've always loved Bobby."

Theirs became a relationship that helped define both men. Valentine was called the ultimate Lasorda protégé—feisty and fearless and full of himself. Valentine had a successful major league hitting career, though he rarely hit home runs. He did it with hustle and smarts. This was just how he played in 2000, when he led the New York Mets to the World Series. People would look at Valentine's amazing progress and endurance and see a great example of Lasorda's managerial prowess. Lasorda would look at him and see a beloved child. Valentine talked the game like Lasorda, loved the game like Lasorda, even tried to manage the game like Lasorda. Once, as a Mets manager, he was ejected early in the game. He later returned to the dugout wearing a fake mustache but was immediately caught. All around the league, old-timers laughed. "That's something Lasorda would have tried," they said.

The first time Lasorda spotted Valentine, the shortstop was being recruited to play baseball at USC. When Valentine was on campus, Lasorda visited USC coach Rod Dedeaux, who was also a close friend. Lasorda was so impressed with Valentine's attitude, he sat next to Valentine and pulled out a radio with the Dodger emblem on it.

"I'm going to leave this radio behind. You can pick it up if you want it," Lasorda told him. "But I want to leave it here to remind you that you will one day be a Dodger."

Lasorda knew the kid was talented. And he knew the Dodger brain trust agreed with him. Soon after receiving his Dodger radio, Valentine could turn it on and hear that he was a first-round pick of the Dodgers. As soon as he signed his contract, he was sent to Ogden, where he met the manager who would change his life.

"He walked into my office his first day and said he would do anything," Lasorda remembers. "And soon I got the chance to test him."

He promptly ordered Valentine, who had just graduated from high school, to buy him dinner. During that dinner, Valentine quietly asked for his first piece of advice from Lasorda.

"Tommy, I don't have any chest hair," he said. "And it's really starting to bother me. What do you think?"

Lasorda had to stifle a smile. He had no idea how to respond to this. He looked at the top of Valentine's chest, looked down at Valentine's steak, and came up with his answer: "It's all about fat. You eat more fat, it will put hair on your chest."

Lasorda began cutting into Valentine's steak, separating the meat from the fat, heaping all of the meat on his own plate and leaving Valentine with the fat.

"Dig in," Lasorda said, and he ate Valentine's steak as well as his own.

Lasorda forgot about the incident until, nearly a month later, Valentine rushed into his office and unbuttoned his shirt, revealing a couple of tiny hairs. "Look, Tommy, you were right!"

"That showed me this kid was a believer," Lasorda remembers. "Who else do you know who could will himself to grow chest hair? This kid was a born leader."

As Valentine rose through the minor league ranks, Lasorda rose with him. They found themselves on the triple-A Spokane team, where Valentine continued to impress him with his willingness to do anything to please the boss. Once, during a three-game series in Vancouver, Lasorda heard a commotion in the stands during batting practice. When he ran upstairs, he discovered Valentine climbing into a pen with the stadium's two growling guard dogs.

"We bet him he wouldn't do it," one player said.

"Get out of there!" shouted Lasorda.

"Relax," said Valentine, petting the suddenly docile animals. "These bums don't know that I've been feeding the dogs all week."

That was the kind of trick Lasorda would have tried, and the manager proudly cheered. Valentine was traded by the Dodgers before he could play for Lasorda in the majors, but Lasorda supported him throughout his career as a player and a manager. He surely would have chosen Valentine as his full-time replacement in the winter after the 1996 season, but Valentine was managing the Mets at the time.

A year later, when Lasorda went into the Hall of Fame, his greatest love became one of his greatest embarrassments. After his induction speech, when asked by the *New York Post* reporter Tom Keegan to name his favorite manager, he mentioned Valentine, which was considered a snub by the current Dodger manager, another Lasorda protégé, Bill Russell. The ensuing dustup drowned out everything else he said that day. How could the newest Dodger Hall of Famer publicly ignore his hand-picked successor?

"I wasn't snubbing nobody," Lasorda says. "When Blumpy [Keegan] asked about my favorite manager, I thought he meant somebody who was not managing the Dodgers."

The public didn't buy it, and turned on Lasorda for being so catty. The Dodgers didn't buy it, and briefly distanced themselves from a guy they deemed a loose cannon. Worst of all, Bill Russell didn't buy it, and his relationship with Lasorda was never the same again. Turns out, Lasorda loved Valentine so much that he was willing to create a national controversy over it.

"The whole thing was blown way out of proportion," Lasorda says. "All I was doing was backing my guy."

From embarrassing to comedic, Valentine created another memorable Lasorda moment a couple of years later, after inviting his mentor to serve as an honorary coach in the 2001 All-Star Game. This was during the period when Lasorda was being quietly phased out by the Dodger organization. It was a thank-you letter from a student that Lasorda will never forget.

"When the league called and told me that Bobby wanted me on the bench with him, I couldn't believe it," Lasorda remembers. "It was like I was dreaming."

In the sixth inning of that game, everyone was emotional for a different reason. With Lasorda coaching third base for the only time that night, the American League's Vladimir Guerrero broke a bat that splintered down the third-base line. Trying to avoid the flying barrel, Lasorda somersaulted backward in a pratfall seen by millions. The crowd held its collective breath, waiting to see if he would get back up. When he did, he was given a standing ovation, followed by a visit from Barry Bonds, who was carrying a catcher's chest protector. The crowd kept cheering, and Lasorda kept basking, and for the first time since his retirement, it was clear.

"I was worried that everyone forgot about me," Lasorda recalls. "For the first time that night, I realized that wasn't going to happen. The love that I gave to baseball for all those years—I realized that it was all going to come back to me."

He walks out of his office and outside the stadium, where his Cadillac is parked near the doors. He is going to do some more managing of fresh-scrubbed kids today, the ones from the office, and he is taking them downtown to Paul's Kitchen for a Chinese lunch. It's a rite of passage for young Dodger employees to accompany Lasorda to Paul's, where he's been eating for forty years. It is here they learn that, no matter how much the Dodgers have become a big business, the team's roots remain in small, unkempt corners of Los Angeles. It is here they learn that, no matter how much fans cheer for Eric Gagne or Jeff Kent, no Dodger will ever have more influence than Lasorda.

He drives down a litter-filled street, past boarded-up warehouses and grimy auto repair shops behind giant black fences. He turns into an aging building with dirty windows and a tiny parking lot.

"I once took Kirk Douglas down here," Lasorda recalls. "We pull in the parking lot and he gets this real scared look on his face and says, 'We're gonna eat here?' And I tell him, 'No, we're gonna eat inside.'"

Inside is a dark room with a linoleum floor and big Formica-topped tables and waiters who approach Lasorda with bows and handshakes and no menus. You eat here with Lasorda, you sit down and wait for the food. It just shows up. Huge, steaming platters of kung pao chicken and moo shu pork and Mandarin beef.

Lasorda won't eat anything that doesn't have steam coming out of it. He once sent back a single bowl of chicken soup five times because it wasn't hot enough. The waiters hustle out the food while it is hot, plates and plates of food that overwhelm the twelve young workers, whose eyes grow wide.

"Oh, c'mon, don't be afraid," Lasorda announces. "Have you ever seen any fat Chinese?"

The only thing Lasorda likes as much as hot food is spicy food, so he mixes some hot mustard with soy sauce in a small bowl and passes it around, and the kids seem afraid to eat it.

"I've heard about you and spicy stuff, Tommy," says a young female marketing employee. "There's no way I'm eating that."

"Oh, c'mon, try it," he says.

And, of course, she tries it. To fail to eat something offered by Lasorda is akin to snubbing him in the hallway. When you are hired by the Dodgers, it's part of the deal. The women giggle, the men sigh, but they all eat, and eat, and eat, stuffing themselves as the food keeps coming. Growing uncomfortable, they clearly cannot stop eating until Lasorda stops. When somebody dares to ask if there is a name for this precise combination of food and sauce, Lasorda begins shouting.

"What are we eating? What are we eating?" he says. "We're eating the Tommy Lasorda Special. They've named this stuff after me, and I'm proud of it. Other people get bridges and roads named after them, but you'll be a heckuva lot happier eating the Tommy Lasorda Special than driving the Lincoln Tunnel."

He starts to preach, and the forks drop.

"There are three ways we learn in life," he says. "We learn by conversation. We learn by observation. We learn by participation."

Everyone solemnly nods as if he's just recited the Gettysburg Address. He starts eating. They start eating. He suddenly stops. They suddenly stop.

"There are three types of people," he shouts. "A guy who makes it happen, a guy who watches it happen, and a guy who wonders what happened."

He points to a young ticket salesman and asks, "What kind of guy are you?"

The young man says, "Mflfldldldld." He is caught chewing on some chicken. Lasorda smiles like a proud father. He enjoys speaking to these kids as much as they enjoy listening to a $40,000 speech for free. He is happiest, perhaps, leaning back in his rickety chair in Paul's Kitchen, a dozen sets of young eyes focused on him, careers being shaped in front of him, a minor league manager once again.

"Be like the old owl!" he says. "The more he saw, the less he spoke. The less he spoke, the more he heard. And the more he heard, the more he learned."

At this, one of the workers begins to tell a story about an actual owl, but Lasorda isn't listening, and his coworkers scowl at the guy until he stops talking. In return for the free advice Lasorda offers the kids, he requires the entire stage, the entire time. To him it is one of those old-fashioned signs of love and respect. Many years ago in Norristown, when his father told stories down at the social club, the younger guys never spoke, so why should these kids? Once he has their attention, he returns that respect.

"These people in the upstairs offices don't get the credit they deserve, but I appreciate them," he announces. "I always wanted to win this thing for these people upstairs. I'm always thinking of them. I know they work hard. Nobody knows it, but I know it, and I appreciate it. That's all part of being a family."

Some of these kids may have long and illustrious Dodger careers, but Lasorda will undoubtedly be the only one to ever refer to the organization as family. He will be the only member of the baseball operation who says he wants to win for them. He will be the one they remember while working long hours for low pay. All the morale-boosting in the Dodger office begins with Lasorda, and for that the team cannot pay him enough.

The lunch ends, and as the dishes are cleared the newer employees ask if they can help with the check. The more seasoned ones scowl again. Of all the rules surrounding eating with Lasorda, this is the most important: you must never, ever pick up the check.

As Lasorda ushers everyone out to the parking lot, he gives the waiter several signed baseballs.

"I consider our front-office employees like my kids," he says. "I've been trying to motivate kids like this all my life. These kids are like my players now."

• • •

He unwrapped all sorts of new motivational tools in those minor league days, not only for the players but for the fans. While managing the rookie league team in Ogden, he once printed up cards inviting fans to visit the Stadium Club. There was, of course, no Stadium Club. On the same cards he would also invite fans to park in lot A, although there was only one small lot. He would invite fans to submit their name so it could be displayed on the message board. But, yeah, no message board.

"It was all about dreaming big," he recalls. "I wanted everyone around me to dream big, to act like we were Dodgers at Dodger Stadium, to believe they could do anything."

Then there were the players who, on their first days with the team, would ask about using the whirlpool.

"We have a nice one in the back. It's called a toilet," Lasorda said. "If you want a hot whirlpool, just put your foot in and flush."

The fans and players would laugh, but Lasorda's message was serious. One of the players who keenly understood it was a pitcher named Billy Graves, who constantly complained about a sore arm even though medical exams showed nothing. Because Lasorda knew his family, he knew that Graves was very religious. So he summoned the player to his office one day to talk about pain.

"When does your arm hurt you?" Lasorda asked.

"Only when I'm actually pitching the ball," Graves said.

"And how long does that take each time?" Lasorda asked.

"About one second for each pitch."

"Exactly. Which means that if you throw a hundred pitches in a game, you will endure pain for one minute and forty seconds, right?"

"I guess," Graves said.

"Do you know how much pain Christ endured when he was crucified?" Lasorda asked. "Do you think that was longer than one hundred and forty seconds?"

In his next start, Graves threw a shutout. It was not a coincidence. Such things happened throughout Lasorda's minor league career, little miracles purchased with big dreams.

An outfielder on his team once refused to soak his sore foot in a bucket of water because he said it was too hot. Since he wouldn't soak his foot, he couldn't play. Lasorda heard about this and made a bet with him. If Lasorda could keep his own foot in the scalding water for a minute, the guy had to play.

"So I kept my foot in there so long, I couldn't walk the rest of the day," Lasorda recalls. "But the guy never heard me scream. And the guy played."

Perhaps his crowning minor league moment came in 1968 when his Ogden team won the pennant on the final day, despite having one star player asking to go home because of a death in the family, and another star refusing to play because he was ill.

The first star's uncle had died. Lasorda knew the player well and had never heard him talk about his uncle. He hugged him and softly asked, "When is the last time you saw your uncle?"

"Four years ago," the player said.

"Four years ago!" Lasorda screamed. "If your uncle didn't see you when he was alive, he sure ain't gonna mind not seeing you when he's dead."

The guy played. So did the other star, catcher Pat Burke, who reported that he was so sick, he couldn't get out of bed. Lasorda quickly made a bed for him on the bench, covers and pillow included, and asked him to get into his uniform and sleep there during batting practice. As the game began, Lasorda tore off the covers and challenged Burke to give it a try. Burke played.

In the bottom of the ninth, with the grieving player on first base, Burke hit a two-run homer to win the pennant. It was a delightful finish. As the Ogden kids celebrated with buckets of water and shaving cream and tears, Lasorda knew that this was not just about good luck, it was about good managing.

"Seeing the two guys who didn't want to play score the tying and winning run," Lasorda says, "seeing how they only played because I talked them into it . . . that made me realize that maybe I could do this job."

He was just getting started. A couple of years later, he was promoted to the triple-A Spokane Indians, where he immediately made his mark by relaying the team's spring training scores back to the Spokane newspaper. Only, they weren't the real scores. After every game, he reported that the Indians had won, even when they had lost. When he was caught in the lie by club officials, he shrugged.

"Hey, spring training is a time for raising hopes, right?" he says. "That's all I was doing."

Another time, in trying to revive his Spokane team during a seven-game losing streak, he reminded them of the 1927 Yankees. "They had Babe Ruth, Lou Gehrig, all those guys. Maybe the greatest team that ever played, right?" Lasorda told them. "Well, guess what? That team once lost nine straight games. So you shouldn't feel too bad about losing seven straight."

The inspired Indians rattled out of the clubhouse onto the field, and returned with a victory and the start of a six-game winning streak. Later, during the quiet of a postgame meal at home, Jo Lasorda casually asked how the 1927 Yankees could have lost nine games in a row.

"I don't think they did," Lasorda said. "But it sure sounded good to those players, didn't it?"

The same thing happened when Lasorda tried to persuade Joe Ferguson to move from the outfield to the less glamorous position of catcher. He mentioned that several great catchers—Gabby Hartnett, Mickey Cochrane, and Ernie Lombardi, among others—had started as outfielders. That was enough to convince Ferguson to put on a mask, but it was not enough to convince Lasorda's boss, Al Campanis. When Campanis heard about the speech, instead of congratulating Lasorda, he needled him.

"Tommy, none of those catchers were ever outfielders."

"I know that and you know that, Al, but Fergy didn't know that," Lasorda said. "And he's wearing a mask now, ain't he?"

The best part of Lasorda's triple-A managing career were the times when he could tell players they were being promoted to the major leagues. He loved calling them into his office and giving them the good news, handing them the phone to call their family, offering them a towel to dry their tears. He would then recount the story he told them at the beginning of every season.

"There's a kid musician playing for the first time in Carnegie

Hall, and when he finishes, and everyone is standing and cheering, he can only see the old man in the back with a tear in his eye," Lasorda would say. "That was the guy who molded him, guided him, sacrificed for him. That was his father. It was a moment they shared forever."

To many of the countless players he promoted to the majors, he retold the story with a twist.

"When you guys get to Dodger Stadium and do something special, look up in the stands for the spirit of a guy who helped you get there, a guy with a tear in his eye," Lasorda would say. "Look up at old Tom."

The speech was more than motivation; it was self-preservation. As always, Lasorda was smartly laying the groundwork for support if he was ever recalled to the major leagues. He was doing more than molding lives; he was buying insurance. And in the winter after the 1972 season, it paid off when he was called to be Walter Alston's third-base coach.

He not only knew most of the players, he was beloved by them. By the time he was promoted to manager in 1976, an amazing seventeen of his twenty-five players had played for him in the minor leagues. After all these years of working to know the players, he was being rewarded with a clubhouse full of men who knew him and supported him.

"That's how you work life, isn't it?" Lasorda asks. "Be nice to people on the way up, because one day you may be joining them."

At first he didn't want to be a coach, for two reasons. First, he thought it would be more difficult to become a manager from a coaching box instead of a minor league manager's office. "Is the next president usually a senator, a governor, or a congressman?" Lasorda told his bosses. "I would rather stay as a senator than risk getting lost as a congressman."

The other reason for his reluctance was that he would be working for his old nemesis, Alston. If the Dodger manager didn't appreciate Lasorda's antics as a player, how would he ever stomach him as a member of the coaching staff? If Alston thought Lasorda was flaky *before* Lasorda had his players fall to their knees and pray to the Big

Dodger in the Sky, well, what now? And how would Alston handle Lasorda's well-cultivated clubhouse following?

"No, I didn't really want that coaching job. I wanted to go from the minors to a big-league managing job," Lasorda remembers. "But in the end they didn't give me a choice."

When he arrived in Los Angeles, Lasorda decided that if he was going to be under Alston's thumb, Alston better have a pretty strong thumb. Because Lasorda was going to be more than a coach—he was going to be a leader, whether Alston liked it or not.

In spring training, Lasorda started the 111 Percent Club for the team's nonroster scrubs, rewarding a novice's hard effort by letting him pose for a photograph in front of the locker belonging to his favorite Dodger player. It was corny, but it worked. Lasorda began to pitch batting practice, screaming at the players to hit him and his funky curveball. Again, corny, but successful.

The tighter Alston became, the looser Lasorda acted. He once allowed a little-known club executive, Fred Claire, to pose as a prospect in a spring training game, and when he was found out, everyone laughed. The more conservative Alston became, the more chances coach Lasorda took on the base paths, sending guys into big outs or big victories. And in the end, the quieter Alston became, the louder Lasorda got, with the manager slowly disappearing and his vibrant coach growing larger than life.

It was no surprise when, at the end of the 1975 season, the Montreal Expos tried to steal Lasorda. It was the closest he came, in his nearly sixty years with the organization, to voluntarily leaving the club. In his entire career as a manager and coach, it was the first time someone outside the Dodgers would make a serious effort to hire him. His loyalty was being put to the test. And, surprisingly, he passed.

Lasorda was making $17,000 a year and living in Fullerton. The Expos offered him a three-year deal worth a guaranteed $250,000, and he could live in a town where he had become a minor league legend. It seemed like such a slam dunk that when Expos boss John McHale phoned to give Lasorda the good news, he didn't mind that Lasorda took the call at Peter O'Malley's desk, with O'Malley, the Dodgers' president, listening in.

Said McHale: "Congratulations, you are the new manager of the Expos. We'll announce it a couple of weeks after the World Series."

Said Lasorda: "Not so fast."

This is when Lasorda showed the same loyalty that he demanded of his players. This is where he walked the walk—and a crazy walk it was.

Said Lasorda: "I'm sorry, I love the Dodgers, and I want to stay here."

He had been made no such promise, but he could see Alston's influence waning, and he could feel the clubhouse support coming to his side. He also remembered when the club agreed to transfer him from Pueblo to Greenville, where he met his future wife. He remembered the loan that helped him get married. He remembered the job opportunity as a scout, the managerial promotion from the rookie leagues to triple-A, the coveted coaching position. He remembered all the incredible ways that the Dodgers had tried to keep him happy. "If it wasn't for the Dodgers, maybe I wouldn't have gotten a job after my playing days were done," he says. "If it wasn't for the Dodgers, I wouldn't have anything. I felt like I owed them."

Lasorda did more than just talk about Dodger Blue. This time he really bled it. He turned down Montreal, and for the rest of that summer, he worried about losing all that money.

"After turning down their great offer, I was in so much emotional pain that I asked Peter O'Malley not to tell anyone what I had just done. I spent the season standing in that third-base coaching box thinking, 'I stayed here to make seventeen thousand dollars and do what?'"

There had never been an indication that Lasorda was promised the manager's job if Alston retired. There was never even an indication that Alston would retire. But Lasorda read the landscape like he read the base paths. His street smarts told him that he was well liked and in a position to be the next Dodger manager. And his heart knew that, when the time came, the O'Malley family would take care of him.

When Lasorda was managing in the lower minor leagues, he would send daily updates to Walter O'Malley's wife, Kay, who was thrilled that someone would take the time to explain the inside game. As their son Peter grew up in the organization, Lasorda grew up with him. The two men made an unlikely combination, the buttoned-down O'Malley and the rough-edged Lasorda, but they knew they needed each other. They each possessed what the other was lacking: O'Malley was the businessman, Lasorda was the baseball man. They formed a brotherhood that was stronger than the outside pressures that pushed them both.

And so, in the riskiest move of a risk-filled managerial career, Lasorda turned down the Montreal money, bet his life on his bond with the O'Malleys, and stayed.

He filled his final season with pregame pep talks in which he would boldly predict his players' success. He filled his evenings boldly directing traffic at third base. He unwittingly put the full-court press on Alston's legacy, winning friends and influencing victories and finally going speechless on September 28, 1976. That was when, while sitting in front of his locker after a game, he heard that Alston was retiring. Later that night, O'Malley found Lasorda and told him that he was the leading candidate and that a decision would be made by the next morning.

The drive to Fullerton was never longer. The drive back to Dodger Stadium the next morning was like torture. The meeting with Peter O'Malley was mercifully quick.

"Tommy, we'd like you to become the manager of the Dodgers," O'Malley said.

Lasorda was speechless no more. Thirty years have passed, and some would say he still hasn't stopped talking. Lasorda used his inaugural press conference to throw a ceremonial first quote that will be remembered forever.

It was a quote born of years of climbing uphill, the words of a guy who was never rich enough or connected enough or just plain good enough, who had reached his dream through an improbable combination of hard work and good sense and great cheer. It was the voice of a guy who, having spent nearly a half century of his life scaling an impossible mountain, was hereby announcing that he was absolutely not coming down without a fight.

Vin Scully: "You're replacing a legend. Don't you feel a lot of pressure on you?"

Tommy Lasorda: "No. I'm worried about the guy who is going to replace me."

Tommy Lasorda as a rookie pitcher for the Brooklyn Dodgers

Lasorda with
his wife, Jo

Lasorda with his four brothers. From left: Harry, Morris, Eddie, and Joey.

Lasorda when he was manager of the minor league Spokane Indians

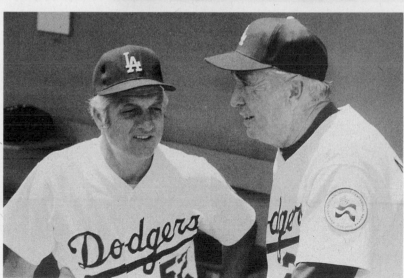

Lasorda as a Dodger coach, with manager Walt Alston

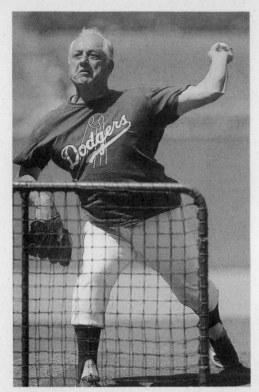

Lasorda throws batting practice at spring training in Vero Beach, Florida.

The professor of Lasorda University gives a lecture on bunting.

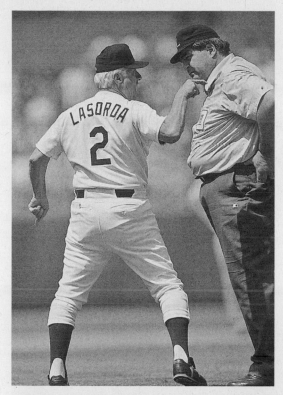

The disputatious manager pursues a point with the ump.

In deep despond after a loss

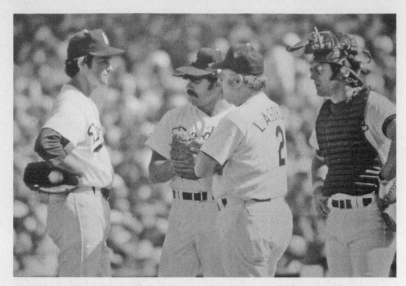

Lasorda removes Doug Rau from the mound during the 1977 World Series.

Even at the height of Fernandomania, Lasorda has to tell Valenzuela it's time to leave the game. Fernando takes it well.

The manager lines up with the crack Dodger infield of Ron Cey, Davey Lopes, Bill Russell, and Steve Garvey.

Lasorda with his close friend and batboy Don Rickles

Frank Sinatra sang the national anthem for Lasorda's first home opener as Dodger manager.

Lasorda with Los Angeles's original wizard, UCLA basketball coach John Wooden

Lasorda gives a former Yale first baseman, President George
H. W. Bush, some Dodger apparel.

Lasorda salutes the flag with another California commander in chief,
Ronald Reagan.

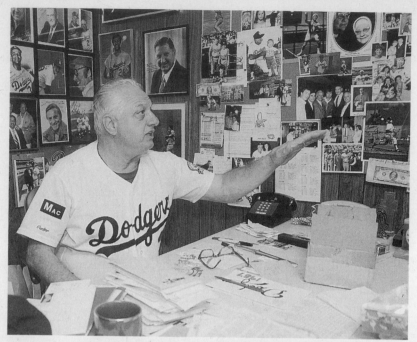

Every picture tells a story: Lasorda is surrounded by memories in his office at Dodger Stadium.

The Dodger brain trust: Fred Claire, Al Campanis, Lasorda, and Peter O'Malley

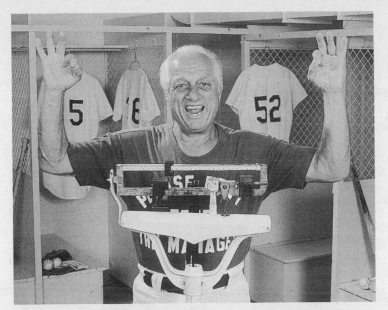

After losing more than fifty pounds on an Ultra Slim-Fast diet, Lasorda happily mounts the scale.

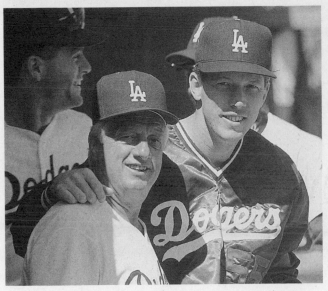

Lasorda in the dugout with his "Bulldog," pitcher Orel Hershiser

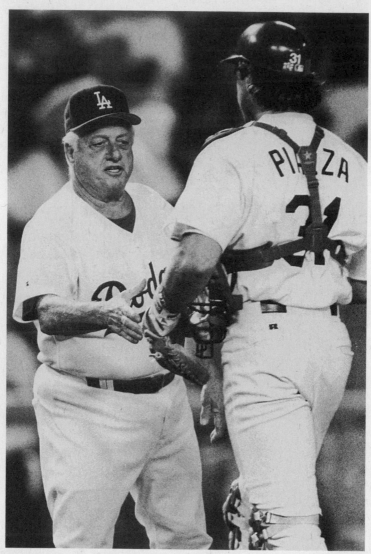
Lasorda greets his godson, catcher Mike Piazza.

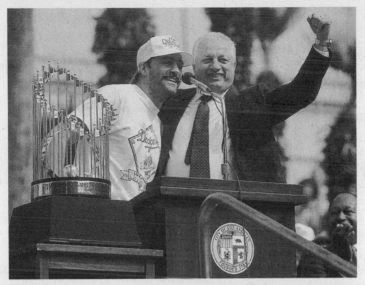

Lasorda celebrates the 1988 World Championship with Kirk Gibson.

Lasorda and his protégé Bobby Valentine

Lasorda weeps at his retirement announcement.

Motivation 101: Lasorda delivers the winning message to a group of Japanese major leaguers.

As manager of the U.S. Olympic baseball team, Lasorda's goal was to beat the undefeated Cubans.

Lasorda celebrates the Dodgers' enduring success with the team's owner, Frank McCourt.

The march of a champion

6

. . .

I WAS BORN FOR THIS

Who's there? Who's there?"

It's 10 A.M. in the narrow kitchen of the modest Fullerton house. The large television on the cluttered counter is blaring a talk show. The smell of toasting bread envelopes the aging cupboards. The bell outside the metal front door rings.

It's September 22, so Tommy Lasorda is hoping.

"Who's out there?" he wonders, walking to the door. "Who could this be?"

It's his birthday, so he knows who he *hopes* it will be. He hopes it will be someone bearing a cake, the kind with the thick bakery icing that he can pull off with his finger. Or maybe it will be someone with a big tub of chocolate ice cream; it wouldn't be the first time he's had chocolate ice cream for breakfast. Really, just a couple of women singing "Happy Birthday" would be fine. Considering Lasorda's parents could rarely afford to throw him a birthday party when he was growing up, he's appreciative of anything that will remind him of what he still considers the luckiest day of his life.

Today he walks outside and sees three things.

They are SUVs. They are filled with giant hunks of colorful plastic. There is a delivery person at the door with a clipboard and an explanation.

"Mr. Lasorda? We have some gift baskets here for you."

"Gift baskets?"

"For your birthday."

"How many gift baskets?"

"Seventy-nine."

Lasorda gasps. Today he is seventy-nine. He gasps again. This is surprising in itself. For a guy who has been through so may tough times, he is never shocked by anything good in his life. He anticipates good, he expects surprises, he demands happiness. Watch the old films of him jumping out of the dugout with his arms waving after a game-winning home run. There is a reason he is always the first one on the field to celebrate. He will later say he expected that home run to be hit. He will later claim he even called it. He has spent seventy-nine years expecting miracles, and each day is just one more.

But this time he gasps.

"Oh my," he says as five workers begin unloading the gift baskets, filled with Disney animals and toys. "Who sent this?"

He is told it is Bobby Valentine.

And now Lasorda weeps.

When Lasorda took over his first Dodger team in 1977, about the only person missing from his family was Valentine, who had been traded several seasons earlier and was now playing for the San Diego Padres. His surrogate son was gone, but seventeen of his former minor leaguers were part of his first major league roster, so Lasorda felt comfortable being Lasorda. They were too young to win a world championship, but he didn't believe that. They lacked the clubhouse leadership to win a ring, but Lasorda would work on that.

In his previous two seasons, the Dodgers had blown leads and lost pennants to the mighty Cincinnati Reds, so the first thing Lasorda did was announce that he was outlawing the color red. No red in the clubhouse, no red in civilian clothes, no red in anything but Red Man chewing tobacco, and only because that was brown. He also countered red by using the phrase "Dodger Blue" again and again.

"It sounded goofy, but it was all about a mindset," Lasorda says. "If we hated red, we would eventually learn to hate the guys wearing it."

Lasorda then wrote each of his players a letter, informing them that it was a privilege to be their manager. It was the first time any of them had ever received such a letter. After that, he phoned each of them, telling them his expectations. That was also a first. When the phone rang in the Kansas home of his quiet shortstop, Bill Russell, the voice on the other end ordered Russell to pick up a pencil.

"Are you standing near a wall?" Lasorda asked him.

"Um, yeah," said Russell.

"I want you to write the following numbers on the wall: thirty to forty-five."

"Why?" said Russell.

"Because that's how many bases you are going to steal this year."

Yet when he called his moody outfielder Reggie Smith, he made no such predictions or demands. In fact, he made an earnest appeal. "I really need your superstar talent this year. I need you to help me survive my first year of managing," he told Smith, who couldn't believe his ears. Usually managers scolded him. Here somebody was embracing him.

Russell stole only sixteen bases that season, but he scored a career-high eighty-four runs and was always forcing the action with his feet. Smith, meanwhile, hit a career-high thirty-two home runs. Lasorda had again showed that the secret to his managing success was simple. He knew his people. He knew who would react to a swift kick and who needed a long hug. He knew that often those people were used to just the opposite. Russell told reporters that he couldn't believe he was writing on his wall. Smith told reporters that nobody had ever said that he was needed.

When his first spring training started, Lasorda did something else unusual. He ordered that his eight starting position players play together, practice together, and even be benched together. Considering that spring training is a time of massive and chaotic substitutions, a time when the eight starters are generally not on the same field until the final week, Lasorda's strategy was widely criticized. Folks said his starters would get tired playing so much, and his reserves would not be ready because they didn't get to play enough.

When Sparky Anderson, the Reds' manager, saw the starters running on the field together before a spring game, he said, "By September, they'll all be running in different directions."

It was the first shot in a season-long verbal war between the managers.

"Sparky's right," replied Lasorda. "They're going to be running in eight different directions—to get to eight different banks to deposit the money they receive for winning the world championship."

Early in the season, after the Dodgers had taken a lead over the Reds in the standings, Anderson said, "It doesn't bother us. They always come back to us in July. Don't ask me why, but they always come back to us."

Replied Lasorda: "Sparky is entitled to his opinion. Opinions are like rear ends. Everybody's got one."

Countered Anderson: "Tommy is like a walking eagle. He's so full of it, he can't fly."

It was indeed a new day in the stuffy Dodger organization. This was a team whose previous manager had been overshadowed by the groundbreaking front office, the likable players, and the diehard fans. This had never been a manager's team. Walt Alston had been so quiet, you'd be hard put to find his tiny office in the Dodger Stadium clubhouse.

Then Lasorda arrived, and everything changed, including the office, which he moved down the hall into a cavernous training room. He brought in couches, laid down carpet, put up photos on the cinderblock walls, and, of course, brought in the postgame buffet so the players could hang out with him. If Lasorda were an executive at a Fortune 500 company, he would be right at home, with the huge couches, ESPN on his TV, and giant jars of candy bars on his desk.

"Your office says everything about you as a manager," Lasorda says. "My office was not only going to be my home, it was going to be their home."

Lasorda imposed a few rules, mostly about hair length and autograph signing, and had interesting ways to enforce them. When a player refused to get a haircut, Lasorda said, "Fine, but next time we're on the road, don't ask me if you can fly home on a day off." When Davey Lopes and Joe Ferguson refused to sit at autograph tables, Lasorda said, "Fine, but not one member of your family will ever fly on the Dodger plane again." Needless to say, both issues were put to rest.

"I had no real hard-and-fast rules, but if you wanted something from me, you had to give something to me," Lasorda says.

Most of the players, having come up in the ranks with Lasorda, understood. One player did not. He was the starting pitcher for Lasorda's first game. He was the only Hall of Fame pitcher Lasorda ever managed. He was, it turned out, also the biggest headache of Lasorda's career.

To play for Lasorda, you had to buy a belief so big and blustery it often sounded like blarney. Don Sutton never bought. When Lasorda arrived, Sutton was a ten-year veteran with five consecutive top-five Cy Young Award finishes on his résumé and a certain cynicism in his eye. For the first pitch of Lasorda's first game as Dodger manager in 1977, Sutton served up a fastball that the San Francisco Giants' Gary Thomasson knocked over the fence for a home run. For Sutton and Lasorda, it was all rocky from there.

"If I had to pitch one guy in a Game 7, it would be Don Sutton," says Lasorda. "I loved him. But sometimes I was one of the only ones."

Sutton sometimes followed his own rules, which could alienate his teammates. For instance, he would want to run instead of shag fly balls with the other pitchers during batting practice. Once in San Francisco during batting practice, Sutton and Doug Rau were trotting around the stadium in their sweats. Lasorda summoned Rau, whom he had nurtured through the minor leagues, to his office, and played the loyalty card.

"Why do you do this to me?" he said to Rau. "You've been like a son to me."

"Sutton made me do it," said Rau.

Lasorda then summoned Sutton, and reminded him that he

could run all day as long as he finished before batting practice. Sutton told him that he would continue to run during batting practice.

"Fine, you want to change the rule, we'll change it right here," Lasorda said, locking the office door. "Let's fight right here, you and me. If I beat you, the rule stays. If you beat me, I'll change it."

Lasorda knew that Sutton was many things, but he was not a fighter, and sure enough, the pitcher backed down.

"Sometimes you have to let your people know that you will fight to protect your team, even from itself," Lasorda says. "You know they won't fight you. But you know they'll get the message."

It was Sutton who once wryly chronicled one of Lasorda's postgame tirades, later announcing, "Congratulations, you have just set the all-time record by using the f-word 124 times in 14 minutes."

Lasorda thought that was funny. What he didn't think was funny was that Sutton continued challenging the few rules that existed. He soon proved himself to Lasorda as every player did, on the field. Once on the mound, Sutton was a portrait of concentration and competitiveness. While he was never quite like Fernando Valenzuela and Orel Hershiser, who would never ask out of games because they didn't want to incur Lasorda's wrath, Sutton nonetheless competed with every pitch, and Lasorda appreciated every drop of sweat.

Not that Sutton didn't drive him crazy. Once in Cincinnati, upon learning that Sutton was asking out of a game, Lasorda jokingly locked himself in the dugout bathroom and pretended he couldn't hear the request. When he finally left the bathroom, pitching coach Red Adams was waiting for him, and made the request again. Lasorda immediately brought in a reliever, who proceeded to blow the game. Afterward, when Los Angeles journalist Tom Singer asked Lasorda why Sutton didn't pitch longer, the manager lost his sense of humor.

"Why don't you ask him?" Lasorda said of Sutton.

Sutton was furious when he read the quote, and confronted Lasorda, who screamed, "I'm sick and tired of making excuses for you. From now on, if you want to come out, I'm telling them you wanted to come out."

While Lasorda tried to be patient with Sutton, the other Dodgers weren't always so forgiving. This was demonstrated through Steve Garvey's left hook. The trouble occurred in New York in the summer of 1978, on the morning after Sutton had been quoted in newspapers as saying, "All you hear about on our team is Steve Garvey, the All-American boy. But Reggie Smith was the real MVP. We all know it. [Smith] has carried us the last two years. He is not a façade. He does not have the Madison Avenue image."

Sutton was right, but his timing was all wrong. That morning, holding the offending newspaper, Garvey met Lasorda for breakfast in a Manhattan hotel.

"What would you do?" Garvey asked him.

In such situations, it is a manager's job to put out the fire. But as Lasorda knew, sometimes it was more important to start one. Garvey had the reputation among his teammates of being soft. Sutton had the reputation of being arrogant. Lasorda wondered whether he could kill two reputations with one stone.

"I ain't going to tell you what to do," Lasorda told Garvey. "But if it was me, and somebody said those things in the paper about me? The first time I saw him, I would deck him."

With that, Lasorda pushed away his coffee, plopped down the newspaper, and left Garvey sitting at the table. He didn't see his star first baseman again until a couple of hours later, at Shea Stadium. Standing on the field before the game, Lasorda was approached by a frightened equipment worker.

"Um, Tommy, there's a fight going on in your clubhouse," he said.

"Who's fighting?" Lasorda asked.

"It's Garvey and Sutton."

Lasorda just smiled.

Inside, Garvey had confronted Sutton about the comment, and Sutton had responded with a derogatory phrase about Garvey's wife, and soon they were rolling around on the dirty carpet, swinging and kicking and shouting.

"They'll kill each other," one bystander said.

"Good," said catcher Joe Ferguson.

Lasorda's ploy had worked. The two players who were most disliked by their teammates had beaten each other into humility. They never bothered any of their teammates or each other again. Two problems had been fixed without Lasorda having to lift a finger.

There was, however, another matter to be resolved. Before the team returned to Los Angeles, Sutton met with Lasorda and threatened to call a press conference so he could lay into Garvey.

Lasorda warned him against it. "He's too big for you. The fans love him. Don't do it."

Sutton called the press conference anyway. With the rest of the team gathered around the television set in Lasorda's office, waiting for the fireworks . . . Sutton took Lasorda's advice and had nothing but praise for Garvey.

"How did that happen?" asked second baseman Davey Lopes.

"No idea," said Lasorda, smiling.

Ask him today and he'll tell you that, if he could start one pitcher in a game to save his life, he would start Don Sutton. Time has helped Lasorda appreciate Sutton's willingness to take the mound under any conditions. Age has helped Lasorda understand that Sutton wanted to win just as badly as anyone else—he just wanted to win in his own fashion.

"Bottom line, Don Sutton was a gamer, he was a horse, he answered the bell every time, and I would put him at the front of my rotation anytime," Lasorda says.

Despite dealing with Sutton and Garvey the way he did, Lasorda managed to hold the Dodgers together through his rookie managerial season, leading the team to the 1977 Western Division title and a playoff series against the Philadelphia Phillies. This being Lasorda, it only figured that the Dodgers would lose the first playoff game. But, this being Lasorda, it only figured that they would bounce back in a most unusual way: they laughed their way back. In the first truly big game of his managerial career, with the Dodgers trailing one game to none in a best-of-five series, how did Lasorda motivate the team? With Don Rickles, of course.

"You would have had a better idea?" Lasorda says.

The acerbic comedian was one of Lasorda's many new Hollywood friends, which included Milton Berle and Gregory Peck, among others. The stars were enamored of Lasorda because he was, like them, an entertainer. Lasorda was enamored of the stars because in Los Angeles, nothing gave a new guy credibility like his friendship with stars. The Hollywood people used Lasorda to get closer to the team they loved, and Lasorda cleverly used them to boost his reputation with the fans and players. It was a relationship that worked well for everyone.

During the season, Rickles served as an honorary batboy. Then, after the opening game loss in Philadelphia, he was asked to be a savior.

"I said, 'Don, these guys are down, their backs are to the wall, they need something to make them smile and believe again. I think right now they're getting tired of listening to me. Maybe you can say something different.'"

Oh, did Rickles say something different. He began by telling the team that Lasorda was so fat, if the Dodgers didn't win, he was going to tie a string around his neck and use him as a balloon. He made fun of the older players for their blue long johns, and the African Americans for trying to move into his neighborhood. Before he was through, he had ripped the entire team, leaving them stunned and laughing. And, oh yeah, inspired. The Dodgers took the next three games, winning the playoffs and carrying Lasorda to his first World Series. The third game of that Series featured a bunt single by aging pinch hitter Vic Davalillo and a double by aging pinch hitter Manny Mota in a three-run ninth inning, great Lasorda decisions that led to a one-run win. So it wasn't all Rickles. But for once Lasorda gladly shared the spotlight.

"Not a bad year, huh?" Lasorda says. "Started it with Sinatra and ended it with Rickles."

As new Hollywood friends go, none was bigger than Frank Sinatra, whose association with Lasorda added yet another dimension to the new manager's clubhouse pull. Some of the jaded players wondered, if Lasorda was so full of bull, why would the most famous singing star on the planet hang around him so much?

"That's why I put up a whole wall of his photos in my office," Lasorda says. "Because nobody would believe it."

He first met Sinatra in Palm Springs, through former Dodger manager Leo Durocher. Sinatra liked Lasorda's humor. He liked the fact that Lasorda did not try to curry his favor. He imagined that if he had gone into baseball, he would be just like Lasorda.

In 1976, when the Dodgers were on a road trip in Chicago and Sinatra was playing a concert there, Lasorda, who had not yet become manager, was summoned to meet him in the back of a dark bar.

"The guy barely knows me," Lasorda said to Jilly Rizzo, Sinatra's longtime friend.

"The old man loves you," said Jilly.

Once they gathered at a back table, Sinatra looked at Lasorda and said, "You know, Tommy, I've been thinking about it. You should be the manager of the Dodgers."

Lasorda was stunned that Sinatra followed baseball that closely. "Thank you, sir. God willing, maybe one day I could be manager."

"Tell you what," said Sinatra. "The first day you manage the Dodgers, I will come out and sing the national anthem for you."

Sinatra left the table. Lasorda turned to Rizzo.

"Is he serious? He can't be serious, right?"

"He's dead serious," said Rizzo. "The old man says something, he means it."

And so it happened that, for Lasorda's first home opener, in 1977, Frank Sinatra sang the national anthem. It was the beginning of a friendship that included frequent Los Angeles dinners and visits to Sinatra's Palm Springs estate. Sinatra would get his baseball fix by hanging out in Lasorda's office. Lasorda would get his entertainment fix by hanging out backstage at Sinatra's concerts.

One winter Sunday, Lasorda played the best golf round of his life on the course behind Sinatra's home. He'd forgotten his clubs, but Sinatra had opened his garage, revealing thirty bags of clubs. Lasorda had forgotten his golf clothes, but Sinatra opened a closet filled with all sorts of clothes.

"Turns out, when you go to Sinatra's house, you don't have to bring your toothbrush," Lasorda says.

The round began just after they awoke, at 1 P.M., the players assembling in golf carts that were air conditioned and contained tiny liquor cabinets. Lasorda, who rode in Sinatra's cart, sliced his first shot far to the left, off the fairway. Sinatra climbed into the cart and drove down the fairway.

"Frank, my ball is over there," Lasorda said, pointing to the weeds.

"No, it's right here." Sinatra dropped a ball in the middle of the fairway.

For the entire eighteen holes, Sinatra ignored Lasorda's shots and simply dropped a ball in the middle of the fairway or green.

"What if you run out of balls?" Lasorda asked.

"I've got enough balls to cover you for the rest of your life," Sinatra said.

After the round, in which Lasorda set a course record, the golfers were drinking whiskey in the cart when Sinatra said, "You know, I was thinking, I bet you've got a great mother. Can I call your mother?"

"Call my *who?*" said Lasorda.

Moments later, Sinatra was on the phone to Lasorda's mother, back in Norristown. Upon hearing his introduction, she promptly hung up, believing it was a prank call. Lasorda phoned his sister-in-law, told her the story, and soon Lasorda's mother was back on the phone with Sinatra.

"Mom," said Sinatra to Carmella Lasorda, "I'm going to be playing at the Valley Forge Theatre pretty soon. Can I stop by your house and eat some of that Italian food you cook for your son? Just don't tell anybody I'm coming, OK?"

Sinatra hung up the phone and smiled. Lasorda laughed nervously, then thought about the words of Jilly Rizzo: *The old man says something, he means it.* But could Sinatra mean what he'd said on the phone?

A couple of months later, during spring training, the phone rang in Lasorda's Vero Beach office. It was Sinatra. He was lost.

"What do you mean, lost?" Lasorda said. "Are you in Vero Beach?"

"No," said Sinatra. "I'm in Norristown."

True to his word, he was driving around Lasorda's old neighborhood looking for his mother's house. Lasorda gave him directions, but Sinatra became confused and went to the house next door.

"Sorry," he said to the stunned neighbor at the front door. And, you guessed it, the woman couldn't get to her phone fast enough. By the time Sinatra had settled into Carmella Lasorda's house, eating her food and talking about her son, there was a mob outside. Police were summoned. Traffic was diverted.

After dinner, Sinatra carefully wheeled the infirm Mom Lasorda through the crowd and down the driveway and into the limousine. Once at the Forge Theatre, she was wheeled to the front row, handed a bouquet of flowers, and introduced to a cheering audience.

Said Sinatra: "I dedicate this show to Carmella Lasorda."

Said Lasorda later: "And people wonder why I take such good care of everyone else's mother. Look what Frank did for my mom."

Lasorda was with Sinatra at a restaurant several months before his death in 1998. The singer was so sick, he didn't recognize his old friends. When he died, Lasorda did not go to his funeral. He doesn't attend a funeral unless the deceased is a member of his immediate family or of the Dodger organization. He doesn't want to be reminded of his own mortality.

"Somebody is dead—what do they need me there for?" Lasorda says. "I want to be remembered for helping them live."

Despite the new dugout celebrities and the new clubhouse office and the new Dodger Stadium excitement, Lasorda's first Dodger team did not win a world championship. They were defeated, four games to two, by the powerful New York Yankees.

But for a manager still searching for a firm footing, the World Series was a success, if only because of a surreal scene in Game 4 that cemented his credibility not only with the Dodgers, but with the entire sports world.

It was the top of the second inning. The Dodger pitcher was the left-hander Doug Rau. He had just allowed three consecutive hits to Yankee batters, two of whom were left-handed. The Dodgers, already behind two games to one in the best-of-seven series, now trailed 1–0 in a must-win game.

Rarely is a pitcher pulled after just one full inning of a World Series game. No manager is ever that overtly desperate. No manager ever gets that impulsively mad. But never before had the World Series seen the likes of Tommy Lasorda.

He jumped out of the dugout and ran to the mound to replace Rau. It was a move so spontaneous, he knew he would have to kill several minutes on the mound to allow reliever Rick Rhoden to warm up in the bullpen. He forgot that he was wearing a microphone that picked up his comments for the radio broadcast. The following exchange begins with Lasorda asking pitching coach Red Adams to let him know when Rhoden was ready.

"Give me a sign, Red, when I get out there," says Lasorda as he leaves the dugout. "I'll mess around for some time, OK?"

As Lasorda walks out on the field, somebody behind him asks if he's going to leave Rau in the game.

"BLEEP no. He can't get the BLEEPING left-handers out, for BLEEP al-BLEEPING-mighty," Lasorda says.

When he arrives on the mound he discovers that Rau does not want to leave the game. "I feel good, Tommy," Rau says.

This leads to perhaps the most memorable mound exchange in World Series history. With the ballpark organ tootling pleasantly in the background, in the middle of the diamond in one of the most picturesque ballparks in America, Lasorda screams as if in a back alley.

"I don't give a BLEEP you feel good. There's four BLEEPING hits up there!"

"They're all BLEEPING hit the opposite way," Rau says.

"I don't give a BLEEP," Lasorda shouts.

"They've got a left-handed hitter. I can strike this BLEEP out."

"I don't give a BLEEP, Dougie . . . I may be wrong, but that's my BLEEPING job."

"I ain't BLEEPING hurting."

"I'll make the BLEEPING decisions here, OK?"

"There was three runs on the BLEEPING board yesterday," Rau says.

"I don't give a BLEEP. I don't give a BLEEP. BLEEP-BLEEP, I make the BLEEPING decisions. Keep your BLEEPING mouth shut, I told you!"

At this point, with the fans looking on in astonishment, second baseman Davey Lopes steps in and pleads for peace.

"Back off the mound," Lopes says. "If you want to talk about it . . . talk about it inside. This is not the place, OK? . . . I'm just trying to avoid a BLEEPING scene out here, that's all."

Lasorda agrees and then turns back to Rau, who clearly should have left the mound by now, but will not move.

"It's BLEEPING great for you to be standing out here talking to me like that," Lasorda says.

"If I didn't feel good, I wouldn't say nothing," Rau says.

"I don't give a BLEEP, Doug. I'm the BLEEPING manager of the BLEEPING team, I've got to make the BLEEPING decisions, and I'll make them to the BLEEPING best of my ability. It may be the BLEEPING wrong decision, but I'll make it . . . Don't worry about it, I'll make the BLEEPING decisions . . . I gave you a BLEEPING chance to walk out of here . . . I can't BLEEP around, we're down two games to one . . . I can't let you out here in a game like this. I've got a BLEEPING job to do. What's the matter with you?"

By the time Lasorda left the mound, the scolding was ringing in the ears of his entire team. As of that moment, there was no doubt that, despite spending the past several years acting as many of these players' surrogate father, housemother, and cheerleader, Lasorda was now their manager. The decision to remove Rau proved to be hasty and ill-considered, since Rick Rhoden allowed two more runs and the Dodgers lost the game, and eventually the Series. But the decision to fight to remove Rau proved monumental.

At this point in his young career, everyone knew Lasorda was cute and funny and loved to hug and lived to preach. But few knew that he could also be tough. Few understood the passionate and profane drive that consumed him, even when the cameras were off and the clubhouse doors were closed. In this incident, in the middle of the Dodger Stadium mound, in the middle of the most important game of his life, the intensity of his inner fire was revealed.

Lasorda had established himself in his players' eyes, and in the organization's eyes, as the Dodger boss. Not their mascot, not their good-luck charm, not their motivational speaker. He was, now and forever, their boss.

"I don't know why everyone makes such a big deal out of that mound visit," says Lasorda. "So I talked to one of my pitchers. So what?"

As he finishes the story on this September morning, he suddenly remembers it is his birthday, and looks around at the seventy-nine gift baskets that fill his living room. He cried because they were from Bobby Valentine, and when he looks closer, he cries again. Each basket contains a note from one of his former players or current associates. From Buzzie Bavasi to the new Dodger owners Frank and Jamie McCourt, from Peter O'Malley to a former player named Eric Karros.

"You know how Bobby got this idea, right?" Lasorda says, his eyes red. "I once told my players that one day they would all forget me. I told them that I would mold their careers and, in the end, they wouldn't even send me a gift basket. Well, look at this."

He is opening the notes now, one of which is from Bill Buckner: "You made me love the game. You were like a father to me."

Here's the one from Valentine himself, which reads, "I learned to be a better baseball player from you . . . I learned to be a better person from you."

Lasorda is crying again, surrounded by the lives he has touched, love notes from grown men attached to baskets filled with stuffed animals, and he thinks about when he was a child, how he longed for someone to make him feel this important.

"Every Christmas we would get the same present, gloves and a scarf," he remembers. "One Christmas we didn't have enough money, and my father went outside and shot his gun—*bam! bam!*—and came in and said, 'Sorry, boys. I just killed Santa Claus.'"

Lasorda maneuvers around the baskets, finds an empty living room chair, sits down, and starts thinking about birthdays, how he never understood their significance. Jo smiles, because she knows what story is coming.

"Jo came down to Dodger Stadium once and decorated the office for my birthday," he recalls. "But we lost the game, so when I came back inside, I was so mad I tore up all the banners and balloons."

He looks at Jo with a sad smile, then looks around at the piles of baskets, then looks back at Jo.

"I'm sorry, Jo," he says.

"That's just you, Dad," she says.

This birthday shows that Lasorda has changed, softened, finally appreciating the importance of the life he's been chasing. It's not enough to be in the Hall of Fame. It's not enough to have two World Series rings and one Olympic championship. Receiving seventy-nine baskets and seventy-nine notes from the people whose lives he touched? That's all he needs?

"Every season I used to say that if we won a hundred and two games, that would be a lot. But that would also mean that we would lose sixty games," he says. "So every year on January first, I knew I would be the most miserable guy in the world sixty times a year. That was a horrible feeling. What other job can give you that feeling?"

He sighs. "Then I remember the time I was walking home from the ballpark in Philadelphia after a bad loss. I'm in a bad neighborhood at three A.M. and a paddy wagon pulls up. The cop says, 'Tommy, what are you doing?' And I tell him, 'I'm waiting for somebody to kill me.'"

He shakes his head. "Nothing was more important to me than winning. But now I'm starting to see that in some ways winning was the least important thing I did. To have some player say I was like a father to him — is there anything more important than that?"

He goes to his bedroom to dress for his birthday celebration at Dodger Stadium. Since retiring, it has been his favorite day at the ballpark. For one day a year he is the manager again, the boss, the center of attention. On those dark days when he wonders whether his difficult journey has been worth it, the standing ovation that accompanies his birthday reminds him that it has. Getting congratulated simply for being born. Imagine that.

After his 1977 rookie season, Lasorda negotiated his one-year contract with Peter O'Malley the same way he always did. He walked into O'Malley's office on a November afternoon. O'Malley gave him a number. Lasorda agreed to that number, signed the deal, and walked away. Lasorda never had an agent, never had a contract dispute. He rarely had more than a one-year deal, but he never complained.

"What did I need an agent for? I always trusted the O'Malleys to pay me what I was worth," he says. "Too many people today are letting their agents come between them and the ballclub. It was the Dodgers who raised me and my family, and the Dodgers who were going to feed me, and I didn't want anything to come between us."

The 1978 season was almost a repeat of the 1977 season, with the Dodgers defeating the Reds for the National League West title, then defeating the Phillies for the National League title, then playing the Yankees in the World Series.

Once there, in Game 2, there was another potential Lasorda mound moment. It was the ninth inning, and the Dodgers were leading one game to none, with 4–3 on the scoreboard. Lasorda went to the mound with his heart on his pine-tarred sleeve. This time, instead of boldly removing a pitcher, he was going to boldly bring one in.

His name was Bob Welch. It was only his second year of professional baseball. It was only his fourth month in the major leagues. And the Yankees had runners on first and second with one out, and two power hitters, Thurman Munson and Reggie Jackson, were coming to the plate.

A year earlier, in this sort of situation, the world saw the crazy Lasorda. Now they saw the cunning Lasorda. He loved Welch's arm, loved that Welch had been good enough to earn seven wins and three saves during the regular season, but there was something else. Having dealt with many young players in both the major and minor leagues, Lasorda recognized the look in Welch's eyes: the kid had no idea where he was, no clue about the importance of the situation. The kid was perfect.

Lasorda summoned Welch from the bullpen, and instead of giving him a pep talk, he handed him the ball, shrugged, and uttered two words: "Throw strikes."

That's exactly what Welch did. He fooled Munson into lining out, then stared down Jackson in what became a classic World Series confrontation. Fastball, strike one. Fastball, ball one. Fastball, foul. Fastball, foul. Fastball, foul. Fastball, foul. Fastball, foul. Fastball, ball two.

The Dodger crowd was standing and clapping and hoarsely screaming. The players on both benches were leaning out of the dugouts in stunned awe. The only person who seemed cool was Welch, which is what Lasorda had expected. Jackson was one of the greatest fastball hitters in history and was at the height of his career, but Welch didn't care. He mindlessly threw fastball after fastball, each one rising higher, each one cutting deeper.

Then it happened one more time. For the ninth consecutive pitch, Welch threw a fastball. This time Jackson's mighty swing missed. Strikeout, game over, the crowd roars, Lasorda hugs the world, the Dodgers lead two games to none.

And it never got any better than that.

The Dodgers lost Game 3 in New York when Graig Nettles made four incredible plays at third base, which cost the Dodgers as many as six runs.

"We don't hit the ball to that guy, we win," Lasorda says.

They lost Game 4 in New York when Reggie Jackson swung his hip into a double play throw from Bill Russell and knocked the ball away long enough to allow a run to score. The play should have been ruled interference, and Jackson should have been ruled out, but the umpires were hesitant to make such a controversial call in a big game.

"I will never forget the name of the first-base umpire that day—Frank Pulli," Lasorda says. "I will never forget the sight of Jackson cheating us out of a run. I will never forget how I told Bill Russell, 'Next time, throw the ball at Jackson's head.'"

The Dodgers lost that game in extra innings, were blown out by ten runs in Game 5, then returned to Dodger Stadium to lose Game 6 and the Series when Brian Doyle, a reserve player who was hitting .192, had three Yankee hits. Afterward, Lasorda could only mutter three words.

Those words weren't "Good job, Yankees." Those words were "Brian bleeping Doyle."

"We had them," Lasorda says softly, the thought still hurting him thirty years later. "I was so certain we had them."

Lasorda will never give credit to the other team. Listen to five seconds of the Dave Kingman tape and you'll understand. It's against his nature. Lasorda forever feels that there was always a way the

Dodgers could have won. For him to admit that somebody else was better would be to admit that he wasn't good enough. If he ever thought that, he may never have made it out of Norristown.

The Dodgers lost the World Series, but Lasorda kept getting bigger. On a trip to New York to play the Mets, Lasorda and his publicity director, Steve Brener, were walking the streets at 2 A.M. after a loss, looking for the next day's *New York Times*. Two policemen in a cruiser saw them, picked them up, and drove them to the *Times*'s loading dock. In return for that favor, Lasorda promised to speak to the city cops—on the spot. So he was ushered down to a subway station, where he addressed the transit police. Then he moved on to the subway lockup where, at 4 A.M., he gave a rousing "God Bless America" speech to inmates who were chained to a wall. He couldn't sign autographs afterward because the chains didn't extend far enough.

"I'll spread the Dodger news anywhere, anytime," Lasorda says. "Especially early in my L.A. career, I wanted the players to see that I not only spoke it, I lived it."

The next couple of years were without a championship, but not without controversy, as Lasorda made the first of several managing decisions that were widely criticized. It was bound to happen. Unlike many managers, he always took chances, and so has always been exposed to second-guessing. The guy who had sent runners home from third base on foul pops in the minor leagues was the same guy who rolled the dice with pitching rotations in the big leagues. For all his memorable triumphs, it only makes sense that he would be in the middle of a number of memorable gaffes.

They only made him stronger. But at the time, they drove him crazy.

In the Dodgers' one-game playoff against the Houston Astros for the 1980 Western Division title, that dice roll came up craps. Instead of starting nineteen-year-old Fernando Valenzuela, who had pitched only ten games at the end of the season, he started veteran Dave Goltz, who was rocked in a 7–1 loss.

"I didn't know if the kid was ready," Lasorda says today. "He had just pitched two innings in relief a couple of days earlier, and I didn't know about his arm then. I wanted to go with the veteran."

Indeed, Valenzuela had pitched two innings three days earlier, but he had pitched two scoreless innings, and he had a 0.00 ERA in ten appearances for the Dodgers. Goltz, meanwhile, had a 7–11 record with a 4.31 ERA during the season.

It was the first time Lasorda ever showed any fear in playing a youngster. But Valenzuela was still a relative unknown, and there were probably few managers who would risk starting a nineteen-year-old in a playoff game. Valenzuela would be the opening day starter in 1981, setting off a season of Fernandomania, but who could have predicted that?

"Yeah, and if Goltz had thrown a shutout, I'd be considered a genius, right?" says Lasorda. "That's why I'll respect second-guessers —because they get two guesses. Me, as a manager, I only get the first guess."

Lasorda admits to managerial mistakes as easily as he spends money. He always has reasons for his decisions, and, like the results of his controversial decisions, those reasons endure forever.

Ask him about sending in a pinch hitter for Valenzuela in the seventh inning of the final game of the 1982 season, against the San Francisco Giants, with the Dodgers needing a victory to possibly tie for a division title. The score was tied, 2-all, the bases were loaded, and Valenzuela was considered by some to be a better hitter than Lasorda's pinch-hitting option, Jorge Orta. Yet Lasorda pulled Valenzuela anyway. Orta made an out, and in the bottom of the seventh the Giants' Joe Morgan hit a game-winning homer against Terry Forster to knock the Dodgers out of contention.

"I thought Fernando was getting tired. I still think he was getting tired," Lasorda says. "And if Fernando bats and makes an out and gives up the winning runs later, then I'm also criticized, so I can't win."

No criticism of Lasorda has been buried as deeply, or has hurt as badly, as a two-word curse that will live with him forever: Jack Clark.

"Those words don't bother me," Lasorda says. "Why should they bother me?"

It was Game 6 of the 1985 playoffs against the St. Louis Cardinals. The Dodgers led by a run, with two out in the top of the ninth and runners on second and third base. Up stepped Clark, the Cardinals' leading power hitter, who was batting .381 in the playoffs. On deck was Andy Van Slyke, a kid who was hitting .091 in the playoffs. On the bench as a possible pinch hitter was Brian Harper, who was hitless in the playoffs.

With first base open and only two struggling options available, you would walk Clark and pitch to Van Slyke, right?

Lasorda may have been the only person in Dodger Stadium who did not agree. He had seen his pitcher Tom Niedenfuer strike out Clark two innings earlier. He believed in his veteran. He believed in history. And he used every bit of his baseball savvy to make the decision.

And it ended up in the bleachers, Clark hitting a three-run homer to send the Cardinals to the World Series. "Man, did that hurt," Lasorda says. "That still hurts."

With one swing, every old attack against Lasorda surfaced. *He overworks his pitchers.* It was Niedenfuer's third inning, a marathon for a short reliever. *He doesn't look at statistics.* Van Slyke was clearly less capable of hitting the ball out of the ballpark.

"None of that matters," Lasorda says today. "Niedenfuer struck out Clark two innings earlier. Why couldn't he have done it again? And if he had struck him out again, I'd be a genius."

Lasorda's reasoning back in 1985 was the same as that in 1995 and 2005. He made the right move. Clark hit a bad pitch. End of story. And if you keep arguing with him, well, he always has a hole card, and it is bronze.

"I remember Whitey Herzog saying I messed up in 1985, and you know what I say to that? I'm in the Hall of Fame."

Lasorda's perceived mistakes have been like everything else in his life: just more fuel for Cooperstown.

All of this talk of decisions and second-guessers has Lasorda a bit angry, and he doesn't want to be angry on his birthday. When he arrives at Dodger Stadium in the early afternoon, he gets out of his car and starts singing.

"Did I ever tell you you're my he-ro?" he croons. "You are the wind beneath my wings!"

When he sings, it's time to change the subject, and the subject is now him. He is serenaded by congratulations as he walks toward the media dining room. It is a room large enough for dozens of writers and scouts, but Lasorda bypasses the half-dozen long tables and several small tables and slips into a windowless room in the back, behind the serving line. This cubbyhole, with only four tables, is the executive dining room. While Lasorda likes to mingle with the media outside, he always eats in here, where no jaded reporters will roll their eyes at his old stories, where his voice still carries.

By the time he arrives, the serving line is closed for the afternoon. No matter. The workers always open it back up for Lasorda. A waiter hustles in with a placemat and silverware. Another waiter hands him a Sprite. They give birthday greetings in Spanish. They take his order for food, which will be unwrapped and reheated.

A longtime cafeteria employee, an aging Mexican-American woman, brings him a brightly wrapped gift. She wants Lasorda to take it home to his wife. He doesn't understand and immediately opens it. It is a book about meditation. Lasorda looks at it warily. "This ain't for me, is it?" he says. "The only meditating I ever did was about what umpire I wanted to kill."

The woman is embarrassed. Lasorda realizes that he may have insulted her, and he puts his arm around her in thanks. She takes this as her cue to begin singing "Happy Birthday" to him in Spanish.

The song is interrupted by an earnest-looking young Dodger executive. "Tommy, Ned Colletti wants to see you in his office," the man says. Only Lasorda could have a birthday celebration that includes a song sung by blue-collar immigrants one minute and a surprise party in the executive suite the next.

When he enters the executive suite, the entire front office is waiting for him, gathered around a large white-frosted cake, everyone singing "Happy Birthday" in English. Lasorda hoped for this, even expected it, but still, he is moved.

"This is why we win . . . *You* are why we win," he says to the employees. "I cannot tell you how much I cherish this cake. Thank you, thank you, thank you." Lasorda is so moved, he will cut the cake for the staff and eat none of it himself. His cell phone rings, and he is summoned back to his office.

"Hey, Tommy," says his assistant. "Bobby Valentine is calling from Japan."

And Lasorda's eyes redden again. He picks up the phone.

"Bobby, I don't believe it, I don't believe it, I am still in awe," he says. "I cannot believe them carrying seventy-nine baskets into my house. Gawd almighty. How about the guys you got to write those things? Boy oh boy. Boy oh boy. Bobby, I thank you from the bottom of my heart. You are something, you are really something. How in the hell can you have a birthday like that? Nobody has that! Nobody! I love you Bobby. I love you."

Before the 1981 season, at a Los Angeles Chamber of Commerce luncheon, Lasorda announced that his team was going to win the world championship. He guaranteed it. A young reporter hustled back to his office to write the hot and bold news story. Only after he had checked the files did he realize: Lasorda had publicly guaranteed a championship every year.

But 1981 was going to be different. That year, Lasorda had the best combination of youth and experience, of smarts and power. His team had the childlike wonder of Fernando Valenzuela coupled with the veteran toughness of Steve Yeager. In the outfield he had the free spirits of Pedro Guerrero, Kenny Landreaux, and Dusty Baker. In the infield he had the solidity of Garvey, Lopes, Russell, and Cey. The players knew one another. They knew Lasorda. They bought his belief. And when a baseball strike suspended the season for fifty-two games, unlike other teams, they stuck together.

"It was the perfect season for my kind of managing," Lasorda remembers.

And beginning with the playoffs, it had the perfect ending. In the first round, a divisional playoff mandated by the strike, the Dodgers trailed the Houston Astros, two games to none, before winning three straight games, with Jerry Reuss pitching a shutout in the finale. Then, in the National League Championship Series, the Dodgers fell behind the Expos, two games to one, and were faced with having to win two games in Montreal to advance to the World Series.

Before the first game, Lasorda's team relied on God. Dusty Baker gave Lasorda a Bible verse that the manager read to the team:

"Suffering produces endurance, and endurance produces character, and character produces hope, and hope does not disappoint us."

The words led to a Game 4 victory, but more was needed in Game 5, when they stepped onto Montreal's outdoor field on a cold, windy day. Lasorda made one of the best motivational moves of his career when he ordered all of his players to get rid of their warmup jackets. "Whatever you do," he told his players, "don't shiver." The Dodgers didn't, the Expos did, and Rick Monday's two-out ninth-inning home run gave the Dodgers a 2–1 victory and sent them on to the World Series.

Once again their opponent was the New York Yankees. And once again Lasorda would engage in a dispute with a pitcher. This time it happened before the games began. The pitcher's name was Rick Sutcliffe, who a couple of years earlier had won 17 games and been named Rookie of the Year. He had been injured at the end of the current season, so he was left off the postseason roster, which infuriated him.

Sutcliffe stormed into Lasorda's office and threw a fit. In previous years, Lasorda might have punched him. But he didn't need to punch him. He didn't need to say a word. Everyone, including Sutcliffe, knew what was coming.

You can laugh at Lasorda. You can play jokes on Lasorda. You can treat him like a nutty uncle or a wacky grandfather. You can do things to him that players on other teams would never dream of doing to their managers. But there is one thing you cannot do to Lasorda. The manager with no rules has one sin, and it is a mortal sin.

You must not be disloyal. You must never turn your back on him or the franchise. You must never do anything that would show a lack of respect for all he has done for you. From the moment Lasorda joined the Dodgers, those who were disloyal disappeared. And so after the World Series, even though he was entering the prime of his career and would later win a Cy Young Award in Chicago, Rick Sutcliffe was traded to the Cleveland Indians. Lasorda had nothing to do with the deal. But few believed that.

"It's simple, really," Lasorda says, not for the first time. "I show you the loyalty of a father, you show me the loyalty of a son."

The World Series began, and the Dodgers lost both games in New York, falling behind two games to none, but they had two things in their favor: they would be returning to a place rocking with Fernandomania, and Valenzuela would be their Game 3 starting pitcher. After being kept in the bullpen while Dave Goltz blew the season, Valenzuela would have a chance to save the team after already saving the season. The wide-eyed, chubby young Mexican had been filling Dodger Stadium with Los Angeles's long-ignored Mexican-American sports fans. He whipped up the excitement called Fernandomania for good reason: in 1981, Valenzuela became the first player to win both the Rookie of the Year and Cy Young awards in the same season. Fernandomania wouldn't have been possible without Lasorda, who was seeing the embodiment of the American dream that he had long preached.

"Where else but in America could a Mexican kid from a dirt-poor farm become Hollywood's biggest celebrity?" Lasorda asks. "You couldn't help but love him."

Lasorda loved him because Valenzuela could speak only Spanish, meaning that often he could talk only to Lasorda. Once, on a national morning news show, Lasorda translated for Valenzuela, saying, "Fernando feels that Tom Lasorda is the greatest man he has ever seen. He's the finest manager ever in the history of baseball. When Fernando was a youngster, all he ever hoped and prayed for was that he would grow up someday to play for Tom Lasorda."

When the show's host wondered if Valenzuela had actually said all that, Lasorda smiled and said, "I didn't tell you what he said. I was just telling you how he feels."

Lasorda also loved Valenzuela because he would pitch until his arm dragged. Which led to Valenzuela's memorable Game 3 start at Dodger Stadium. By the third inning, he had allowed two home runs. By the fourth inning, he had allowed four total runs. If this were Doug Rau, he would have been gone. But Valenzuela stayed in the game, struggling and scuffling and battling until everyone looked up and it was the ninth inning, and somehow the Dodgers had won, 5–4. It was one of the grittiest games in World Series history, with a kid throwing 146 pitches to finish a win.

It may also have been the start of the heavy use that led to Valenzuela's release in 1991, which led to a grievance being filed against the Dodgers, which led to Lasorda's testimony that it took Valenzuela ten years to forgive. But at the time it was magic, and the Dodgers were back in the Series.

In Game 4, showing that he reacted differently to different players, Lasorda pulled a struggling Bob Welch in the first inning. Four years after he struck out Reggie Jackson, Welch had been through hell, admitting to being an alcoholic and spending time in a treatment center. Lasorda always backed any player who owned up to a problem, no matter what it was, because to hide it would be disloyal. As he backed Bob Welch, he later backed Darryl Strawberry, saying both men were afflicted with a disease and deserved pity, not scorn.

"So I always thought Bobby Welch was one of the most courageous people I knew," Lasorda remembers. "I've never had a longer walk to the mound than when I had to pull him from that World Series game."

The Dodger bullpen survived, though, and funnyman Jay Johnstone hit a pinch homer, and the Dodgers tied the Series. A day later, they led three games to two after Yeager and Guerrero beat Ron Guidry. Lasorda was now just nine innings from his first world championship. As if honoring his playing career, he decided he was going to try to win it with a managerial curveball.

It was the fourth inning of Game 6, the score was tied at 1-all, the Yankees had a runner on first base with two out, Larry Milbourne was at the plate, and pitcher Tommy John was on deck. John had pitched seven shutout innings against the Dodgers in Game 2, and with his sinker getting stronger as the game progressed, he was going to be tough to handle. So Lasorda lowered the bait. Even though it was unconventional in this situation, he intentionally walked Milbourne to put two runners on base for John.

He didn't do it to test John's hitting; he did it to test Yankee manager Bob Lemon's guts.

"Twice before in the Series I walked Milbourne, and each time Lemon sent up a pinch hitter for the pitcher," Lasorda recalls. "I really wanted John out of the game. So I walked Milbourne just to see if Lemon would do it again."

There was no way the Yankee manager would pull a successful pitcher in the fourth inning of a World Series game, would he? This one did. Lemon bit. He pulled John for pinch hitter Bobby Murcer, who flied out to end the inning.

"Bob Lemon is a great manager, and I would never second-guess him," Lasorda says. "But obviously everyone was happy to see Tommy John leave the game."

When a mediocre reliever, George Frazier, replaced John, everyone was ecstatic. The Dodgers scored three quick runs off Frazier en route to a 9–2 victory and Lasorda's first world championship. Yes, he was the first one out of the dugout, leaping onto the field before the final fly ball dropped into Landreaux's glove. And yes, he later told the world that his team had made the biggest comeback in sports history, rebounding from deficits in three postseason series before winning the championship. The bluster was spraying like champagne, Lasorda clamoring to play in a *real* World Series, shouting, "Bring on the Tokyo Giants!"

Someone asked him what it was like to be a world champion after only five years as a major league manager. Lasorda thought back to the long nights in Greenville, the long years in Montreal, the chilly summers in Spokane, the endless days in the Dominican Republic.

"Five years?" he says today, laughing at the notion. "That first world championship was the culmination of the trip of a lifetime."

Shortly after the World Series, following a victory parade, Lasorda, in his final act as manager of the 1981 Dodgers, addressed a huge crowd in front of Los Angeles City Hall. Every player stood behind him except Fernando Valenzuela. Fans shouted for the young pitcher, wondering why he didn't show up.

"Fernando has a bad cold and can't make it," Lasorda said.

The fans did not know that a few hours earlier, a frightened Valenzuela told Lasorda he did not want to attend the parade for fear he would be mobbed and trampled. Fernando was still a kid, and he felt overwhelmed.

Lasorda understood this, and saw that he would need Valenzuela's heart for the next decade or so. In exchange, he knew he had to support his pitcher, even if it meant failing to fully explain his whereabouts. The fans would give Lasorda love, but only Fernando could give him wins, and despite his image as a peddler of bluster, Lasorda was all about the wins. Because nothing sells like wins.

So Lasorda ended his first world championship season the way he started his managerial career—loyal to a fault, loyal to the end, backing his players because he knew they would back him.

"Fernando had a cold," Lasorda insists today. "Who told you he didn't have a cold?"

Later on his birthday night, from his seat in Frank and Jamie Mc-Court's dugout box, Lasorda will be asked to stand, and thousands of fans will sing, and for the umpteenth time this day, he will cry.

"What did I do to be so lucky?" he says in a choked breath after sitting down to bask in a glow that grows stronger each year. "What did I do to deserve all this?"

7

. . .

I PREACHED FOR THIS

What's that noise?"

Station 1 of the Los Angeles Fire Department is alive with the honking of horns and clanging of bells. Several of the twenty firefighters gathered around long tables in the cramped kitchen jump up and race for the door. Before they do, they grab Dodger caps and pause to thank their speaker, Tommy Lasorda, who shakes his head and shouts.

"Where you guys going? What's the emergency? Can I go with you? I thought that was the dinner bell!"

The remaining firefighters look at each other and smile. This visiting Hall of Fame manager has spent the past hour acting like a giddy kid. He has tried on fire hats. He has climbed around fire trucks. And now he wants to join them on a job, or maybe eat their lunch — they're not certain.

"We have an opening for fire chief, Tommy. Why don't you apply?" one asks.

"Those fires wouldn't stand a chance with me," Lasorda says.

"You'd be a great firefighter!" says another one.

"I heard this place has the best food in town, so I know I'd be a happy firefighter," Lasorda says.

He arrived at this aging station about a half hour ago. It's right down the street from Dodger Stadium, his first and only stop of the day. The reason he is here is as simple as the reason he does any of his two hundred speeches a year. Somebody called and asked him.

"I don't know who the hell called and asked me, but *somebody* did," he says.

That's all it takes. It's one of the great secrets in sports. To hire one of the most popular motivational speakers in sports history, all you have to do is dial his cell phone and give his assistant your date, and if Lasorda is available, he'll do it. No cover letter necessary. No faxes required. No reason needed.

"When the guy from the fire station asked me to come here, he says, 'Tommy, every time we watch you on TV, you never fail to mention how proud you are to be living in the greatest country in the world. You definitely believe in free speech, right?' And I say, 'Yeah.' And he says, 'Good, because you're gonna have to make one.'"

The firemen howl, the first of many laughs for a speech that Lasorda has given more than a thousand times. But each one is a little different, because Lasorda never has a script. He never brings notes. He never asks why he is speaking. He never asks to whom he is speaking.

"I just show up, check out the kinds of people in the audience, and talk from my heart," Lasorda says. "Ain't that what motivational speaking is all about? Your heart?"

He never intended to be a speaker. His voice was raspy and his delivery was crude and he couldn't stop cursing. But he played in so many small towns, groups requested him because he was often the loudest voice around. Realizing that his left arm wasn't going to carry him very far, he decided to try his charm. At first he was terrible, forgetting jokes and botching names. Then one night in 1964, in Pasadena, he found his calling. He was a lowly Dodger scout then, but was nonetheless asked to join a judge and a retired admiral on the dais of a dinner for Eagle Scouts. Thinking he might find some future players among those boys in crisp uniforms, he accepted the invitation.

"But when I heard the judge and the admiral talk, I knew I was screwed," Lasorda remembers. "What could I possibly say that was more important than what they said?"

Standing in front of the Scouts, sweating profusely, he had an idea. And his first real speech began with an old favorite: "On my honor, I will do my best to do my duty to God and my country . . ."

Unable to think of a better opening, he had begun by reciting the Boy Scout oath. It was corny. It was brilliant. When he finished, he was given a standing ovation, and Lasorda knew he could do this.

"Public speaking is just like managing," he says. "You eventually figure out who you are speaking to, then you just speak their language."

On this winter afternoon, before the firemen of Station 1, he gives a sermon that begins with props. His assistant passes out Dodger caps, which is the springboard to a first story.

"These hats, you might not think they're very valuable, but they could be," Lasorda tells them. "I once spoke at a dinner in Baton Rouge. Guy comes up, name of Dr. Leisner, and he says that all he ever wanted was a Dodger cap. I ask for his address, tell him I'll send him one. He says that's great and asks if he can do something for me. I asked him, 'What could you do for me?' He says, 'I'd like to give you a fifteen-thousand-dollar gallbladder operation.'"

The firemen are laughing, and Lasorda knows he has them, so he moves in slowly for the kill.

"Hold on to those hats, men. One day they could be worth a triple bypass!"

Lasorda's timing and delivery in his speeches, unlike in his baseball career, are impeccable. He not only knows which stories are funny, he also knows which words are funny, always placing those words at the end of a sentence. He knows that if he uses a curse word as a modifier to that last word, the laughs will be even bigger. He changes his voice to fit his story, adopting an accent for Spanish-speaking players and southerners alike. He sometimes changes the story to fit the audience. When he told the Dr. Leisner story to President Ronald Reagan, he used a Dodger jacket instead of a cap, because he'd given the president a jacket.

After his opening joke, he warms up his group with a compliment, just as he once warmed up new players with compliments. Today he is talking about the firefighters' hearts.

"I have respect for all of you. People don't realize how valuable you are until big fires occur. They don't know how important you are until they need you, and you are to be congratulated for what you do. Sometimes we take people for granted. We don't realize what a tough job it is. The time comes and you're called, you're ready, you're there, ready to save lives. I just wanted you to know how I felt about it, the appreciation I have for you."

The firefighters are quiet and staring now, appreciative of the kind words, feeling the sincerity fill the room, settling in for a nice flowery . . . Wait. Lasorda stops. He can feel them growing too comfortable. This always happens at the beginning of a speech. He starts being nice, and folks start to nod off, and that's when he hits them. Without a transition, seemingly without any thought, he jumps into a string of stories intended to make them laugh. It happens every time. He's been nice to them, and now it's their turn to be nice to him.

"Wherever I go to speak, I always meet an Italian there named Tony," he says, changing gears. "My wife and I are the grand marshals of the Columbus Day parade in New York City, and behind us are marching thirty-three thousand Italians, and fifteen thousand of them are named Tony. Everybody in this country has an Italian friend named Tony. So I did some research, and I found out why. When they shipped them over from the old country, they stamped on their forehead, 'TO NY.'"

The firefighters laugh and look at each other with amazed grins. After all these years, this old manager is still down to earth, still hilarious, still one of them.

"Let me tell you about these two Italians, Angelo and Tony. They made a pact that whoever dies first, he has to come back and talk about where he is. So Tony dies first, and for three years Angelo waits for the sign. One night, Angelo sees a ball of red fire and hears Tony's voice: 'Angelo, Angelo, it's me, Tony.' And Angelo cries out, 'You said you'd come back, and you did! How is it?' And Tony says, 'Every morning I have sex, then breakfast, then sex, then lunch, then sex, then dinner, then sex.' And Angelo says, 'Man, it sure sounds great in heaven.' And Tony says, 'Heaven? I ain't in heaven. I'm a rabbit in Colorado.'"

More laughter, fists pounding on tables, hands slapping thighs. The joke might not look so funny in print, but Lasorda's delivery is priceless, as he gives different voices to each man, with Angelo speaking like a regular guy and Tony speaking in falsetto, as if he's a ghost. It is a typical Lasorda joke, too, in that it's racy without being dirty, the kind of joke he can tell before any crowd. Lasorda is smart enough not to talk about something as explicit as sex without throwing in something cute like rabbits. Now he coughs and shrugs and starts another story, same Italian theme but veering slightly.

"So the pope comes to New York, lands at La Guardia, rushes to a limo, tells the driver, 'Take me to this address, and hurry.' The driver says, 'I can't drive that fast.' The pope says, 'I *have* to get there fast. Let me drive and you get in the back.' So the pope goes flying down the highway, and a cop stops them. He walks around the car, then runs back to his radio and calls the station and says, 'Chief, you won't believe who I just stopped. This guy is big, big, big.' And the chief says, 'Bigger than the president?' And the cop says, 'Yes!' And the chief says, 'Bigger than Sinatra?' And the cop says, 'Yes!' And the chief says, 'My God, who *is* this guy?' And the cop says, 'I don't know, Chief, but he's got to be big, because he's got the pope driving him!'"

The joke is old, but coming from Lasorda it sounds fresh, and the laughter continues. The firefighters loved the line that put Sinatra above the president, and loved the punch line even though they surely knew it was coming. Once again Lasorda filled the joke with the sort of dialogue and mimicry that made it seem more like a campfire tale than a stock speech. The secret of his success as a speaker is the same as the secret of his motivational technique as a manager: he makes you feel as if he is talking directly to you.

After his 1981 world championship, Lasorda entered a low period when he questioned his ability to motivate the team. His comeback in 1982 fell short on the final day, when he controversially batted for Fernando Valenzuela against the hated San Francisco Giants, and aging second baseman Joe Morgan—in his final insult against the Dodgers—homered off reliever Terry Forster. In 1983, the Dodgers won the West Division but were outclassed in the National League Championship Series against the Phillies. Over the next four years, the Dodgers had three losing records and one lost playoff series, which ended when Lasorda decided to pitch to Jack Clark.

All around him, the family that accompanied him to the big leagues was disappearing. Steve Garvey left for San Diego when the Padres offered him more money. Reggie Smith went to San Francisco. Davey Lopes and Ron Cey were traded when their careers began to decline. The guys who had grown up listening to Lasorda's shtick were gone, and everyone wondered whether he would have the same effect on new players who didn't feel so intimidated or indebted. Although he had been to three World Series in five years, Lasorda still had to prove that he could manage as well as he motivated. With a new and uncertain cast, the mid-1980s were his chance. And, at first, with average teams and late-season folds, Lasorda felt his first bit of major league frustration.

"We were so young, and some of our guys didn't come up with the right fundamentals," Lasorda says. "We were teaching them in the big leagues. It was a difficult time."

Nobody epitomized this frustration more than Steve Sax, a hustling young second baseman who replaced Davey Lopes on the field, and replaced Don Sutton as Lasorda's nemesis. Sax was one of only four Dodgers to play for both world championship teams in the 1980s, and Sax was Rookie of the Year in 1982. But from the time he joined the team, his mental and physical clumsiness drove Lasorda nuts. Steve Sax was the first player to make Lasorda wonder whether he could truly meld a man's mind. At first, as hard as he tried, he could not fix his struggling infielder.

"Steve Sax played the game like my wife shops—all day," Lasorda says. "The problem was, his intelligence never reached his playing ability."

Lasorda remembers lecturing Sax about not hitting the ball in the air, because he didn't have enough power. He would constantly remind him to hit it on the ground and use his speed. One day Sax said he finally figured it out.

"Skipper, I've got this hitting theory down pat," he told Lasorda.

"Eighty percent of the balls I'll hit down the middle, twenty percent I'll hit to the left, and the other twenty percent I'll hit to the right."

Lasorda remembers sitting on the team bus in Chicago, reading the *Wall Street Journal,* when Sax passed his seat.

"Hey, Skip," he said. "When you're finished with that, can I have the sports section?"

Things were even more confusing on the field, where Sax had difficulty understanding the signs. Lasorda once had a steal sign that consisted solely of the first-base coach shouting the player's last name. In the middle of one game, with Sax leading off first base, Reggie Smith yelled Sax's name several times, but Sax would not budge. Sax then called time-out and went into a huddle with Smith. After the inning ended, Lasorda asked Smith about the discussion.

"I can't tell you, Tommy, or you'll get really mad," said Smith.

"Tell me!" said Lasorda.

"OK. Saxie came over to me and said, 'Reggie, how long have you known me? Don't you think you should be calling me by my first name?'"

Another time, the steal sign was a wink. Coach Manny Mota winked several times at Sax, but, again, he never budged.

"So after the inning I said, 'What happened?'" Lasorda remembers. "And Manny said that Saxie just kept winking back at him."

Sax's mind and body collided on the field, where he was unable to consistently complete the short throw from second to first base. In 1983, he made a deplorable thirty errors at second base, many of them on thirty-foot throws that seemed to sail thirty feet high. The Dodger coaches would hit pregame grounders to Sax for hours, and he always threw them perfectly to first, but once the game started, the balls would go directly into the stands.

This was an important moment for Lasorda. It was a bigger moment for his critics. Lasorda was known for being able to light a fire under the chilliest of dispositions. But he was not known for being able to change the way a guy played. He could bring out greatness in a guy who possessed greatness. But could he do it with a guy who did not? Could he really make chicken salad out of chicken droppings? Sax was his crucial test. The world was watching. Lasorda, as usual, was screaming. Before one game in St. Louis, he grabbed Sax and led him around the infield.

"Lemme ask you a question, Saxie. How many people in this country can hit .280, which is what you're hitting?"

"Not many," said Sax.

"Now, how many people can steal fifty bases, which is what you're gonna steal?"

"Not many."

"OK, now, how many people can throw the ball from second base to first base?"

Before Sax could answer, Lasorda started screaming.

"I'll tell you how many, Saxie. Millions. Millions! Millions of people out there can make the simple throw from second base to first base! Everyone but you! How can you not figure that out?"

That wasn't exactly a manager's pat on the back, but it was typically brilliant Lasorda. He had crossed first, second, and third base building Sax up as one of the best players in the game. And then, for the last 90 feet, walking from third to home, he had torn him down and challenged him to rise to the level of the previous 270 feet.

Lasorda's final lesson to Steve Sax about his bad throws to first could be put into four words: "You're better than this." They were four words Sax had never heard before. This time he finally listened. After that talk, he never made thirty errors in a season again. In fact, he once made fewer than thirty errors over a three-year stretch.

Once again Lasorda had an answer. In the mid-1980s, this was good preparation for the times when he did not have one.

"I always go to the ballpark with a smile, no matter how I feel, because my team gets its mood from me, and if I ain't happy, they ain't happy, and if they ain't happy, they ain't winning," he says. "As a kid, I remember reading the back of a Carnation milk can where it said, 'Contented cows give better milk,' and I've always believed that about people."

But sometimes, in the mid-1980s, beneath the smiles, Lasorda felt such great pain that he would close his office door and turn on a television Western and put his head in his hands. Sometimes the smile couldn't even get him through batting practice, and would disappear inside the cinderblock clubhouse walls. Sometimes he would remain behind his closed office door for nearly the whole pregame period, with officials claiming he was in a meeting, when in fact he was in a funk.

It started in Houston's Astrodome on opening night in 1987, after the game. While Lasorda was out having dinner, his boss and mentor, Al Campanis, was at home plate being cooked. As part of an ABC *Nightline* show on the fortieth anniversary of Jackie Robinson's breaking the color barrier, Campanis, the Dodger general manager, was asked about the scarcity of blacks in management positions in baseball.

Campanis, who was seventy, had just finished a postgame cocktail. He was tired after flying from Los Angeles earlier that day, and uncomfortable sitting alone at home plate while looking into a single camera and listening to Ted Koppel in his earpiece.

"Looking back, seeing the situation in hindsight, you just figured something bad was going to happen," Lasorda says.

It was worse than bad. The next thirty-five words changed the Dodgers, and thus Lasorda, forever.

"I truly believe they may not have some of the necessities to be, let's say, a field manager, or, perhaps, a general manager," said Campanis of blacks. "Why are black people not good swimmers? Because they don't have buoyancy."

This was the same Al Campanis who had been Jackie Robinson's minor league roommate, the man Robinson considered one of his guardian angels. Campanis had helped Robinson make the switch from shortstop to second base. Campanis had later taught him various ways to avoid the tough slides of racist base runners.

This was also the same Campanis who promoted the Dodgers' involvement in Mexico and Latin America, a general manager who supported everyone from Fernando Valenzuela to Pedro Guerrero, a boss whose starting eight position players in 1981 included four minorities.

The statements were startling in their stupidity. But even more startling was that Campanis was the one who said them.

"That man didn't have a racist bone in his body," says Lasorda. "Al did more for blacks and Latins than anyone in baseball history. Al did more than Branch Rickey. There used to be only two photos hanging in Al's dining room, and one of them was of Jackie Robinson. That man was just trying to cover up for baseball, and he was tired, and he said a stupid thing."

Lasorda didn't hear about it until the next morning, when Peter O'Malley summoned him to breakfast with Campanis to discuss the issue. Lasorda remembers O'Malley's disappointment and Campanis's shame, but no indication that any punishment was forthcoming.

"Al got up to use the bathroom and I said, 'Peter, when he comes out, you've got to put your arm around him and tell him you support him,'" Lasorda recalls. "'That man has given his life to this team. He has earned your love.'"

So when Campanis returned, O'Malley stood up and hugged him.

"And I thought that was the end of it," Lasorda recalls.

But it was only getting started. After news of Campanis's statement swept through Los Angeles, local groups vowed to boycott the stadium if he was not fired. The pressure on O'Malley mounted. Two days after the incident, he decided he could no longer support Campanis, who was asked to resign—a pioneer in race relations forever branded as a racist.

Lasorda closed his office door and wept.

"They told me they couldn't handle people boycotting the stadium, so they had to get rid of Al," Lasorda says. "I told them, 'You've hung an innocent man.'"

From that moment, everything on the Dodgers changed. An organization that had been run by a long line of old-fashioned baseball men was suddenly being run by a former publicity guy and longtime Dodger employee Fred Claire. He was smart, honorable, and sensitive to the Dodger legacy, but he was not a good ol' boy, and Lasorda's status with the team lost some of its swagger. His voice wasn't as loud in the front office anymore. His bluster was not embraced like before. His credibility as a manager wasn't as strong anymore.

Remember, Campanis was the Dodger executive who had pointed to Lasorda during that spring training bus trip and predicted great things for the boastful minor league pitcher. Campanis was like Lasorda's second father. Claire, on the other hand, was like Lasorda's little brother.

In the spring of 1969, when Claire was a reporter for the *Long Beach Independent Press-Telegram,* he once mentioned that he used to play baseball, and wondered whether he could take spring training, go out on the field with Lasorda's Spokane Indians. Lasorda, as he usually did with writers, buttered him up by letting him play in an exhibition game. When Claire stepped up to the plate, Lasorda shouted to umpire Billy Williams, "Wait till you see this guy. We paid him a $100,000 bonus." After Claire struck out, Williams shouted back, "You paid that guy $99,999 too much!"

So while Lasorda and Claire were friends, Lasorda always thought of Claire as a newspaper guy who couldn't hit a fastball, and Claire considered Lasorda a great manager who nonetheless wasn't above criticism or help.

With Claire arriving and the Dodgers coming off several disappointing seasons, it was almost as if Lasorda had to prove himself all over again. Then, in the summer of 1987, questions about his managing were overshadowed by questions about his mortality.

Sitting in his office during batting practice one hot July afternoon, he was summoned by a coach yelling, "McMahon's down! McMahon's down!"

Lasorda raced from his office down the concrete tunnel to the Dodger Stadium steps, where he found scout and instructor Don McMahon lying on his back. McMahon, a former big-league pitcher, was throwing batting practice in the summer heat when he collapsed of an apparent heart attack. Lasorda dropped to his old friend's side and gathered him in his arms and did the only thing he knew how to do. He gave him a pep talk.

"Don't die, Don, dammit, don't die! Please don't die. Please don't die."

Then, with a *pfffft* sound that Lasorda will never forget, McMahon took his last breath. Efforts to revive him failed. Don McMahon, three years younger than Lasorda and in much better shape, died in a Dodger uniform after throwing the same sort of early batting practice that Lasorda often threw.

"As they carried him away, I thought, 'That's me,'" Lasorda says. "I thought, 'I'm not ready to die. I got more things I want to do. I got another championship to win.'"

The Dodgers finished the 1987 season with a 73–89 record, the second consecutive year of subpar baseball. The two worst records in Lasorda's career had occurred back to back. The team's future looked bleak. The manager's future didn't look much better. Instead of spending a winter surrounded by welcomes, Lasorda was surrounded by whispers. Was 1988 going to be his last year? Was Fred Claire going to do what Al Campanis would never do—remove him?

Tommy Lasorda had to win another championship to keep his job. He wasn't the only one who believed he had to, but he was the only one who believed he could.

The firefighters of Station 1 in Los Angeles are hungry for lunch. There is a huge stainless steel salad bowl on the counter. There are huge chunks of chicken in the refrigerator. But Tommy Lasorda, thirty minutes into a free speech that was supposed to last five, is still talking.

"I've been with the Dodgers fifty-eight years and been married fifty-seven years, and my wife and I still go dining and dancing three times a week."

"Ahhh," say the tough firefighters.

"Yeah," Lasorda says. "My wife goes on Mondays, Wednesdays, and Fridays, and I go on Tuesdays, Thursdays, and Sundays."

Lasorda has them laughing again, and off he goes with another story about poor Jo.

"One night I was speaking to a group of FBI agents in Los Angeles. I drive home, look at the dashboard clock, it's three A.M. I sneak inside and take my shoes off to be quiet—you guys know what I mean—and take six or seven steps and then, boom, the lights go on and Jo is shouting at me. 'Where have you been?' she says. I say, 'Whoa, hold the phone.' I reach up into the cabinet and take down a bottle of vodka. I pour some into a tiny cup. I tell Jo, 'Drink this.' She says, 'I ain't drinking that. I don't drink vodka. Why should I drink that?' So I'm begging her to drink it, and she finally takes one sip and spits it out and goes, 'Ohh, that stuff is terrible.'"

Lasorda pauses. Time for the big swing.

"So I tell her, 'You see? And you think I'm out enjoying myself?'"

As the laughter dies, it becomes clear that in this typical Lasorda story, he's talking about using common sense to outsmart someone.

In the 1988 season, that theme became a reality. It started when Fred Claire, the stuffy new general manager who couldn't possibly be as scrappy as Tommy, won a series of fights that should have made Lasorda proud. In the summer of 1987, Claire acquired two utility men, Mickey Hatcher and Mike Sharperson; two outfielders, John Shelby and Danny Heep; and a pitcher, Tim Belcher. Then, that winter, negotiating as tough as Lasorda once pitched—only with more control—Claire acquired shortstop Alfredo Griffin, catcher Rick Dempsey, relievers Jay Howell and Jesse Orosco, starter Don Sutton, outfielder Mike Davis, and, in an inspired move, outfielder Kirk Gibson.

"It was a tremendous winter, and Fred Claire did a tremendous job," Lasorda says. "He knew the pulse of the team. He knew I needed a guy to run things in the clubhouse. He knew we needed Gibson."

Lasorda has always believed that even a clubhouse-wandering manager like himself needed someone to carry his torch among the players. He needed someone who could support his baseball values and work ethic when he wasn't around. This player could scold his teammates for not hustling, and they would listen. This player could corner other players in the shower or on the bus or in a hotel lobby and preach Lasorda's gospel, and they would respond. Gibson wasn't only Lasorda's toughest player, he was his disciple.

"In every walk of life, a manager needs guys like that, employees who will watch the boss's back and spread the boss's word," Lasorda says.

Winning teams have those players; losing teams do not. From the first game that spring, it was obvious that the 1988 Dodgers had one of those players. He was a former Michigan State football star and a Detroit Tigers World Series hero, famous for running over second basemen the way he once ran over safeties, a guy known for being a football player in a baseball uniform.

While sprinting in the Holman Stadium outfield before the first spring game of 1988—he never did anything halfway—Gibson lost his cap. When he put his hand to his forehead, he felt clumps of eye-black, the nasty stuff that players wear under their eyes to reduce the sun's glare. Somebody had smeared eyeblack on the bill of his cap. It was a joke. At least, on previous Dodger teams it might have been considered a joke. But Gibson wasn't laughing. He stormed off the field and disappeared for the day. When he returned the next morning, he demanded to speak to the players.

"It was the speech that set the tone for the season, and I didn't have to say a word," Lasorda remembers.

Gibson berated the players for not having a winning attitude, warned them that it would be a long summer if they continued to play jokes like this, and scared them enough that Jesse Orosco admitted he was the culprit.

"I knew then that my star player and I were on the same page," Lasorda says. "When that happens, when your best employee thinks just like the boss, then miracles can happen."

And so the Dodgers and Gibson stormed through the summer, blowing past the rest of the National League West with an ordinary team that cared extraordinarily about winning. Lasorda loved this team more than any of his others, because this team played the way he played, with bits of brilliance strung together with long stretches of hustle and smarts. For the first time since Lasorda turned the franchise into Hollywood's team, the Boys in Blue wore collars of blue, with one group of players becoming famous for not being famous. The Dodger reserves made such a stunning contribution in difficult circumstances, they were known as "the Stuntmen," led by the nutty Mickey Hatcher. Where Gibson enforced dedication, Hatcher enforced humor, and Lasorda sat back and watched with pride.

"It was the most fun I've ever had with a team, because they all wanted to win so much," he remembers. "It was hard to find egos. I couldn't see any selfishness. They were all about winning."

The team was so much like Lasorda, he spent the regular season in the background before taking over in the postseason. But it only seemed like these Dodgers could do it all themselves, like Gibson was the final piece to a championship. In fact, that final piece was Lasorda, who spent October showing the world, once and for all, that the motivator could manage.

The National League Championship Series pitted Lasorda's Dodgers against the powerful New York Mets, who had beaten the Dodgers in ten of eleven games during the season. The Mets beat ace Orel Hershiser and stopper Jay Howell in Game 1, and it looked as if this misfit outfit had finally hit the wall. And then the *New York Daily News* hit the streets. On the day after the Game 1 victory, the paper ran a column by Mets pitcher David Cone. He used the forum to tear down the Dodgers, writing that Howell was a "high school pitcher" and that Hershiser was "lucky."

Such barbs are often traded between teams in a postseason series. And while the press calls them "bulletin board material," the actual words rarely end up on a bulletin board. Most managers believe that if the players need this sort of extra motivation to play the biggest games of their lives, they don't deserve to win anyway. Most managers just ignore this stuff.

Tommy Lasorda, of course, was not like most managers.

"Are you kidding me? Players are human beings. Players react to everything. Everybody thinks they're robots, but players live in fear of being embarrassed. And that's what happened here. David Cone tried to publicly embarrass my players."

So instead of ignoring it, Lasorda embraced it. He printed copies of Cone's column and placed them in every home locker in Dodger Stadium. He posted copies on walls. He handed copies to friends. He did everything but insist that the article be shown on the big-screen scoreboard.

"Don't you see?" Lasorda asks. "This was better than any clubhouse speech I could have given. For one day, anyway, David Cone did my job for me, and I thank him."

Sure enough, the Dodgers racked around Cone that night, scoring five runs in two innings and in the end knocking him for a 6–3 Dodger victory. By the time the teams met for Game 3 at Shea Stadium in New York, Cone had apologized to every Dodger he could find.

"He didn't need to apologize to me," Lasorda says. "I thought it was great writing. I was going to nominate it for a Pulitzer."

In Game 3, Lasorda was back in the news: Howell was thrown out of the game when umpires discovered pine tar on his cap. The

Dodgers then blew an eighth-inning lead and lost, falling behind two games to one in the series. Lasorda was so angry he left the clubhouse without telling anyone, avoiding the team and returning to Manhattan by car. He wasn't angry at Howell—hey, maybe the guy was cheating, but at least he was trying. He was angry at reliever Jesse Orosco, who essentially cost the Dodgers the game after Howell was thrown out. Orosco lasted only three batters, allowing a single, hitting a batter, and walking a batter. Orosco couldn't get an out, eventually allowing two runs, and the next morning Lasorda made a promise.

Sitting at breakfast with his coaches, he vowed that he would never trust Orosco again that season. He looked at his coaches, looked up at the ceiling, and said, "God, if I ever pitch that bleep Orosco again, may you hit me with a bolt of lightning and kill me dead."

He said it in the solemn tone of a priest giving last rites. Coming from any other manager, it would have been a joke. Coming from Lasorda, it was serious, and his coaches knew it.

"Darn right I meant it," he recalls. "Everyone knows how I like to use my pitchers. If I didn't make that promise, I would have used Orosco in a minute. I was going to rely on God to keep me from using the one guy who could kill our season."

The mood became more desperate when it was announced that Howell had been suspended by the league for three games—later reduced to two—for the pine-tar incident. The Dodgers would now have to beat the National League's most powerful team at least two more times without its star reliever. Two of those games would be at Shea Stadium. Nobody thought they had a chance.

Lasorda gathered his team together before Game 4 and did what he did best. He screamed the lessons of his father. He screamed the hardships of his past. He screamed belief.

His team expected him, like most managers, to comfort them about the loss of a key player and perhaps inspire them to win in honor of that player. Instead Lasorda basically told them to forget about Jay Howell and focus only on themselves.

"We're not going to let one person determine our fate," he said to his stunned team. "We love Jay Howell, but this team is bigger than him. This team is bigger than any one person. If we all tug on the same side of the rope, we can move mountains. We're going to win this thing with or without Jay Howell."

The speech was so emotional that Hershiser, who had thrown 110 pitches the previous day, approached Lasorda afterward in his tiny Shea Stadium office.

"I'll be Jay Howell," Hershiser said.

"Get out of here, you're crazy, I'll never use you so soon," Lasorda said.

Yet a few hours later, it was Lasorda who was going crazy. Within a span of ten minutes, in two of the most important managerial decisions of his career, he broke a promise both to God and to the Bulldog.

It was the bottom of the twelfth inning. The Dodgers had tied the game with a dramatic Mike Scioscia homer in the ninth, then taken a one-run lead on a Kirk Gibson home run in the top of the twelfth. But now the Mets had runners on first and second base with one out and two left-handed hitters coming up. There was nobody left in the bullpen but Orosco, who had been ordered chained to his chair for the evening. It was the perfect situation for the left-hander. But everyone on the bench knew about the promise.

Turning to pitching coach Ron Perranoski, Lasorda said, "Dammit, if I'm going to manage this team right, I've got to bring in Orosco."

Said Perranoski: "You can't bring him in. He's the only guy we've got left."

Said Lasorda: "I'll take care of God. You just go out there and bring in Orosco."

As Perranoski walked to the mound to make the pitching change, Lasorda stuck his head out of the dugout and looked up to the sky.

"God, you know about this morning?" he said. "I was just kidding."

Once he was back in the dugout, the phone rang. It was bullpen coach Mark Cresse.

"Hershiser just showed up down here. What do I do with him?"

Having already broken his word to God, Lasorda figured, aw, what the hell.

"Get him warmed up," he told Cresse.

Orosco took the mound and promptly walked Keith Hernandez on four pitches. Then he threw three consecutive balls to Darryl Strawberry. The entire Dodger season rested on the arm of a weary pitcher who was on the verge of walking home the tying run. Hershiser wasn't warmed up yet. Orosco was their only hope. And he had just thrown seven straight balls.

Lasorda couldn't take it anymore. He jumped up and ran to the mound. It was time for his second pep talk of the day. A personal pep talk. He moved Orosco to the side of the mound so the television cameras couldn't read their lips. Then he began screaming.

"Can you throw a bleeping strike?" he yelled at Orosco. "Can you just throw the bleeping ball over the plate? I am sick and tired of looking at your bleep. Throw a bleeping strike!"

If you watch the video of this discussion, you can see the dark-skinned Orosco's face turn white. Watching it live on television, Jo Lasorda saw the eerie transformation and later wondered what her husband had said to him.

"I was cheering him up," Lasorda told her later.

Now he returned to the dugout and started praying again.

"Do you think God would actually let Orosco throw a strike?" he asked Perranoski.

The answer came with the thud of a catcher's mitt. Strike one. The answer came with the dull ping of a ball grazing wood. Foul ball, strike two. Then the answer was finalized with a weak pop fly to second base.

Orosco had retired Strawberry. The Dodgers were one out from surviving the game. It was time for Lasorda to . . . pray again?

"I'm sorry, God, but now I'm bringing in Hershiser," he said.

"You can't do that!" said a voice.

It wasn't God, it was Perranoski, who was making the point that Hershiser was the last Dodger pitcher in uniform and could face only one or two batters before risking an injury to his arm.

"He'll get this out, the game will end, and it won't matter," said Lasorda.

Hershiser came into the game. Lasorda started praying again. Truly, if Hershiser did not retire Kevin McReynolds, the Dodgers would have to bring in a position player to pitch, and they would surely lose the game.

But as he had done all season, Hershiser threw the big pitch. He fooled McReynolds, who hit a fly ball into shallow center field. As John Shelby chased it, Lasorda began jumping up and down as if riding a horse.

"C'mon John, c'mon John!" he shouted.

Shelby made the catch. And for the first and only time after a big win, Lasorda did not charge out of the dugout. Instead he retreated to the bench and collapsed. He couldn't move.

"I was so sapped out, I was like a wet dishrag. I've never felt that way in my entire life."

The Dodgers won the game, and the series stretched to a seventh and deciding game, leading to one last Lasorda pep talk.

"We're like the guy whose boat capsized a mile offshore," Lasorda told them. "He swam to within one yard of shore and then drowned. He should have drowned at sea when his boat capsized. It's worse when you get so close and don't make it. We're only a yard away. We can make it!"

Some of his players later wondered whether there was ever such a guy who swam away from a sinking ship only to drown in the shallow surf. Then again, years before, some of Lasorda's minor leaguers must have wondered whether the 1927 New York Yankees had actually lost nine games in a row.

"Hell, I have no idea if any fool ever drowned in ankle-deep water," Lasorda says. "But does it matter?"

It didn't to his players, who easily defeated the Mets, 6–0, to win the pennant in the most grueling fashion.

"We saved a lot of people a lot of money by winning this series," Lasorda says. "See, a lot of people spend a lot of money every year to go all the way to Our Lady of Lourdes in France to see miracles. All they had to do this year to see miracles was watch us."

Lasorda admits it was a miracle that his increasingly rotund body survived the ordeal.

"Of all my sixty-three playoff games, those seven against the Mets were the toughest by far. It wasn't even close."

But not everyone was so thrilled. At the victory party, in a Pasadena restaurant, Jesse Orosco, looking fierce, approached Lasorda.

"You know, I've never had a manager talk to me like you talked to me on the mound out there," he said.

"And what happened?" Lasorda said.

"Well, um, I got the guy out," said Orosco.

"Exactly."

Today at the Station 1 firehouse, it is question-and-answer time. Lasorda keeps eyeing the big bowls of sliced chicken and lettuce. He's ready to eat. He's not thrilled with the idea of questions. He likes to control his stories as much as he liked to control his games.

One of the firefighters pulls out a list. Lasorda sighs.

"You managed nine players who won Rookie of the Year honors. The Los Angeles Fire Department is hiring more rookies than ever before. How can we be as successful with our rookies?"

Lasorda smiles. That is not a question, it is a compliment. Somebody wants to compare his managing to the business of fighting fires? He longs for that sort of respect, but feels it is rarely given. He worries that people on the outside can't understand that beneath his bluster is a methodology that would work as well on summer interns as on kid pitchers.

"I remember when I won ten games in a row at Montreal, and I get called up to the Brooklyn Dodgers, and I only played in one game the entire time I was there," he recalls. "That guy Alston never gave me a chance, and I never forgot it. So when I get young players, I play them. I never gave a darn about how old they were. I only cared if they could play. It should be the same here. Bring 'em up, let 'em know their duties, tell them that you believe in them, then let them do their jobs. It's the only way they learn."

The firefighter has another question. Lasorda wants to hear it. He fancies himself as a Lee Iacocca in chaps and spurs. Imagine a poor kid from Pennsylvania telling the nation's second-biggest fire department how to run its shop.

"Ever since Jackie Robinson arrived, the Dodgers have been one of the most diverse organizations in baseball. The Los Angeles Fire

Department is also diverse. How did you get so many different types of people to bond?"

Lasorda gladly explains: "I once had a starting rotation of five pitchers from five different countries. Mexico, Korea, Japan, the Dominican Republic, and the United States. When you can't speak the language, the main thing you use is gestures. An embrace or an arm over the shoulder speaks louder than any words. You also use food. I would eat with different guys on different days. And I would give them their choice: their native food or pasta. In the beginning, they chose their native food. In the end, it was all pasta. Every day I told them I would be their father away from home. And that's how I acted."

Sometimes he was the boisterous father who jokingly chides his teenage son about girlfriends until the boy covers his ears and runs for the car. Other times he was the hot-tempered father who, when his daughter stands up to leave the dinner table without asking, slams down his fork and scares her back into her chair.

Lasorda was at his best, though, when he was being the protective father, the father who would call the fifth-grade teacher when the son complained about an unfair test, or send a warning to the cheerleading sponsor when the daughter complained that practices went on too long. The media grew tired of the stance, opponents made fun of it, but the players always appreciated it.

In the 1988 World Series, Lasorda was at his protective best. The Dodgers were heavy underdogs to the mighty Oakland Athletics, a team that had won 104 games in the regular season, 10 more than the Dodgers. The A's had swept the Boston Red Sox in the American League Championship Series and were rested and strong, featuring some of the best players that muscle supplements could buy, including Jose Canseco and Mark McGwire.

"Those guys were so huge, their forearms were bigger than some of our players," Lasorda remembers. "Everybody was in awe of them. I worried that even we were in awe of them."

And the Dodgers were, until the bottom of the ninth inning of the opening game, with the A's leading 4–3, with future Hall of Fame pitcher Dennis Eckersley on the mound, with two out and nobody on base.

Everything changed when clubhouse attendant Mitch Poole ran over to Lasorda on the bench.

"Gibby wants to see you," Poole whispered.

Kirk Gibson had to miss the opening game because he'd suffered a leg injury in the playoffs against the Mets. He had spent the evening sitting on a table in the trainer's room. Lasorda had dashed down the tunnel and into the room after every inning.

"Feeling better?" he'd ask Gibson.

The Dodger slugger and team leader flashed a thumbs-down each time.

So when Poole whispered to Lasorda in the bottom of the ninth, the manager jumped up and ran to the tunnel. In the trainer's room he found Gibson standing on one leg.

"I think I can hit for you," Gibson said.

"Follow me," said Lasorda.

Being careful to hide him from the Athletics in the other dugout, Lasorda sat Gibson down next to him on the bench. With Mike Davis batting, Lasorda instructed light-hitting Dave Anderson to stand in the on-deck circle.

"I figured if they thought Anderson would bat next, they would pitch carefully to Davis," Lasorda says.

The scheme worked: Davis walked. Lasorda smiled. The old curveball pitcher was now throwing curves from the bench. Then Lasorda turned to Gibson.

"OK, big boy," he said. "Get your ass up there."

To the amazed cheers of the Dodger Stadium crowd—and the amazed stares of the A's—Gibson hobbled past Anderson and dug into his stance at home plate. When Eckersley got two strikes on Gibson, Lasorda threw another sweeping curve. He signaled Davis to steal second base, setting himself up as the tying run. Davis stole easily, then Lasorda held his breath. With first base now open and a tough hitter like Gibson batting, wouldn't you think Eckersley would intentionally walk him?

"That's why I waited for two strikes before I ordered Davis to steal," recalls Lasorda. "Because I knew about the pride of a pitcher and the pride of a manager, and neither of them will ever intentionally walk a batter with two strikes on him. They just don't do it."

Some say having Davis standing on second base unnerved Eckersley. Others say the mere distraction of the steal hurt his concentration. Still others say he should have just sucked up his pride and walked Gibson. Whatever the case, on the full-count pitch Eckersley threw what he always threw on a full count—a backdoor slider. The Dodgers had been warned about it. Gibson was waiting for it. He swung. The ball sailed toward right field.

Lasorda started screaming: "Where is it? Where is it?"

It was the most dramatic home run of his managerial career, the most defining home run of his career, a home run he had set up with the most deft sleight of hand of his career. Yet Lasorda never saw it. He never saw the ball off the bat. He instead watched right fielder Jose Canseco go back, and back, and back.

"And when he stopped going back, I knew it was out." Lasorda then stormed the field, in another trademark jog-with-tiny-arms-pumping.

Five minutes after the ball was gone, he also knew that this World Series, just one game old, was over.

"We're finally leaving the dugout after all the celebrating, and I look up and some of those Oakland A's were still on the field," he recalls. "You knew right then, the hit had paralyzed them. The hit had finished them."

But Lasorda's work in the Series wasn't finished. After the Dodgers won Game 2, the A's stole Game 3 in Oakland on a ninth-inning homer by Mark McGwire, setting up a Game 4 that could have tilted the Series back in the Athletics' favor.

The A's were going to start the veteran Dave Stewart against the Dodgers' young Tim Belcher. A couple of hours before the game, however, with Gibson already out with the leg injury, the Dodgers were dealt another blow when fragile Mike Marshall said he couldn't play because of a headache.

Lasorda heard the news and lost his temper. After surviving an incredible postseason of bad luck, the Dodgers were going to blow it all because of a headache?

"A headache!" he shouted, his words filling the Oakland Coliseum tunnel. "A man can't play the biggest game of his life with a headache?"

Marshall's absence meant a different Dodger lineup: Steve Sax, Franklin Stubbs, Mickey Hatcher, Mike Davis, John Shelby, Mike Scioscia, Danny Heep, Jeff Hamilton, Alfredo Griffin.

It was a lineup with only a handful of players capable of starting for another major league team. It was a lineup marked by bench players, underachievers, and disappointments. Lasorda looked at the lineup card and knew. He immediately called his players together for another meeting. He made certain Marshall was sitting in the middle of it. While waiting for the players to gather, he idly reached up and turned on a clubhouse television set. It may have been the best decision he made in the Series.

"How can you tell me you can't play in the World Series with a headache!" he shouted at Marshall, in front of everyone. "I don't understand that. How can you do that to us!"

Then he turned to the team and gave a speech they had already heard in this postseason.

"We're not about one man, we're a team. We can still do this. We can pull together and—"

Lasorda was interrupted by two players who were watching the television set behind him.

"Tommy, look up there," said one player. "Costas is saying something bad about us."

Lasorda turned around to see the NBC announcer Bob Costas standing on the field, talking about the Dodgers. Everyone quickly quieted enough to hear him call the team one of the worst lineups ever to play in a World Series. Costas was right. But Lasorda felt wronged. And you know what happens when Lasorda feels wronged. He turned to face his team again.

"Did. You. Hear. What. That. Bleeping. Guy. Said. About. You? What. The. Bleep. Are. You. Going. To. Do. About. It?"

The Dodgers charged onto the field to start the game. As they walked past Costas, they cursed him in every form imaginable. Curse words used as nouns, pronouns, adjectives, adverbs, interjections, entire declarative sentences. Hey, whether it was profanity or baseball, they had learned from the best. They scored two runs in the first inning and never again trailed, winning the game and proving again the effectiveness of another Lasorda motivational tool.

"It was David Cone against the Mets, and Bob Costas against the A's," Lasorda remembers. "I used both guys to make us feel like we were fighting the world. Who doesn't get fired up to fight against the world?"

All of this set up one more Lasorda-induced miracle. The following night, Game 5, the Dodgers were leading, 2–1, in the fourth inning. Davis was standing at the plate with a 3-and-0 count, and Mickey Hatcher was on first base. Davis had only four home runs in the previous year and a half, yet, inexplicably, Lasorda gave him the green light to swing at the next pitch.

"It's all about showing your players you trust them," Lasorda says. "It's amazing what a player can do if he thinks he's being trusted."

In this case, the player can hit the ball a mile. Davis knocked the ball into the right-field seats, to give the Dodgers a 4–1 lead that eventually became a 5–2 victory and a world championship. Lasorda cried on everyone's shoulder and hugged everyone's waist and kept repeating, "If you believe it, you can achieve it!"

Until that moment, many in the baseball world thought those were the words of a glorified salesman. Many thought Lasorda wasn't so much a manager as a positive-thinking guru. Many thought, simply, that he was full of it.

But with the victories over the Mets and the A's, his critics finally began hearing those words differently. They believed in him as a baseball man. They believed in him as a guy whose strategy matched his speeches. They no longer believed in lucked-into championships. They believed he achieved them.

At last, lunch at Station 1 is served. Lasorda plops down on a bench, and the firefighters place a giant chicken ceasar salad in front of him. He begins eating, but then one more question is asked, and he just has to answer.

"Tommy, I'm thinking about going to Dodger fantasy camp. What do you think about that?" a firefighter asks.

Fantasy camp is where adults pay big bucks for the chance to spend a week playing and learning under former Dodger players and coaches. It's supposed to be a fun experience. Lasorda puts down his fork and scowls.

"Tell you what, man. When I was pitching in those camps, I would make guys like you earn it!" he says. "I'd throw at you guys. You're darn right I would. I knock those bankers and lawyers on their butts. I'd say, 'You better be ready, man, because this ain't a fantasy!'"

The firefighter slinks away, having been reminded that, for baseball's last true believer, the game will never be just a fantasy. The other firefighters, however, gather closer, because Lasorda is riled up again, ignoring his food and talking his love.

One of them wonders if Lasorda will ever return to managing.

"No way. I couldn't do it. It wouldn't work," he says. "There's been a change in attitudes today. It's like the salesman who has four kids. He has to sell his product or else his family goes hungry, so he sells his butt off. Then there's the guy with a rich father and no kids, and he doesn't feel the need to sell anything. I managed that first kind of salesman. But today's players are that second kind. They're like, 'I hit .220, so what, I don't care as long as I'm getting paid.' Multiyear contracts have hurt the game. Free agency has hurt the game. You ask a guy to run through a brick wall, he says, 'Are you crazy? I'm not running through that wall. I'm getting paid enough that I don't need to run through that wall. I play four or five years, I'm set for life, so I'm not going through anybody's wall.'"

Lasorda was asked how, in this climate, he managed to survive from the late 1980s to the mid-1990s, when the Dodgers acquired expensive egos like Darryl Strawberry and Kal Daniels.

"I used to beg the players," he says. "I asked the owner to let me make more money than one player on the team. Then, to the rest of them, I'd say, 'I need you guys. I've got a family, I've got to stay around, can you please win for me?' Seriously, I had to beg."

He was asked, finally, whether that 1988 season was his greatest motivational achievement. He laughs so loud he almost drowns out one of the emergency buzzers.

"Hell no," he says. "That day happened back in Spokane."

He tells the story of how, while managing the Dodgers' triple-A franchise, he approached his rattled pitcher, Bobby O'Brien, on the mound in the last inning of a crucial game, with the Indians leading Tucson, 2–1.

"Bobby," Lasorda told the kid, "imagine the heavens coming apart and you're hearing the voice of the Big Dodger in the Sky, and he says, 'Bobby, this is the last hitter you will face on earth, then you will come to heaven with me.' Well, Bobby, how would you like to go face the Lord on that day? Would you like to face him getting an out or giving up a hit?"

O'Brien looked at Lasorda and said, "Well, um, getting an out, of course."

Lasorda glared back, "All right, then, dammit, pitch like you are going to die."

No sooner had Lasorda returned to the dugout than O'Brien gave up a two-run homer that cost Spokane the game.

"What happened?" Lasorda asked as O'Brien trudged off the mound.

"I was so afraid of dying, I couldn't concentrate on pitching."

Lasorda smiled then, and, four decades later in the firehouse, he smiles again.

"Forget about 1988," Lasorda tells the laughing firefighters. "Making a guy truly believe that on his next pitch he's going to die? Now that's motivation!"

8

. . .

I NEARLY DIED FOR THIS

L ook at the poles!"
Tommy Lasorda is swerving to the right and pointing to
the left, driving down desolate blocks of South Los Angeles
like a bubbly tour guide, slowing to point out the poles.

"You see 'em? Look at all of them."

It's not exactly the poles that have Lasorda excited. It's what is
flapping from the poles.

"Look at my face up there!" he says. "You ever seen so many of
my faces before?"

His face is imprinted on flags that flap from a dozen concrete
poles that stretch high above barred windows and junk-filled yards.
This crowded, failing neighborhood would be an odd place to celebrate a baseball manager, but the flags are not celebrating Lasorda as
a manager. They are celebrating him as a human being.

"The Tommy Lasorda Heart Institute," the flags read. They direct
visitors to the wing of the Centinela Medical Center that bears his
name.

Lasorda often jokes that he doesn't get heart attacks, he gives
them. But perhaps no single structure in Los Angeles—not even the

dugout at Dodger Stadium—gives him more pride than the place he was treated for his heart attack in 1996. It is a modest building that squats amid the chaos of a blighted part of the city. The doctors here, especially Dr. Tony Reid, saved his life. Four years later, he gave them his name, attaching it to the third-floor heart center in hopes of raising money and gaining exposure. It worked as well as his heart. It worked so well, the name "Tommy Lasorda Heart Institute" is now on a huge banner that hangs from the side of one of the Centinela buildings. The name is on the ambulances that bring patients here. The name is on so many billboards and flags that Lasorda treats the heart institute as his home. And so, being his home, he figures he can drop in whenever he pleases.

Often on the way home from Dodger Stadium, he will make a detour to visit the patients here, checking on them like a benevolent uncle, making sure they are being treated properly for illnesses he can't even pronounce, giving them advice that only family members would give. When they added Lasorda's name to their treatment center, the Centinela folks thought they were getting a celebrity endorser. They had no idea they were enlisting a property manager.

"Hey, when it's your name on the building, you want to make sure everything is running smoothly inside," Lasorda says. "If these patients are staying in my place, I want to keep them happy."

So on this Sunday afternoon in July, he pulls up to the gated parking lot, reaches into his wallet, and smiles. This is his favorite part. He pulls out a card, swipes it across a black pad, and the gate opens, allowing him access to the doctors' parking lot, across from the front door.

"See that?" he says. "I've got the same privileges around here as a doctor. Not bad for a guy who barely got through high school, is it?"

Of all the pomp and circumstance surrounding Lasorda's endorsement of this place, leave it to Tommy to be most excited about having access to doctors' parking. Not that he has much use for doctors. Lasorda has never much bothered with his health. He always felt he could fight through illness as well as he fought through the 1988 World Series. Heart disease paled in comparison to the Oakland Athletics. The pain of sickness was something that could be handled much more easily than the pain of defeat. His mind was indestructible, so why not his body?

Even when he started a national campaign that changed the weight-loss industry, it wasn't about dieting. It was about a bet. It was the spring of 1989, and Lasorda was sitting in his closet-size Vero Beach office eating a huge bowl of pasta with Kirk Gibson and Orel Hershiser. Strengthened by his success the previous season, fairly certain that his manager wouldn't chase him out of the room, Hershiser looked at Lasorda and said what everyone was thinking.

"Tommy, you're getting fat, and we're getting worried about you."

Lasorda didn't chase, but he didn't retreat. He reacted the way he always reacts, even when the criticism is constructive: he took a swing at it.

"Hey, I'm fat because I choose to be fat," he said with a straight face. "I can lose weight anytime I want to."

While some businessmen create empires built on cars or computers, Lasorda created an empire built on food. In every town he visited, he knew a limo driver who would take him and his coaches to that city's best restaurant. He knew the maitre d' of that restaurant, who would seat him at the best table in the house. Most important, he knew the owner of that restaurant, who would feed him. All of this would happen at about midnight.

It was an honor for America's eateries to fill such a famous belly. So, in a way, it was incumbent on Lasorda to live large.

"That was my world, and I was proud of it," Lasorda says.

On that spring day in 1988, Lasorda boldly lied to Hershiser when he claimed he had complete control over his eating. And Hershiser knew it.

"You can lose weight anytime you want?" Hershiser asked. "Fine. Then prove it."

"Prove it how?" said Lasorda.

"If you can lose twenty pounds by the All-Star Game, Gibby and I will each give ten thousand dollars to your favorite charity," said Hershiser.

"Yeah," said Gibson. "Prove it."

Lasorda felt he was being bullied, and he hated being bullied. So, with as much thought as he'd used back when he threw fastballs at batters' necks, he quickly stood up and fought back.

"You got a deal," he said. "Let's go over to the scale."

Lasorda went into the training room and stepped on the scale: 218 pounds. He was five foot nine, 218 pounds. He shrugged, figuring he could probably sweat off 20 pounds by July.

"Get your checkbooks ready," he told his two stars.

"Have another bite," Hershiser said with a smile.

Four days later, noticing that Lasorda was doing nothing to lose the weight, Hershiser returned to his office, more serious this time.

"OK, if you lose eight more pounds, I'll give you another ten thousand," Hershiser said. "You really do need to lose this weight."

"Now it's thirty thousand dollars?" said Lasorda. "OK, OK, I'll do it."

He spoke with the same bravado, but inside, Lasorda was becoming increasingly worried that he wouldn't be tough enough. In his belly, he may have finally met his match.

"I had never been able to conquer that one area of my life," he says. "And that scared me."

News of the bet reached the newspapers, and Lasorda feared that his one vulnerability would become fodder for public ridicule: *The man who can motivate others to win championships can't even convince himself to stop eating.*

"The way I figured it, I had two options," Lasorda remembers. "One of my coaches would have to punch me in the jaw so I'd have to drink from a straw for three months. Or Hershiser and Gibson would have to forget about the bet."

Understanding the persistence of his two best players, Lasorda knew that they would never forget the bet.

"So I pulled aside one of my coaches, Joe Ferguson, and told him to get ready to punch me out."

Then, out of nowhere, it appeared.

A milkshake from heaven. An incredible milkshake that would both shrink Lasorda and make him larger than life. America's most famous fat man was about to become even more famous because of a diet.

"If I told you how I started drinking that Slim-Fast stuff, you'd never believe it," Lasorda says.

It began with a phone call to his spring training office from a guy who had been reading newspaper accounts of his wager. The guy worked for a quirky diet company called Ultra Slim-Fast. At the time, in the spring of 1989, the diet food aisle in stores was considered a place for desperate losers. Nobody bragged about using diet drinks, and few public figures would agree to endorse them.

"I heard about your wager," said the voice on the other end. "You need to lose a lot of weight fast. I've got some stuff you've got to try."

"I ain't taking no stuff," Lasorda said.

"It's called Ultra Slim-Fast," the voice said.

"Never heard of it, don't want it," Lasorda said.

"We'll come to Vero Beach on Tuesday and talk to you about it."

"On Tuesday, I'm making a commercial for Budweiser in Spanish, and I won't be done until midnight."

"See you then."

Sure enough, when Lasorda returned to Dodgertown's room 112 at 12:30 A.M., he was met by five Ultra Slim-Fast representatives bearing cans of diet milkshake. This was more than a voice. They were real. The manager greeted them with a wary smile. He was so impressed with their dedication and willingness to work late hours, he could think of only one thing.

"I wanted them to get the hell out of there," Lasorda remembers. "I was tired, and they were strange."

But the Ultra Slim-Fast representatives persisted.

"You really won't even try it?" asked one.

"I don't see how you can lose weight drinking a milkshake out of a can," Lasorda said.

"But it tastes good," said another.

"Nothing tastes good out of a can," Lasorda said. "I'm not trying it."

As Lasorda ushered the representatives to their car, S. Daniel Abraham, the owner of the company, played one last card.

"Wait a minute, Tommy. Aren't you trying to build a convent?" he asked.

It was a question that would reshape lives and make fortunes. Yes, Abraham had done his homework: Lasorda had been working on building a new convent for the Sisters of Mercy in Nashville, Tennessee. He had visited there the previous winter and discovered that the present convent had been condemned and that nine bedridden nuns would have to split up and find new quarters. He had talked about his plans in the newspaper, but had no idea how he could raise the money.

Then, on this spring night at around 1 A.M., he did.

"Yeah, I'm building a convent," Lasorda said.

"Here, I want to help," said Abraham, who pulled out his checkbook and wrote a $20,000 check.

"Whoa, I can't take that check. I can't be beholden to you," Lasorda said, his fingers nonetheless tightening around the script.

"No strings attached," said Abraham. "You take the check. You don't have to try our drink."

Lasorda shrugged and kept the check. But he also took a case of the Ultra Slim-Fast milkshakes, which he later sent to the team's trainers.

"The guy who owns this company just gave me twenty thousand dollars for doing absolutely nothing," Lasorda told the trainers. "Guy that rich, there must be a lot more gold where that came from. Check this stuff out and make sure it won't kill me."

After a quick inspection, the trainers assured Lasorda that the milkshakes would not kill him any faster than eating five servings of veal marsala. So Lasorda phoned Abraham and told him he would try Ultra Slim-Fast, and asked him if he'd like to be even more charitable.

"Sure, I'll match the players' bet," said Abraham.

This pushed the convent fund up to $80,000. The pressure was now clearly on Lasorda. His toughness was being tested, but more important, his integrity was too. He wouldn't renege on a promise to the nuns, would he?

"Heck no, I wouldn't do that to the sisters," he says. "That's what pulled me through. A fear of embarrassment, and a bigger fear of letting down the poor old nuns."

It was hell around Dodgertown and tense during the early part of the season, but Lasorda swallowed his Ultra Slim-Fast and started losing weight. He would drink a milkshake in the morning, a milkshake at noon, and eat a healthful dinner at night. The coaches who once followed him from restaurant to restaurant also tried the drink and began losing weight. Even stocky players like Mike Scioscia lost weight. It was a testament to Lasorda's influence over the organization that, for the 1989 season at least, the Dodgers led the league in low body fat.

And it was a testament to his nationwide popularity that the rest of the nation followed suit. The commercials that Lasorda made in which he proudly showed off his lost weight weren't just cute, they were real. "If I can do it, you can do it!" he exclaimed, and looking at his bodily transformation, who wouldn't believe him?

"That was the secret to those commercials," Lasorda says. "If you see a guy who says he lost fifty pounds, you never know if it's true because you never really saw him before. But me, everybody saw me fat. Everyone believed me."

He began hearing about it from the stands, with paunchy middle-aged men now ridiculing him with, "Hey, Lasorda, thanks to you, my wife makes me drink that crap!"

He began hearing about it in the dugout, when one day pitching coach Ron Perranoski got up and moved to the opposite end of the bench.

When a family member asked why, Perranoski told her, "Ever since that guy started drinking Slim-Fast, he farts all the time."

Lasorda lost thirty-eight pounds by July and reveled in his new look. For the first time in thirty years, he was able to comfortably wear a bathing suit and sit by the pool. For the first time in a long time, his shirts didn't bulge out of his pants, and his pants didn't threaten to snap his belts.

Many people thought that because he was so fat for so long, Lasorda didn't care about his appearance. When he lost the weight, he proved them wrong. He wanted to look thin. He hated being fat. But because he chose to spend his career managing other people and massaging their egos, he never had the time or energy to do the same for himself. So food did it for him. Food wasn't only his fuel, it was his reward, his lifeblood; it was the one thing that even losing couldn't ruin. He not only ate to live, he ate to love and laugh.

"When I realized I could still have fun as a thin person," he says, "I felt so much better about myself."

So did the Sisters of Mercy, whose convent would be rebuilt with Lasorda's donations, and who lined up in the Nashville convent's narrow hallways to meet with Lasorda in the middle of the campaign.

"We prayed for a miracle, and God sent you to us," said one.

Another nun gave Lasorda what he still considers his greatest compliment: "If only I could have met you before I went into the convent . . ."

Also thrilled were the Ultra Slim-Fast folks, whose revenues doubled, going from $10 million to $20 million in the first year of the ad campaign. By the time Lasorda's relationship with them ended five years later, Ultra Slim-Fast had gone from a small company to a thriving big business that was sold in 2000 to Unilever for $2.3 billion.

In his life as a salesman, it was Lasorda's greatest moment. It was also, quietly, his biggest flop. When he agreed to do the commercials, his contract called only for a fee for the daily work. It provided no equity in the company.

"I helped make them one of the biggest business success stories in American history, and I never saw a penny of that success," Lasorda says.

Nevertheless, Lasorda feels rich today as he struts through the barren lobby of the Centinela Medical Center, home to his heart institute. Unlike other local hospitals that cater to the stars, Centinela is for regular Angelenos, the Dodger-fan folk, Lasorda's people. The lobby is filled with large families gathered around crying babies and empty fast-food wrappers. A guard at the door searches everyone who enters. Everyone except, of course, Lasorda.

"Aren't you gonna search Tommy?" someone asked.

"Nah," said the guard. "Everyone knows Tommy."

He is certainly known at his own heart institute, as he breezes up the elevator to the third floor, stepping into a hallway lined with huge photographs. There are pictures of Tommy and Jo, Fernando Valenzuela, and others. Several photos that depict Dodger history line a hallway leading into the actual heart institute, which is a hospital ward with thirty beds in rooms surrounding a large nurses' station.

A nurse standing at the station looks a bit like Jo, with short blond hair and a big smile, and she greets Tommy with that smile.

"Lots of people who come in here think I'm your wife," she tells him. "I tell them, 'He has his name on the place, his wife doesn't have to work here.'"

Lasorda gives her a hug and then, without seeking permission or approval, ducks into one of the rooms, where an elderly woman is attached to a heart monitor. Her gray hair is twisted in knots, her tortoiseshell glasses are smudged, and her gown has stains on it. Yet when she sees Lasorda, there is no shyness or embarrassment. She immediately sits up in her bed. Above the oxygen tube that runs to her nose, her eyes redden.

"Ohhh, ohhh, Mr. Lasorda, ohhhh," she says, startled to tears. "Oh, Lord, I need a camera. Why don't I have a camera?"

"You feeling OK, honey?" Lasorda asks.

"I'm better now," she says.

The woman, named Joyce, was brought in the previous night with chest pains. She said she complained that nobody knew her here, and worried that she might not receive the proper care.

"I guess they heard my complaints," she says to Lasorda, in all seriousness. "They sent you to see me. I'm feeling much better now."

"You take care, honey," says Lasorda, handing her his card. "You call me if you ever feel lonely again."

He does this with all the patients here. He hands them his business card with his office number at Dodger Stadium. If they call him, he will answer. It is more than most doctors will do. It is something no celebrity has ever done. Lasorda treats this place the way he treated his teams. He is not merely the hospital's namesake; he is their protector and motivator and friend.

"This is my place, my house," Lasorda says. "If people here need me, they should be able to find me."

"But it's only your name on the building," somebody says. "It's not your building."

"Try telling that to the people who come in here."

In the next room is Charlie, an elderly, bespectacled man awaiting a heart valve replacement. He waves at Lasorda like a long-lost buddy. Many of the elderly in Los Angeles have seen so much of Lasorda in their lifetimes, to them he feels as comfortable as an old pair of slippers.

"I heard you were here," says Charlie. "Good to see ya."

"They taking care of you?" Lasorda asks.

"Yeah," says Charlie.

"Well, if they don't, you call me right away," Lasorda says, handing Charlie his card.

"You know, I don't like baseball," says Charlie.

"Oh yeah?"

"But I like you, because you argued with umpires."

"I argued for my team, and you know what else?" says Lasorda. "I'll argue for you."

"I know that," says Charlie, and now he is crying.

"God bless you," says Lasorda, still managing and moving after all these years.

Lasorda likes to say that his motivational style can create more than just baseball miracles. He lays claim to several real miracles, and nobody has ever disputed them.

"You'd be amazed what belief can accomplish," he says.

During one of his speaking engagements at the U.S. Air Force Academy, Lasorda was being escorted around campus by a former baseball-playing lieutenant.

"So when are you going to start flying?" Lasorda asked.

"I was hit in the head by a line drive, and the doctors say I can never fly again," said the lieutenant, a man named Bob Wright.

"What is the name of the doctor who told you that?" Lasorda asked. "Was the doctor's name God?"

"What?" said Wright.

"You heard me," said Lasorda. "The only person who can say you can't fly is God. Just because God delays, that does not mean God denies."

Two years later, Lasorda received a photograph of Bob Wright standing next to a plane that he was preparing to fly on an overseas mission.

Nine years later, during a speaking engagement at Maxwell Air Force Base in Montgomery, Alabama, Lasorda was hugged by Major Bob Wright, who was on his way to becoming a colonel.

"If it wasn't for you, I never would be here," Wright said to Lasorda.

"Don't ever say that," Lasorda said. "This was about you and God. Like I said, just because God delays, doesn't mean God denies. Sometimes God just completely takes over."

Another of those times involved Lance Goodman, a teenage baseball player who had been seriously injured in an automobile accident in the San Francisco area. Goodman was in a coma, and his parents were desperate, so Lasorda was summoned to his bedside. With the family standing in a semicircle around the darkened bed, Lasorda launched into another pep talk.

"You've got to get better," he told the motionless Goodman. "You've got to get out of here. People are counting on you. The Dodgers are counting on you. I need a batboy. I need you. You've got to get better. You've got to believe."

Suddenly, tears began pouring out of the boy's eyes. Soon everyone in the room was crying. And shortly thereafter, Lance Goodman did get better, emerging from his coma and eventually returning to his life. And, yes, he became a batboy, joining the Dodgers whenever they played in San Francisco, and later in Denver.

"Have I lived the greatest life or what?" says Lasorda. "To be blessed to help someone?"

He was once asked by a college baseball coach to write a letter of inspiration that parents could read to a Santa Barbara teen who was in a coma after an auto accident.

"Send him a letter?" Lasorda said. "Hell, I'll just call him."

"He can't talk," said the coach.

"So maybe he can listen."

Lasorda called the boy's room, asked the nurse to put the phone to his ear, and began talking.

"You are not to blame for this accident. It was not your fault. You must talk to your parents—they need you right now. You must say something to me, you hear me?"

The boy heard him and began talking. Later, during a speaking engagement in Santa Barbara, the boy's mother recounted the story to Lasorda and hugged him and cried. That sort of thing happens to him often. He'll be in a small town making a small speech and some stranger will approach him with thanks for changing a life. During Lasorda's years as manager, there were honorary batboys in seemingly every city, all of them kids whom Lasorda has helped. In every city his players witnessed little dramas that Lasorda engineered. They were given pep talks without ever hearing a word.

"They would sometimes get tired of hearing about belief from me," Lasorda says. "I wanted them to see it in the lives of someone else."

In Houston once, Lasorda climbed into a hospital bed and gave a pep talk to another boy who was comatose after a car accident. Lasorda promised the boy that if he recovered, he could sit next to Lasorda on the bench. The boy indeed recovered, and when he later walked into the Dodger clubhouse to join Lasorda, he was given a standing ovation.

Among the piles of mail at Lasorda's home are other signs of his impact. There are letters from Eagle Scouts whom he has counseled and thank-you cards from penniless former third-string minor league catchers. For years, that pile included a box of tomatoes, sent annually from the garden of a man who claimed that Lasorda's inspiring words persuaded him not to attempt suicide.

Lasorda moves around the corner of the hospital ward, knocks lightly on the door of another elderly woman.

"Can I see you?" he says in a strangely soft, high-pitched voice from behind the door.

"Sure," says the white-haired woman, who clutches her afghan to her chest when Lasorda appears in her room. "Oh, gracious, it's you!"

The woman, named Sherry, is not a big baseball fan, but Lasorda doesn't mind. He spends the next few minutes talking to her about the weather and the hospital food. Lasorda acts as if he's known Sherry and the other patients for years. They act as if it's no big deal that a Hall of Fame baseball manager strolls into their room on a Sunday afternoon in August. Because with Lasorda, it's not.

"You know, I followed you and prayed for you when you were sick like me," she says.

"That's one of the reasons I'm here," Lasorda says. "Because I know what it means to be sick like you."

It was a Sunday night, June 23, 1996. Earlier in the day, the Dodgers had defeated the Houston Astros by the margin of a Mike Piazza ninth-inning homer. Afterward, Lasorda, who was sixty-eight, and Jo attended a celebrity charity gala at a hotel in Beverly Hills. Lasorda was the master of ceremonies. His job was to occasionally take several steps from his table to the stage, say a few words, then return to his table. It wasn't grueling work, but Lasorda was sweating profusely.

"Is it hot in here?" he asked Jo.

It was then he noticed that, with the air conditioning pumping through the hotel ballroom, his wife was actually shivering.

On the drive home, Lasorda grabbed his stomach through his tight tuxedo cummerbund and moaned.

"I've got the damnedest stomachache," he told Jo.

"I'm calling the doctor," she said.

"Don't call the doctor. I'll be fine."

Jo called Dr. Michael Mellman, the longtime Dodger physician. On the phone, Mellman said it sounded like indigestion and prescribed milk of magnesia. He also ordered Lasorda to come in to the office the next day.

"I've got to go to a black-tie deal on Monday night, so it will have to be quick," Lasorda told Mellman.

When he showed up Monday, initial tests seemed to reveal an ulcer, but Mellman was worried.

"I want you to stay overnight," he told Lasorda.

"I ain't staying overnight, I'm getting back to my team."

Then Mellman said the magic words, words that may have saved Lasorda's life, three words that held ultimate power over him during his time as Dodger manager.

"I'm calling Peter."

Peter, of course, was Peter O'Malley, the Dodger owner who practically grew up with Lasorda, the boss's kid and the bossy young manager forming a bond that transcended the field. They would negotiate contracts on a handshake; they would send each other presents for Christmas; they would talk baseball and life, this Dodger odd couple, the buttoned-down O'Malley and the swashbuckling Lasorda.

O'Malley was the only man in the organization to whom Lasorda felt complete and unconditional loyalty. He was, thus, the only man who could give Lasorda orders.

"You're calling Peter?" said Lasorda, sighing. "OK, then I'll stay."

Because Lasorda stayed, the hospital was able to run further tests, which showed he had suffered a heart attack. On Wednesday, June 26, he underwent an angioplasty procedure that made it official. He was sick. He would miss at least a month of managing. He was scared.

"I thought about my life, thought about how I had always joked about being fat," Lasorda says. "I remember flying to the Mayo Clinic once for an examination, and they got more wires on me than a telephone pole. Then the doctor walked out and said, 'Sir, we've determined you are overweight,' and I said, 'I didn't need to fly all the way to Minnesota to hear that. I knew that when I put on my pants this morning.'"

Lasorda no longer found those jokes funny. He no longer wanted to hear the stories of how he would break couches in visiting managers' offices, or break records by eating a hundred oysters in one sitting. He began thinking about Don McMahon dying in his arms. He thought of Don Drysdale, the Hall of Fame Dodger pitcher who died suddenly of a heart attack a couple of years earlier. He talked to old friends and family members and made a tentative decision.

"I thought, hell, I was going to be different than everyone else," he remembers. "I really wanted to come back and manage. I didn't have any hobbies. I didn't have any other interests. I was a baseball man. I wanted to continue being a baseball man."

When he received a standing ovation from the Dodger Stadium crowd on July 16, his first public appearance since the heart attack, he was inspired even more. Then Dr. Mellman cleared him to return to the dugout, with Lasorda having lost twenty pounds and his cholesterol having dropped from 252 to 175.

When Lasorda and Jo met with Peter O'Malley on Sunday morning, July 28, it seemed clear that Lasorda wanted to return.

"I thought I could have managed the rest of the year, maybe even another year."

According to Lasorda, in that meeting O'Malley allowed him to make the decision, saying, "Tommy, there's a uniform downstairs ready for you. If you want to keep managing, go down and put it on."

Before making it official, Lasorda had to check with one more source. He asked Peter if he and Jo could excuse themselves to talk in private. Once outside the office, overlooking an empty stadium, surrounded only by the occasional *swish* of a sprinkler, Lasorda asked Jo if she had any last-minute advice.

"Yes," she said. "No."

"No?"

"No," she said. "I do not think you should be managing again. I don't think it's healthy. I don't think it's safe. I don't think you need it. It's your decision, but if you're asking me, I say no."

It was at that moment that Tommy Lasorda retired as manager of the Los Angeles Dodgers.

"The decision was mine, but I just couldn't do that to Jo," Lasorda says. "She has stayed in my corner through lots of tough years. She's always been there for me. She's never complained. She's never asked for anything. When she wanted me to quit managing, how could I say no?"

Dodger insiders knew that Lasorda did not want to quit, but they didn't know why he did. One popular theory was that he was pushed out by O'Malley. Another theory was that he was just too scared to return. Neither theory was correct. Turns out, it came from the woman who never asked for anything, the woman who finally asked for something. Jo Lasorda asked her husband to come home, and so he did.

If Lasorda's final decision as Dodger manager was true to his nature, his final act as Dodger manager was true to his legacy. His final move was one of loyalty. When he decided on that Sunday afternoon to retire, the only person he called was a quirky, heavyset *Los Angeles Times* sports columnist named Allan Malamud. It was Malamud who had publicly pushed for Lasorda to replace Alston at the end of the 1976 season. It was Malamud who, because he was unafraid to criticize Alston while supporting Lasorda, was once challenged to a hallway fight by the stern farmer.

"Malamud was with me in the beginning, and I wanted him to have the story in the end," Lasorda says.

Sure enough, the following day, across the front page of the *Los Angeles Times*, Allan Malamud had the scoop, writing that Lasorda would announce his retirement "today." It was precise. It was perfect. It came at a time when his page 2 column was considered a charming antique. It showed that Malamud could still hit a home run. It was the biggest story of his career.

It was also the last big story of his life. Less than two months later, at the age of fifty-four, Malamud died of heart failure in his Los Angeles apartment. At his memorial service, many admiringly discussed his Lasorda scoop. It became part of Malamud's legacy. The simple act of loyalty also made it part of Lasorda's legacy.

"That's how I am, that's what I've preached forever, that's what made our teams work so well," Lasorda says. "You show me loyalty, I will watch your back forever."

And if you don't show loyalty? In Lasorda's black-and-white world, there is a price to pay. In one of the great ironies of Lasorda's life, nobody has paid a higher price for a perceived lack of loyalty than the man Lasorda picked to succeed him.

His name was Bill Russell. He had joined the Dodgers in 1966 as a kid outfielder on Lasorda's minor league team in Ogden. He stunk. He should have been released. Lasorda fought to keep him.

"You could see there was something special with this kid," Lasorda says. "The way he battled, you could see a lot of me in him."

Russell's Dodger career was spared, and he slowly fought his way to the big leagues, where he was moved to shortstop and played for eighteen seasons, eventually representing the steadiest of Dodgers. It was this stability in Russell's demeanor and character that led Lasorda to hire him as a major league coach after his retirement as a player in 1986. With the exception of a brief stint as a minor league manager in triple-A Albuquerque, Russell remained a protégé of Lasorda's until he took the manager's job after Lasorda's heart attack.

While many thought Lasorda's blessing was the single most important reason that Russell succeeded him, that was not entirely true. The Dodger executives liked Russell not only because he and Lasorda were close, but because he and Lasorda were different.

Where Lasorda screamed, Russell glared. Where Lasorda swaggered, Russell stalked. Lasorda spoke in the surly street voice of eastern Pennsylvania. Russell spoke in the soft midwestern twang of Kansas. Lasorda filled his office with photos of celebrities. Russell replaced them all with one portrait of John Wayne.

Lasorda knew that Russell was his polar opposite, but he hoped Russell, out of loyalty, would allow him to stay involved with the team and maintain his legacy. The general manager, Fred Claire, on the other hand, hoped that Russell would bring change to a team that had not won a playoff game since 1988. He wanted Russell to establish a new legacy.

In the end, realizing who was signing his paycheck, Russell slowly shifted his loyalty to Claire and away from Lasorda. And that's where the trouble started.

"Bill Russell hurt me as bad as I've ever been hurt by anybody," Lasorda says. "And I will never, ever forgive him. I will die not forgiving him. I don't care if he says he's sorry. I cannot and will not forgive him."

When asked about Russell today, Lasorda tells the story of his father, Sabatino, and a weekly card game in Norristown. During one of these games, a dispute arose and an acquaintance angrily pulled a gun on Sabatino. No shots were fired, and shortly thereafter the acquaintance left for Italy, where he stayed for eight years. When the acquaintance returned, he resumed playing cards with the gang. After one of their first games together, Sabatino asked the man to join him outside. Once there, Sabatino beat the man senseless while screaming, "I waited eight years for this! Eight years!"

Lasorda feels the same way about Russell. He feels as if, during Russell's brief managerial reign, he essentially pulled a gun on Lasorda.

"The way it worked in my family, I will never forget," Lasorda says. "Eight years or eighty, I will never forget. I treated Bill Russell like a son. I got him clothes, cars, shoes. I took him out to dinner all the time. When somebody like that turns on you, you can't forget that."

From the day Russell became manager, on July 29, 1996, until the end of that season, Lasorda purposely stayed away from the clubhouse to avoid being a distraction, but he thought Russell could have at least met him for lunch or called him for advice. According to Lasorda, that never happened.

"Billy, because you don't have a contract past this year, I'm not going to come down to the clubhouse," Lasorda said to Russell that first summer. "It's your team, you're the boss, it's your clubhouse. But I'll go to lunch with you. I'll talk baseball with you. Just let me know when you need me."

Lasorda was abiding by a baseball tradition: a manager with a one-year contract doesn't need anyone looking over his shoulder. Russell's lack of contract security would have become an issue with the players if they constantly saw Lasorda, wondering whether he was going to take his old job back. So Lasorda stayed out of the clubhouse but made the offer of behind-the-scenes help if needed. According to Lasorda, Russell never acted as though he needed him.

"All the lunches I bought him, and he never bought me lunch, never asked me about the team," Lasorda says.

When Russell signed a two-year deal after the season ended, Lasorda called him again.

"OK, Billy, you've got two years now, you don't have to worry about me. I can come to the clubhouse. I can do whatever you want."

But again, according to Lasorda, Russell never summoned him. In fact, Lasorda heard rumblings that the front-office people wanted Russell to steer clear of Lasorda, to better establish his own credentials.

"Why wouldn't Billy want to hang around me?" Lasorda asks. "All the baseball knowledge I've gained, I'd be glad to help him. Why didn't he ever want to hang out with me and pick up some of that advice?"

When Russell was going through a divorce, he didn't even mention it to Lasorda. Lasorda felt wounded.

"I was like his father, and he goes through these big changes in his life and doesn't even tell me. Why was I suddenly an outcast?"

Lasorda says he wasn't invited to Russell's second wedding. He says he wasn't consulted on player trades or ideas about the mood of the clubhouse. He says that the man who sat next to him for over two decades could not have been more distant.

"I kept saying to myself, 'I know Bill Russell. This is not him,'" Lasorda remembers. "But I guess it was him."

Russell later said that he felt it was Lasorda who was acting distant. He said he felt that Lasorda was subtly undermining him, from the press box to the owner's office. He said he never felt that Lasorda gave him a chance. Lasorda vehemently denied these statements, becoming enraged at the reporter who printed them and shouting down anyone who repeated them.

"I would never do that to Bill Russell," Lasorda says. "He was like my son."

The separation of the Dodger past and present wouldn't have been a factor if the Dodgers were winning championships. But at the end of the 1996 season they were swept out of the playoffs in the first round. Then, in 1997, Russell's first full season, they missed the playoffs even though they led the National League Western Division by two games on September 16. It was a stumble that cut to the heart of the changing Dodger culture. The old Dodgers would have fought to stay in first place. The new Dodgers just quietly disappeared.

If Russell were as loud and gregarious as Lasorda, perhaps he could have blustered his way through his growing pains. But because he was so quiet, each loss made it more painfully clear that he was not Lasorda. There was talk among Dodger insiders that Lasorda was ripping Russell to his superiors. Lasorda was hurt by these rumors.

"Billy Russell was so worried about being undermined, but he had to understand that by not communicating well with the players, he was just undermining himself," Lasorda says.

Lasorda says he talked O'Malley out of firing Russell after his first full season. But after the O'Malley family sold the team to Fox in the spring of 1998, the new owner wanted a complete change of direction. When the Fox folks traded the beloved catcher Mike Piazza without consulting Claire, the signs were clear.

"Things were going crazy, and while everybody thought I had something to do with it, I had nothing to do with it," Lasorda says.

During a mediocre early 1998 season, the buzz around Russell became so loud that Lasorda left town. Ten years earlier, Lasorda was everyone's lucky charm. But by the summer of 1998, some people looked at him like he carried the plague, and he knew it.

"When the team started losing, I got lost, because if something went down, I wanted everyone to know that I had nothing to do with it," Lasorda says. "It's Vero Beach in the summer, triple digits, and I go there for a week. Then I go to Yakima to work with the minor league kids for a week. It wasn't fair. People were afraid of me. I had to stay out of the way. It wasn't right."

Tommy Lasorda hiding? It was so unlike him as a manager. But in his new role as an adviser, he knew that his presence could be seen as a threat. As much as he wanted to be the front man in the dugout, he figured he could accomplish more if he worked in the front office. On Sunday morning, June 22, Lasorda flew home from Yakima to wash his clothes and prepare for another trip. Upon landing, he learned from waiting television journalists that Al Campanis had died. Lasorda broke down in tears. When he got home, he received a phone call from Bob Graziano, the Dodger president.

"He tells me not to go on my next trip," Lasorda remembers. "He tells me to come to Dodger Stadium that night at nine o'clock."

When Lasorda arrived at the ballpark, he learned that Russell and

Claire had just been fired. It was a stunning move, known in Dodger history as Black Sunday. Then Graziano made a request that Lasorda says surprised him even more.

"Tommy, you know how you always said you would do anything for the organization?"

"Yeah?"

"Well, we want you to be the general manager for the rest of the season," Graziano said.

Lasorda gasped. This had always been his dream. But he never wanted it to happen like this, after he'd had a heart attack and in the middle of the firing of two longtime Dodger employees. One moment, he clenched his fist in celebration. The next moment, he wiped his brow in worry. The dream, he feared, could become a nightmare.

Russell was so certain Lasorda was involved in his firing, he refused at first to go into the stadium on that Sunday night when he saw Lasorda's car parked outside. Claire was too classy to ever say anything, but he also had his doubts. The public agreed with both of them, and Lasorda became the villain of Black Sunday.

"I never told anybody to fire Russell," Lasorda says. "He wasn't a good manager, but I never told anyone to fire him. Al Campanis didn't want me to hire him as a coach, but I did, and I supported him all the way."

When Russell initially asked Lasorda what happened, Lasorda responded, "I didn't fire you, you fired yourself."

When a newspaper story appeared in which Russell implied that Lasorda had engineered his firing, Lasorda cut the last ties with his former protégé.

"I supported this guy for twenty years, and now I have to go all over the country telling people I didn't fire him?" Lasorda recalls. "He put me in a really bad position, and I'll never forget it. We were finished."

Several years later, Russell visited Lasorda's office in an attempt to mend fences.

"I really want to work for the Dodgers again," Russell said.

"That's not my department," Lasorda told him. "But get your ass out of here. Get out now, or I'll come from behind this desk and throw your ass out."

"What's wrong with you?" Russell said.

"You betrayed me, then you told lies about me."

"They told me you don't want me working here."

"No, I don't," Lasorda said. "I told them they can hire you, but I won't talk to you or be near you. I will never forgive you. You can get on your knees and I'll never forgive you."

While it was never proven that Lasorda was involved in the firing of his successor, the perception lingered throughout the Dodger offices. This is what made Lasorda so angry. He understood that, especially in Hollywood, perception is reality.

When he was named general manager for three months, he knew he had to act quickly to show that it wasn't about him, it was about the Dodgers. He decided to run the front office the way he ran a dugout. He wanted to take chances. He wanted to inspire greatness. So he publicly guaranteed that a team with a 36–38 record would make the playoffs, then hustled to make it happen.

But what worked on the field did not always work in the executive suite. Bold was perceived as risky. He traded first baseman Paul Konerko and pitcher Dennys Reyes for reliever Jeff Shaw, only to later see Konerko slug his way to fame with the Chicago White Sox. And he traded Wilton Guerrero, outfielder Peter Bergeron, and pitcher Ted Lilly to Montreal for pitcher Carlos Perez, second baseman Mark Grudzielanek, and utility man Hiram Bocachica, only to later watch Lilly become a dependable starter elsewhere.

In his short time as a general manager, Lasorda worked hard, but he found it impossible to motivate players while wearing a sports jacket. And though interim manager Glenn Hoffman did his best, and the team finished the season with a 47–41 record since Lasorda took over, they did not make the playoffs.

When Kevin Malone was named the new general manager in September, Lasorda was gently escorted back offstage. With many Dodger employees still wary of the perception that Lasorda was a meddler —as if meddling from a Hall of Fame manager was a bad thing—the Dodgers' most important employee was becoming increasingly ignored. The voice that once motivated millions was considered too loud, so it was silenced. The presence that once created championships was considered too large, so it was crushed.

"They forgot about me," he says. "It reached a point that they just forgot about me."

That point began shortly after he was relieved of his general-manager duties in 1998 and continued until Frank McCourt, a Boston real estate developer, purchased the team in 2004. During that six-year exile, Lasorda was sent to Japan to work with the Dodgers' partner teams. He was sent to Vero Beach to check on the kids. He was shipped anywhere but where the Dodgers were playing. His home became anywhere but Dodger Stadium.

"They took advantage of my loyalty," he says. "They knew I would not complain if they shipped me to the ends of the earth, and I didn't. But it hurt. It really hurt to know that an organization that I always loved no longer loved me back. And I could not figure out why."

It was all about Fox, because Fox was all about business. Longtime employees were fired to make room for younger and lower-paid ones. Standing O'Malley traditions, such as the serving of free ice cream in the front office after certain wins, were ended. Fox didn't consider Lasorda an icon, it considered him a liability, an elderly employee with a loose tongue who could only do them harm.

To understand what was happening, one needed only to look at Lasorda's new office. It was a windowless storage closet with just one redeeming feature.

"All I could think was, heaven help the poor guy who had to move out of here to let me in—I couldn't imagine the location of his new office," he recalls. "By the location and look of my office, they made it very clear what they wanted me to do. They didn't want me to do anything."

In the winter of 1999, a year after Lasorda had been sent into exile, he thought he would be rescued by Hollywood tycoon and Dodger fan Bob Daly, who bought a minority interest in the team and became a managing partner. But Lasorda says he was wrong, and wronged.

"Before Bob Daly bought a piece of the Dodgers, I must have had lunch with him twenty-five times," Lasorda remembers. "When he comes in on the deal, I'm thinking, 'This guy is going to lean on me.' But he didn't. Not once did he ever ask me about a player. Not once did he take my advice."

While Daly has long contended that Lasorda was consulted regularly, Lasorda says he was never asked about important baseball matters. He remembers that whenever he offered to help, he was shipped out. Lasorda recalls that there were trade meetings of top club executives to which he wasn't invited. Sometimes they feared that he would reveal to his journalist friends the closely guarded details of a possible trade. Certain club executives just didn't believe that this senior citizen had any idea about today's game. Forget that Lasorda was the last manager to win a Dodger world championship. Forget that he'd always been known as a great talent evaluator. Some insecure Dodger folks grew tired of his giant personality and simply didn't want him around.

"I never want to feel like I'm a burden to anyone," Lasorda says. "But for a while I felt like that, and I couldn't understand it. All that I've given this organization—I was a burden? I couldn't prove myself even by going into the Hall of Fame? It wasn't fair."

The freeze became national news in the winter of 2001, at baseball's annual meetings in a Boston hotel, when the Dodgers and their new general manager, Dan Evans, met for trade talks with the Cincinnati Reds. After large contingents from both clubs had gathered in the room, the Reds' cocky general manager, Jim Bowden, made a loud request that would soon be heard all the way back to Chavez Ravine.

"Where's Tommy?" he asked.

"What?" said one of the Dodger employees.

"You heard me," said Bowden. "I am not starting this meeting without Tommy Lasorda."

The Dodger employees suspected it was a setup. They figured Bowden, a close friend of Lasorda's, knew that Lasorda had been feeling isolated. They guessed that Bowden was trying to make a national statement about the mistreatment of his buddy. Some of them wondered whether Lasorda had goaded Bowden into saying something.

But surely some of the Dodger staffers must have thought that Bowden had a point. All these executives at the meeting, and Lasorda wasn't one of them? He wasn't there because he had not been invited. They quickly phoned Lasorda in his hotel room.

"I knew they had a meeting, but I also knew I wasn't invited, so I waited in my room in case they needed me," Lasorda remembers. "I was always around if they needed me."

By the time Lasorda reached the meeting room, the hotel was buzzing with Bowden's comments. Some folks thought the Dodgers should have immediately canceled the meeting and left the room. Others thought they should be ashamed of themselves for ignoring Lasorda. Bowden later said he was not trying to start a fight; he was only trying to inject some common sense into the proceedings.

"When you think of the Dodgers, you think of Tommy Lasorda," Bowden said.

The incident was instructive for the Dodgers, showing them that, even in retirement, Lasorda was bigger than anyone in the organization and should be handled with care. The incident was actually more embarrassing for Lasorda, who couldn't believe he had to rely on a young opposing general manager to stick up for him in a team meeting.

"That was tough. It told me where I stood in the organization, and it wasn't pretty," Lasorda recalls.

By the time he had flown back to Los Angeles, he was so angry he called for a meeting with Bob Daly. He had never before asked his bosses for a meeting. They were the ones who always summoned him, remember? They were the ones who always called him in for a new contract or congratulations. They were the ones who needed him.

Now, though, it was clear that Lasorda needed them. And so he swallowed his pride and sat in front of Daly and pleaded for his career.

"I said, 'Bob, I must have had twenty-five lunches with you, and yet you come in here and never ask me about one player, and I want to know why.'"

"I didn't know you felt like this," said Daly.

"You bet I feel like this."

Daly explained to Lasorda that in the movie industry the boss relies mostly on his second-in-command; he doesn't take office polls. In this case, Daly spoke mostly to General Manager Kevin Malone.

"That's bull," Lasorda said. "Do you mean to tell me that in the movie industry if one guy knows more than the other guy, that guy is still ignored if he's not high up in the pecking order? Bob, that's a lot of baloney, and I'm very disgusted and disappointed in you."

The conversation ended as most of Lasorda's heated conversations ended, with the two combatants expressing their love for each other. No matter what the nature of the argument, Lasorda always tries to walk away with a smile. He's crossed so many bridges in his career, he knows the importance of keeping them intact.

But he remembered that conversation. And it continued to grieve him when things didn't change.

"Five years," Lasorda says, "and the only time they asked me about something was about Jim Tracy"—the former Dodger manager. "I recommended that they hire Tracy, and they did. But that was it."

Soon they even stopped asking him about the minor leaguers he was supposed to scout. For the first time since he'd been a player, Lasorda thought seriously about quitting.

"I would go down to the minor leagues and motivate and inspire and pick out kids, and they never once asked me about them," he says. "I thought, 'What am I doing? Why should I do this? They don't care about me.'"

Lasorda would look at Red Schoendienst, the elderly former St. Louis Cardinal player and manager who still wears a uniform and wanders around the batting cage before the game, and he'd get jealous. The most confident man in the history of baseball, finally jealous of someone else.

"I watched him bring the lineup card to home plate one day and thought, 'Look at how much respect they're giving him. They're using his experience, his knowledge. They continue to value him as an employee,'" Lasorda says. "Then I look at my own situation and realize that I don't even feel welcome."

• • •

Lasorda moves on to the last room at the Tommy Lasorda Heart Institute, where he visits an elderly woman named Johnnix, leaning over and kissing her on the cheek.

"I don't know what's going to happen to me," Johnnix says from beneath a labyrinth of tubes.

"Oh, I know," Lasorda says. "You're going to beat this, that's what you're going to do."

"Thank you," she says. "I'm glad somebody believes in me."

"As long as you're in here, somebody will always believe in you."

"You really do have a beautiful facility, Mr. Lasorda."

"Oh, it's not mine," Lasorda says, turning and waving to a couple of nurses walking in the hallway beyond the open door.

The nurses stop and wave back. Behind them, a woman in a wheelchair pulls up and waves. Then a man with a walker slows and waves, his hands trembling.

Outside, a siren wails as another ambulance races underneath the flapping likenesses of Lasorda's face. Another stricken man is wheeled into the building bearing Lasorda's name. If the patient survives, he will notice the photos on the wall and wonder whether Tommy Lasorda ever actually shows up here. Then one day the patient will awaken from a nap and a heavyset old man with kind eyes and a strong grip will be standing at the edge of his bed, urging him to be strong. And later, the patient will recall this moment as the one when his healing began.

Out in the hallway, the two elderly people and the nurse are waiting for Lasorda to leave Johnnix's room, waiting for one more touch, one more bit of belief.

"I used to be a baseball manager," Lasorda says.

"Can't you see?" Johnnix says softly. "You still are."

9

. . .

I CRIED FOR THIS

D ad, put your pajamas on."

Somewhere in the clutter of the Lasorda home, a clock is ticking midnight. Tommy Lasorda has just returned from another aching day of being Tommy Lasorda. He doesn't say so, but it's hard and getting harder. How a seventy-nine-year-old man represents the hope of youth on a daily basis, how a man with a doubting body sells belief so irrefutably, is beyond the comprehension of anyone who would see him on this night.

His left hip is sore, his eyes are heavy, but despite Jo's request he is not ready for sleep. He doesn't want the pajamas.

"They can bury me in those pajamas," he says. "But right now I'm still alive."

So he hobbles into the kitchen for an aspirin, then hobbles back out to the family room. He plops down in his white leather recliner and leans back and sighs.

"Are you sure you shouldn't just get dressed for bed?" Jo asks.

"Remember the Olympics?" Lasorda says.

"Can it wait until morning?"

"Times like this, I like to remember the Olympics."

The story begins on a spring day in 2000, when Lasorda received a call at his Fullerton home. He had heard that the U.S. baseball team had qualified for the 2000 Olympics in Sydney, and that it needed a manager. In his trademark whispering style, he had been spreading the word that he would be interested in the job.

It was a crazy idea. Lasorda would be seventy-three by the time the Games were under way. His team would be a bunch of minor leaguers who were not good enough for September call-ups. He would have to beat the powerhouse Cuban team, the gold medalist in the previous Summer Olympics that contained baseball, a team that had an 18–0 record in the Games. In addition, he had fallen out of favor with the Dodgers and had not been directly involved in a major league game for several years.

The very notion of it was nuts. But Lasorda went on whispering, and the Olympic team's organizers knew that those whispers could soon become a buzz, and they felt obliged to at least listen. So Bob Watson and Bill Bavasi (the son of Buzzie Bavasi), appointed by the U.S. Baseball Federation to pick the manager and the team, invited Lasorda to lunch in Long Beach, south of Los Angeles.

"We understand you want to be manager of this team," said Watson.

"You bet I do," said Lasorda.

"We're concerned about your age," said Watson.

"Worry about your own stinking age," said Lasorda.

"We have three other candidates," Watson said, referring to Ray Miller, Jim Lefebvre, and Terry Collins.

"Are you kidding me?" Lasorda said. "I've won more games than those guys combined. Don't you ever put my name in the same sentence with those three guys! Forget this job. I don't want this job. I'm leaving. If you still want to win gold, you'll call me. See ya."

Lasorda bolted out the door and held his breath. He had never given such an ultimatum before, but he had never been in this position before. He was being ignored by the Dodgers. His twenty years of managerial success were being trivialized by players who didn't know him and a front office that didn't appreciate him.

The Olympics were his chance to show the world that he was still Tommy Lasorda. But if he was indeed still Tommy Lasorda, he couldn't beg or plead or negotiate for the job. As Tommy Lasorda, he had to act insulted at the list of other candidates, storm out the restaurant door, and cross his fingers and pray that the officials would chase after him.

Of course, they did. The federation decided that while the United States, embarrassingly, had no chance to win a gold medal, at least Lasorda could make this country feel good about its national pastime's Olympic team. They decided to chase after Lasorda, not so much because he managed a great game, but because he could put up a terrific smoke screen.

They eventually called him in Fullerton and offered him the job. He thought about it for precisely five seconds. He gave a two-word acceptance speech.

"'Bout time," he said.

That was that. America's baseball team was going to be led by America's baseball symbol. It was just what the officials wanted. It was over the top.

On May 5, it was announced that Lasorda would be the manager of the baseball team that would represent the United States of America in the 2000 Olympic Games.

And immediately he began screaming in shades of red, white, and blue.

"I've been the most lucky guy that you could ever imagine—all the good things that have happened to me in my lifetime," he said. "But something like this is really something special to me . . . Thank God I was born in the greatest country in the world!"

He was asked about all those fans across America who disliked his Dodgers and his style.

"As manager of the Dodgers for twenty years, I think a lot of the Dodger fans really love me," he said. "But now the whole country's supposed to love me."

Then he was asked about his team, which at the time had no players or coaches.

"We're gonna beat the Cubans," he said. "That's why I want this job. Because the Cubans have never been beaten, and we're going to beat them."

Members of the media laughed. The Olympic officials blanched.

They thought they were hiring an aging general. They had no idea that Tommy Lasorda still thought he was a trained soldier. They knew he would be motivated to resurrect America's baseball legacy. They had no idea he would also be motivated to resurrect his own.

Lasorda attended baseball's All-Star Game in the middle of the summer to plead with general managers to allow him to use their best young players. This was the first Olympics in which professionals were allowed to play, and no country had as many great professionals as the United States.

The general managers refused. They were worried about sending any of their players halfway across the world after a full minor league season. They were worried about subjecting them to injury and fatigue. They basically told Lasorda that they would recall their best kids to the major leagues so that he would be left with only the scraps.

"Those selfish people," Lasorda said to friends. "They don't care about America. They don't care about the country that made them great. All they care about is themselves."

Lasorda then told reporters that it didn't matter if his players were ragged hand-me-downs with anonymous names and questionable abilities.

"To win an Olympic championship, I require only one thing of my players," he said. "They need to be breathing."

On September 2 in San Diego, he finally met those players, and they were breathing. But just barely.

"Now I know what is going to be the hardest thing about managing this team," Lasorda said. "Trying to remember their names."

The roster was filled with has-beens and never-weres. There was a player who had nearly 1,200 minor league games under his belt but not one major league appearance. There was a player who was still a teenager. There were aging minor leaguers and kid minor leaguers and, mostly, lifer minor leaguers.

Lasorda had heard of only one of them. He was the leather-skinned veteran Pat Borders, a former World Series MVP for the Toronto Blue Jays. But Borders had not been a star for nearly a decade, and was currently playing in the minor leagues for the Durham Bulls.

When the Olympic uniforms were issued, one of the names was misspelled. There were some names that Lasorda never pronounced correctly. There were some names he never knew.

"The whole thing was like a scene out of *Bull Durham*," Lasorda says. "I'd be walking around the field before games saying, 'Now, who the hell are you?'"

After just one practice, in San Diego, the team was scheduled to fly to Australia's Gold Coast, two hours north of Sydney, where they would play a handful of exhibition games. Before boarding the flight, Lasorda gathered the players in a meeting room for what he knew had to be the pep talk of his life.

"I don't know who you guys are," he shouted. "I don't know where you come from. I don't know whether you're married or single. I don't know if you're good, mediocre, or bad. But I do know one thing: when this is over, the whole world is going to know who you are!"

He took a breath, wiped the spittle from his lips, and continued.

"You don't represent your families, you don't represent your teams. You represent the entire USA, and you are going to win. And you know why? Because baseball is America's game, and we're not going to let those donkeys beat us!"

Bystanders grinned. "We're not going to let those donkeys beat us" might not rank up there with "Win one for the Gipper." But it inspired at least one person. Lasorda walked out of the meeting and called Jo.

"Mom, there's gonna be a quiz twenty-five years from now," he said. "Who was the only guy to win a World Series and an Olympic gold medal? And the answer is going to be me."

"That's great, Dad," she said. "But first can you learn the players' names?"

Once they arrived at Australia's Gold Coast, the workouts were uneven and the players were uncertain and Lasorda still couldn't remember anyone's name. Then, on the most unexpected of nights, in the most unexpected of places, the Americans bonded.

"It was the good ol'-fashioned American way," Lasorda says proudly. "Our team came together over a casino fight."

The players were at the blackjack tables in a casino when a patron was seen peeking at Pat Borders's cards, and then he bumped the catcher.

"Hey, buddy, back off," Borders said.

The patron backed off, grabbed a chair, and slammed it into Borders's ribs.

"And that was all she wrote," Lasorda recalls. "It was at that moment that I finally recognized all of our players. They were the ones coming out of the woodwork to beat this guy's butt."

The brawl spilled across several blackjack tables and included people of all ages and genders, including a woman who bit second baseman Brett Abernathy in the nipple, seriously enough that he was taken to a doctor.

"I saw the size of that bit nipple, and I saw Abernathy's pain, and I thought, 'Why didn't I ever think of fighting like that?'" Lasorda says.

Because the fight occurred in such a faraway place, it wasn't reported in the American press, and nobody knew about it but the U.S. baseball officials. The next morning, they ordered Lasorda to ban the players from the casino. Lasorda refused.

"To ban my players would be to imply that they did something wrong, and they didn't do anything wrong," he told them. "If they can't go into the casino tonight, then I can't be their manager."

The baseball officials relented, and the players returned to the casino, with thanks to Lasorda for supporting them. At that moment, this group of strangers became a team, and that team belonged to the old manager. Lasorda's actions resulted in one player, Abernathy, winning $125,000 by hitting a royal flush playing video poker.

"Not a bad payoff for a bit nipple," Lasorda says.

The circus soon headed south to Sydney, where the team and staff were housed in the spartan Olympic Village. It was yet another chance for the players and their manager to bond amid the discomfort of small rooms, narrow hallways, and creaky toilets.

Lasorda lasted about three hours. There had been a mistake in the rooming list, and someone hesitantly asked Lasorda if he wouldn't mind moving to a hotel, and Lasorda was emphatic in his patriotic response.

"Are you kidding me?" he said. "Get me out of here! There's no cable television or telephones in these rooms. How can you have a hotel room with no cable television or telephones?"

Lasorda was soon ensconced in a luxury Sydney hotel, complete with hot tub. But he got up early every morning and spent the entire day at the Village. Every night he would walk with pitcher Ben Sheets, the team's most promising prospect, talking about curveballs and haymakers. During the day, he would tell the players stories of Dodger championships, exaggerations and all.

His players so wanted his approval, they began testing his memory of their names.

"OK, Tommy, who am I?" pitcher Kurt Ainsworth said during one hallway meeting.

"No idea," Lasorda said.

"But Tommy, I just told you ten minutes ago," Ainsworth said.

"All you guys look alike."

By the time of the opening ceremony, Lasorda was perhaps the most popular guy in the Olympic Games. He thought this was neat, until he gathered with the athletes outside the stadium to prepare to march. Once there, athletes from many nations surrounded him hoping for photographs.

"I'm surrounded by people speaking all these different languages, asking for my picture, and I'm looking at their flags, and all I can think of is, I never heard of these countries," he says. "I don't mind taking a picture for your country, but at least I'd like to know if that country actually exists."

Americans back home have fond memories of watching Lasorda march into the giant Olympic stadium with his team, waving a tiny flag and smiling at the fans. Lasorda has different memories.

"Two things about that Olympic march," he says. "One, you are on your feet for hours, so you should not wear new shoes—I wore new shoes, and my legs were killing me. Two, you better go to the bathroom before they start playing your song, because otherwise you've got to hold it out there all night."

Lasorda concludes, "Now I know why the Olympics have the

world's greatest athletes. You have to be the world's greatest athlete to survive that march."

On Sunday, September 17, 2000, the Americans played their first game. It was against Japan. Throughout the pregame media interviews, Lasorda had promised not to harass the mostly amateur Olympic umpires.

Five batters into that first game, he was running on the field, shouting at some poor blue-shirted guy cowering behind home plate.

"You missed the bleeping call!" Lasorda shouted.

"Tom-my, Tom-my, Tom-my," the crowd chanted.

Ben Sheets was the starting pitcher. His Milwaukee Brewer bosses asked Lasorda to use him for only sixty pitches.

"He's never pitched in September before," they told him.

"I'll tell him it's August 31," Lasorda said.

Toward the middle of the game, when Sheets had clearly passed the sixty-pitch limit, Lasorda's dugout phone rang. He ignored it. Up in the stands, Bob Watson began motioning for Lasorda to pull Sheets out of the game. Lasorda shrugged like he didn't understand.

"I made a rule right there that I didn't give a darn about pitch counts," Lasorda says. "I just wanted to win."

A Japanese throwing error had allowed the game to become tied. In the thirteenth inning, a little-known player, Mike Neill, hit a two-run homer to give the United States a 4–2 victory.

"All I can say is, God bless America," Lasorda told the media.

That's not all he would say. He also compared Neill's blast with Kirk Gibson's homer, and his one-win team with the 1988 Dodgers.

"What was I supposed to do?" Lasorda asks. "The only chance we had to be great was to believe we were great. At that point, the truth didn't matter."

Before the team's second game, Lasorda gathered his pitching staff in the clubhouse and told them the story of how Orel Hershiser got the nickname "Bulldog." Then the Americans went out and beat the South Africans, 11–1. The hitting hero, with five RBIs, was John Cotton, the guy who had logged more than a thousand minor league games and no major league appearances.

"We have a really nice team," Watson told Lasorda.

"I don't care about being nice," Lasorda said. "I just want to beat Cuba's butt."

After their third game, a 6–2 win against the Netherlands, Lasorda lapsed into an odd 1970s trance, reeling off the names of his former Dodger heroes.

"Buckner! Garvey! Paciorek! Russell! Cey! Yeager! Ferguson! Joshua!" he shouted to a befuddled foreign press. "The way I felt about those guys, I feel about these guys!"

In their fourth game, they beat Korea, 4–0, on a grand slam in the bottom of the eighth inning, and now even Lasorda was starting to believe. With his pitchers having allowed just five runs in four games, he gathered them together in the clubhouse to give a pep talk with a prediction.

"I'm telling you guys, you just don't know how good you are. Give me this pitching staff in the major leagues, and within two years we'll win the World Series!"

Onlookers shook their heads in disbelief, but as it turned out, Lasorda was only slightly kidding. The pitching staff included current major league mainstays Ben Sheets, Roy Oswalt, and Ryan Franklin.

In the fifth game, on September 22, Lasorda's seventy-third birthday, the Americans played—you guessed it—Italy. A couple of years earlier, the Italians had asked Lasorda how much he would charge to coach their team.

"Not one dime," he told them. "Italy gave me the greatest gift any man could ever have—my father."

Thus the world thought Lasorda would enter this game with his allegiance torn in two, battling with his past, struggling to be competitive. As usual with Lasorda, the world was dead wrong.

"I'm so proud of my father's homeland," he said before the game. "I hope we beat the living bleep out of them."

The Americans won, 4–2, on a bad Italian throw in the eighth inning, and afterward, Lasorda shrugged.

"Everybody thought I'd be nice to Italy, but let's get one thing straight. I was born in the U.S.," he said. "It was my duty to kick Italy's butt."

As Lasorda left the field, he heard someone singing "Happy Birthday" to him from the stands. It was Peter O'Malley, who had long since sold the Dodgers but had never wavered in his support of Lasorda. O'Malley flew to Australia simply to let Lasorda know that, even if the Dodgers were ignoring him, he was not alone.

"I'll never forget hearing Peter singing that song," Lasorda says. "That was exactly the sort of thing the O'Malley family did for me during my entire time with the Dodgers. Even if it meant going to the end of the earth, they would stand by my side and give me their support. They were my ultimate cheerleaders, every night of my Dodgers career."

With five wins and no losses, the Americans now faced the unbeaten Cubans. It was only a preliminary game, not yet the medal round, but it was symbolic of the Americans' uphill climb here, and Lasorda's players showed they had been listening to him.

"We're gonna kick their bleeps!" shouted several players before the game.

Showing his innate sense of diplomacy and self-preservation, Lasorda immediately reverted to the stance he took with his minor leaguers. Back then, when he told them not to fight, it was a direct order to fight. Halfway around the world, the message was the same. Virtually winking with every word, Lasorda warned his players to leave Fidel Castro's kids alone.

"OK, fellas, I've knocked more guys on their butts than you have hairs on your head," he told them. "But this time, for once, you can't fight. Even if they want to fight, you have to back down. Castro wants us to embarrass ourselves. You can't let it happen."

The players didn't believe a word of it, running outside with fists clenched, spikes high, and common sense missing. When a Cuban pitcher hit an American player, Ernie Young, in the shoulder with a fastball, Young shoved the Cuban catcher and accused the pitcher of intentionally winging him, even though the Cuban pitcher was throwing a no-hitter. Doug Mientkiewicz dove at the legs of a Cuban runner at first base, despite the fact that he had no play. Borders was nailed in a clean collision at home plate, yet ran off the field shouting curses at the Cubans. Abernathy walked out of the dugout, faced the Cuban dugout, and pointed to his head, as if threatening beanballs.

The Cubans won, 6–1, and the world's media attacked the Americans for their poor sportsmanship.

"Our players were just trying to protect themselves against the incredible Cuban machine," Lasorda said. "Can't an American protect himself?"

The game had been lost, but the message had been sent. Lasorda's Americans were perhaps the first team in the history of international baseball who were not afraid of the Cubans.

The U.S. team easily beat Australia, 12–1, in the final preliminary game, setting them up for a tough semifinal bout against South Korea. Once again, Lasorda's resiliency was contagious. In the ninth inning of a tie game, with a runner on first, Mientkiewicz was supposed to bunt him to second. But the runner was picked off. So Mientkiewicz shrugged and hit a game-winning homer in a 3–2 victory.

"This team is destined!" Lasorda proclaimed. "I just love Doug Man . . . cha . . . er . . . whatever! I still can't pronounce his name, but I love him."

Time for the gold medal showdown against Cuba, the team that had never lost a game in the Olympics. The morning of the contest, Lasorda sat down in the Olympic Village cafeteria with his starter, the young Ben Sheets.

"Ben, one day you will win twenty games a year and a Cy Young Award in the major leagues," Lasorda said. "But tonight you will pitch the biggest game of your life, because you will be pitching to bring a gold medal to the USA."

Sheets looked up from his cereal with a furrowed brow and asked, "Who are we playing again?"

Lasorda threw up his hands and walked out of the cafeteria. Even if these players would never understand his sense of patriotism, they certainly bought into his passion for victory and his belief in the impossible, the same traits that had been sold countless times to so many Dodger players before them.

"When we took the field against Cuba, I knew we were gonna

beat them," Lasorda says. "The players were going to do it for their country and for themselves, and maybe even for me."

So they did. Sheets was brilliant, throwing a complete game, a three-hit shutout. All the while, the U.S. officials in the stands begged Lasorda to take him out of the game before his arm grew sore. By the middle innings, Lasorda had had enough of their meddling. He stepped outside the dugout and gestured into the stands.

"Sit down!" he shouted at the officials. "I ain't taking this guy out even if God tells me to take 'im out."

Then he turned to his pitching coach, Phil Regan, and said, "Get rid of that pitch counter. Throw it away. Sheets is finishing this game."

When he did, the Americans had scored four times, for a 4–0 victory and an astounding gold medal.

"It's like I told those guys who produced that movie *Miracle,*" Lasorda says. "I told them, 'Fellas, you're making a movie about the wrong team.'"

When the game ended, the players danced and hugged, then later shook hands with the Cubans like all good Olympians. But walking off the field, Lasorda couldn't help himself. He turned and pointed to the Cubans and began yelling in Spanish. A blushing interpreter later translated the diatribe.

"Go back to Havana," Lasorda had shouted. "Fidel is waiting for you, and he's gonna have the whole goddamn bunch of you cutting sugar cane!"

Shortly after the victory, a giant podium was dragged onto the field, and the U.S. team climbed up to the highest level to receive their medals. Lasorda began walking toward the podium with them. Then, when he was about halfway there, he stopped and turned back toward the dugout.

Only moments earlier, he had been informed of one of the quirks of the Olympic Games, a footnote that instantly became one of the sad oddities of his life: Olympic coaches don't get medals.

Only the Olympians themselves receive medals. Even in team competitions, where the coach can be as important as a player, the coaches don't get medals. Which means Lasorda, after spending five months bellowing and braying and pushing his team to win a gold medal, wouldn't get one.

He was strikingly calm about the news. He returned to the dugout and put his hands behind his back. While his team received its medals, his eyes welled up. When the American flag was raised and the national anthem was played, he began openly weeping. He was so moved by the flag, he momentarily took his hand off his heart and pointed to it. He was so struck by watching these anonymous guys draped in gold, he said he felt the weight of the medal across his bare chest.

"Everyone said, 'Oh, Tommy, we're so sorry you didn't get a medal,'" he says. "And I tell them, 'Oh, no, I got a medal. I got a medal when they put it around our players' necks. I got a medal when they raised that American flag. I got a medal when they played our national anthem. I cried that night because I did something for my country, and that meant more to me than any medal.'"

He was OK about not having a medal because he had just been blessed with the shining story of a lifetime.

"This was my greatest championship, my greatest games, my greatest anything," Lasorda said at the time. "When you win a World Series for the Dodgers, the Dodger fans are cheering for you, but Giants fans and Reds fans and all the other teams' fans are not. But when you win an Olympic gold medal, all the fans in the country are cheering for you. You're not winning for one city or team, you're winning for an entire nation."

After the anthem ended, fans began chanting his name again: "Tom-my, Tom-my." Lasorda looked around, wondering whether any of the Dodger officials who had been ignoring him saw that unabashed display of love by fans from around the world. But no. On this night, none of them were there. None of them could be bothered to make the trip to Sydney.

A few days later, when Lasorda was honored with a two-minute standing ovation in the third inning at Dodger Stadium, none of the players could be bothered to leave the dugout to shake his hand. And nobody in the organization, then or later, thought to offer him what would have been a thoughtful gesture of congratulations and appreciation. Nobody bothered to make him even an imitation gold medal.

"I came back home and I was still ignored," Lasorda says now, speaking haltingly as he slips into sleep in his family room's recliner. "But that's OK. I realized that while the Dodgers had forgotten me, America never did."

Epilogue:

I WAS REBORN FOR THIS

The phone call came in the winter before the 2004 season, perfect timing for a man who was slowly staggering into a bitter retirement. It had been four years since he last managed a big-league game, four years since he'd had any real impact on the team. During that time, the club had acquired new players, new executives, and a new culture that did not have room for rotund old guys spinning yarns in the clubhouse.

Then, on a chilly Tuesday at around 10 A.M., his phone rang. Frank McCourt was on the other end of the line. McCourt was a lifelong Red Sox fan who was trying to buy the Dodgers. He was also a lifelong baseball fan who knew that for the takeover to be considered anything less than hostile, it must include Lasorda. Nobody in the organization knew more about baseball. Few current Hall of Famers were as active and accessible. And, after all, no matter what the Dodgers thought, the fans still loved Lasorda. McCourt knew that if he wanted Los Angeles on his side, he needed Lasorda by his side.

The calliope on Lasorda's cell phone sang. McCourt politely introduced himself, then said the one word Lasorda had longed to hear since he retired in 1996. McCourt said, "Help."

Taking the call in his Fullerton home, Lasorda pulled the phone away from his ear in shock and then, trembling, he put it back against his ear.

"My current bosses would barely acknowledge me, and here's a guy who wants to fly me across the country just to pick my brain?" Lasorda recalls. "That was amazing."

It was more than amazing. It was resuscitation.

Lasorda was being given a chance to contribute again. He jumped on the next flight to Boston, walked out of the terminal at Logan Airport, and was greeted by Frank and Jamie McCourt's driver, who told him all he needed to know.

"I asked him how long he's worked for the McCourts, and he says he's worked there forever," Lasorda recalls. "That tells me something right there. Because I had worked for the Dodgers forever."

With their pointed questions and obvious respect, the McCourts made an enormous impression on Lasorda. He knew this wasn't just a publicity stunt. He knew they really valued him.

"If I buy this club, I want you with me," Frank McCourt said.

"Thank you," Lasorda said.

"You're the most important part of this transaction," McCourt said.

"Thank you," Lasorda said.

"I want you to be my right-hand man, my special adviser," Mc-Court said.

This was a job offer, with a new title and new responsibilities for an aging manager. This was something that would require thought and negotiation.

Lasorda engaged in neither. He did not need time to think about it. He did not even pause. He just repeated the same phrase he used throughout the meeting.

"Thank you."

When McCourt officially became the owner, he lived up to his word, giving Lasorda a fancy title and a permanent seat in the owner's box, next to the dugout. Lasorda sits there still, not as an entertainer but as an expert, empowered to give McCourt advice on everything from a young general manager to an aging pitcher.

McCourt returns all of Lasorda's calls. He listens to all of Lasorda's opinions. He publicly recognizes Lasorda whenever possible, on birthdays and anniversaries and sometimes just for fun. He knows Lasorda went a couple of years without a standing ovation. He wants Lasorda to hear them forever.

In return, Lasorda has become the owner's biggest defender, especially during McCourt's difficult early days when some rookie mistakes required much defending. In the first year of McCourt's ownership, one could turn to any Los Angeles sports-talk radio station during the summer and the chances were good that one would hear Lasorda screaming at the hosts or the callers about the greatness of Frank McCourt.

Walking across an empty Dodger Stadium field one winter day after meeting McCourt for a brainstorming lunch, Lasorda suddenly stops, looks up to the executive offices on the fifth floor, and shakes his head.

"You know what the McCourts gave me?" Lasorda says, his throat thickening. "They gave me back my prestige, my honor, my dignity."

He idly picks up a brown-stained baseball from the dugout floor and begins tossing it. "You know what the McCourts gave me? They gave me back my life."

This, then, is where that life will probably end, on a deep green diamond, Lasorda holding a brown weathered baseball, the most improbable of journeys completed in the only place that ever made any sense.

From a freezing Norristown tenement to the entertainment capital of the world. From a third-string high school pitcher to a world champion manager. From the back of a bouncing laundry truck to the Hall of Fame.

That place is baseball, that place is America, and for eighty years Tommy Lasorda has symbolized them both.

There were times when he thought he'd lost them both. But always, the simple belief of a boy standing on a crumbling mound in newspaper-stuffed cleats brought them back. There were also times when he thought he was bigger than both. But then the tug on his cuff of an autograph-seeking child or the flapping flag on a downtown barbershop would remind him he was wrong.

"It's been a heckuva ride, you know?" Lasorda says, still tossing the ball.

He spits forcefully on the grass, as if his pitcher had just walked the leadoff hitter. He hikes up his gray wool slacks, and for a second you think he's about to run out to the mound and grab that pitcher by the tobacco-stained shoulders and order him to throw just one more strike, dammit, one more strike.

But not today. He takes a few hobbling steps and sits gingerly on the dugout bench. He checks to see if the groundskeepers are looking, and when they're not, he gently pumps his fists, and you know he has just seen Kirk Gibson hit another home run—about once a week he sees that home run. He stands up and begins pacing the empty dugout as if Doug Rau is on the mound all over again. Not a month goes by when he is not reminded of Doug Rau. The memories are alive around him. He still wishes he could sit in this dugout and make more memories.

But then he walks outside the stadium and looks around and sees that all the colleagues his age are either dead or watching the game from their living rooms. The crooked-nosed, bigmouthed kid who was one of hundreds in Vero Beach in 1949 has outlasted them all, and he is just thankful to be here. He is amazed every day, to this day, at the simple fact that he is allowed to be who he is.

"Don't tell anybody this," he says, "but sometimes, you know, I can't even believe it myself."

But he does believe, because this is what baseball and America have given him. The limitless possibilities of a game with no clock have allowed him to view the endless opportunities in his own life. The boundless promise of a country with no restrictions on poor children with bad curveballs has allowed him to seize those opportunities.

The journey to becoming baseball's last true believer has broken his heart. But it has also strengthened his spirit. For as long as he is able to climb out of that Fullerton recliner and walk through that cluttered kitchen and climb into that flag-covered car and drive to a field or a classroom or a firehouse or anywhere he can transform doubt into trust and cowards into champions, he will continue to manage.

Baseball. America. He lives for this.

Tommy Lasorda's Managerial Record

Minor League Managerial Record

Year	Team	Standing	W–L
1965	Pocatello	2	33–33
1966	Ogden	1	39–27
1967	Ogden	1	41–25
1968	Ogden	1	39–25
1969	Spokane	2	71–73
1970	Spokane	1	94–52
1971	Spokane	3	69–76
1972	Albuquerque	1	92–56

Major League Managerial Record

Year	Team	G	W	L	PCT.	Standing
1976	LA N	4	2	2	.500	2
1977	LA N	162	98	64	.605	1
1078	LA N	162	95	67	.586	1
1979	LA N	162	79	83	.488	3
1980	LA N	163	92	71	.564	2
1981	LA N	110	63	47	.573	2
1982	LA N	162	88	74	.543	2

Major League Managerial Record (cont.)

Year	Team	G	W	L	PCT.	Standing
1983	LA N	163	91	71	.562	1
1984	LA N	162	79	83	.488	4
1985	LA N	162	95	67	.586	1
1986	LA N	162	73	89	.451	5
1987	LA N	162	73	89	.451	4
1988	LA N	162	94	67	.584	1
1989	LA N	160	77	83	.481	4
1990	LA N	162	86	76	.531	2
1991	LA N	162	93	69	.574	2
1992	LA N	162	63	99	.389	6
1993	LA N	162	81	81	.500	4
1994	LA N	114	58	56	.509	1
1995	LA N	144	78	66	.542	1
1996	LA N	76	41	35	.539	1
Total		3,040	1,599	1,439	.526	

Division Series Managerial Record

Year	Team	G	W	L	PCT.
1981	LA N	5	3	2	.600
1995	LA N	3	0	3	.000
Total		8	3	5	.375

League Championship Series Managerial Record

Year	Team	G	W	L	PCT.
1977	LA N	4	3	1	.750
1978	LA N	4	3	1	.750
1981	LA N	5	3	2	.600
1983	LA N	4	1	3	.250
1985	LA N	6	2	4	.333
1988	LA N	7	4	3	.571
Total		30	16	14	.533

World Series Managerial Record

Year	Team	G	W	L	PCT.
1977	LA N	6	2	4	.333
1978	LA N	6	2	4	.333
1981	LA N	6	4	2	.667
1988	LA N	5	4	1	.800
Total		23	12	11	.522

Transaction Information

Signed as an amateur free agent by the Philadelphia Phillies, 1945.

Selected by the Brooklyn Dodgers from the Philadelphia Phillies in the minor league draft, November 24, 1948.

Sold by the Brooklyn Dodgers to the Kansas City Athletics, March 2, 1956.

Traded by the Kansas City Athletics to the New York Yankees in exchange for Wally Burnette, July 11, 1956.

Sold by the New York Yankees to the Brooklyn Dodgers, May 26, 1957.

Released by the Los Angeles Dodgers, July 9, 1960.

Acknowledgments

I would like to thank, first, my editor at Houghton Mifflin, Susan Canavan, for her undying patience and persistence. She cheered above the silence, believed beyond all reason, and turned a blurry vision into something as sharp as Tommy Lasorda's stare and as hearty as his laugh. She's a wonder with words, a deity of description, a sultan of story arc, and if this sentence were part of the actual book, she would cut it out immediately, because she hates it when I write like this. But it's not. So she can't. So there.

I would also like to thank Bill Goldberg, an art guy who is really an architect, who built the foundation on which this book has grown. It was Billy G on the phone, Billy G at the fire, Billy G in the pothole, Billy G not only living *for* this but living *with* this, and bless him for that.

Thanks also to Grover and Mary Plaschke for their guidance, to Brad, Beth, and Bob for listening, to Tim Brown for his laugh, to Randy Harvey for his understanding, to Gene Wojciechowski for his advice, to Mark Langill for his memories, and to Andrew Ladores for being there.

My gratitude goes to David Fisher, the wonderful coauthor, with Tommy Lasorda, of *The Artful Dodger*—we are forever kindred spirits. And to Fred Claire, the most honest man in Los Angeles, for the inspiration provided, with his coauthor Steve Springer, in *My 30 Years in Dodger Blue*.

Thanks from Tommy and me to the good people of Houghton Mifflin. In addition to Susan Canavan, we'd like to thank Bridget Marmion, Megan Wilson, Sanj Kharbanda, Larry Cooper, Loren Isenberg, Eamon Dolan, Will Vincent, and Dodger historian and fact checker extraordinaire Mark Langill, whom Houghton hired to gather photographs and check the facts.

Finally, thanks to Tommy Lasorda for his time. No, no, Tommy, I'm full. Seriously. I can't eat another bite. Oh, well, OK, just one more . . .

Bill Plaschke

* * *

First, I would like to thank my family, beginning with my wife, Jo. I have often said that if there were ever a Hall of Fame for wives, Jo would be the first inductee and the template for all to follow. I am proud to say that as of this writing Jo and I have been married for fifty-seven wonderful years. My daughter, Laura, has always made me so very proud to be her dad. She has so much beauty, style, and compassion. Laura is always there for others and is a great mother to my granddaughter. My son-in-law and agent, Billy Goldberg, has been essential. His integrity, loyalty, hard work, and love have helped our family and my career immensely. I have always said that we should have grandkids before kids. My granddaughter, Emily Tess, is the "greatess." I love her smile, her "stick-to-it-ness" with everything she takes on, and her innocence and curiosity are beyond reproach. I want to live forever just to watch her grow into the beautiful, talented, smart, and warm young woman I know she will be. I would also like to thank my brothers, Eddie, Morris, Harry, and Joe, and my wife Jo's family — they are my family too — Jean, Gladys, Fran, and, in loving memory, Lee.

I would like to acknowledge the memory of my son, "Spunky." A day does not pass without my thinking of him.

I owe a debt of gratitude to my extended family, which has been like my right arm: the Dodger organization. My thanks go to the O'Malley family and Terry Seidler, who helped make my dreams become reality. It was their belief and vision that gave me the opportunity to manage the greatest organization in major league baseball. And, too, Al Campanis, my mentor and friend. I will always miss you, pal. Vin Scully: Vinny, it all started in Brooklyn for the two of us. Behind the mike, you are the best who ever lived. What a ride it has been! Billy DeLury: Thank you for all you have done for me, the players, and our families for over five decades. And my Dominican brother, Ralph Avila, who has been and continues to be an important part of my life. And of course the McCourt family, who helped me continue my dreams. I believed in you, and you believed in me, and I am so happy for your success with the Dodgers. Thank you for making me such a big part of that success and for treating me like a Hall of Famer.

I would like to take an extra moment to acknowledge a man I met in Los Angeles in 1963. At the time, I was an anonymous scout and he was a big-time coach. Yet USC's Rod Dedeaux took me under his wing and became my best friend, until he died in January 2006. This book is for him, in honor of his nearly fifty years of selfless loyalty. Dedeaux was loyal to USC, where he became college baseball's winningest coach and the author of ten national championships, despite being paid $1 a year and despite constant offers to join the major leagues. Dedeaux was loyal to me, making me his honorary pitching coach when I was still a scout, introducing me to his friends, paving the way for me to become a fixture in Los Angeles. Whatever I achieved, I achieved with Rod Dedeaux's help and support. In later years, we accompanied each other to everything from football games to vacations. Where I was loud, he was quiet. Where I was crazy, he was thoughtful. We were perfect together. Jo has a postcard with our photos on it, and underneath she wrote this inscription: "Three of a kind couldn't beat this pair." And she was right. The football coach I most admired was Vince Lombardi, the basketball coach was John Wooden, and the baseball man was Rod Dedeaux. I'll never forget his wisdom and courage and friendship, and a part of him will live with me forever.

I would also like to single out Michael Milken and the good work he has done for cancer research through his Prostate Cancer Foundation. Together we have traveled the country promoting this cause, and someday, mark my words, his efforts will help bring about a cure.

This book is for all the players who played for me and put me in the Hall of Fame. It is for all the coaches and staff who propped us up along the way, and for every fan who has ever loved the Dodgers as their own. Without you, none of this would have been possible.

I would need every page in a library full of books to include the names of all the people I'd like to thank. I have been blessed: I have lived on this earth for eighty years, a life in which I've been touched by so many people, touched every single day. It's impossible to name everyone here, but when I see you again — and I will — I will thank you personally. Know that you are in my heart.

Tom Lasorda

Index